Critical Studies in Native History

(continues Manitoba Studies in Native History)

Elder Brother and the Law of the People

Contemporary Kinship and Cowessess First Nation

Robert Alexander Innes

UMP

University of Manitoba Press

University of Manitoba Press
Winnipeg, Manitoba
Canada R3T 2M5
uofmpress.ca

Printed in Canada
Text printed on chlorine-free, 100% post-consumer recycled paper

17 16 15 14 13   1 2 3 4 5

Cover design: Marvin Harder
Interior design: Karen Armstrong Graphic Design
Maps: Weldon Hiebert

Library and Archives Canada Cataloguing in Publication

Innes, Robert Alexander
Elder brother and the law of the people : contemporary kinship
and Cowessess First Nation / Robert Alexander Innes.

(Critical studies in Native history ; 17)
Includes bibliographical references and index.
Issued also in electronic format.
ISBN 978-0-88755-746-0 (pbk.)
ISBN 978-0-88755-437-7 (PDF e-book)
ISBN 978-0-88755-439-1 (epub e-book)

1. Cowessess First Nation. 2. Native peoples—Kinship—Saskatchewan.
3. Native peoples—Saskatchewan—Ethnic identity. 4. Native peoples—
Saskatchewan—Treaties. 5. Native peoples—Legal status, laws, etc.—
Saskatchewan. I. Title. II. Series: Critical studies in Native history ; 17

E78.S2I56 2013   306.83089'97071244   C2012-908127-2
                                                     C2012-908128-0

The University of Manitoba Press gratefully acknowledges the financial
support for its publication program provided by the Government of Canada
through the Canada Book Fund, the Canada Council for the Arts, the Manitoba
Department of Culture, Heritage, Tourism, the Manitoba Arts Council,
and the Manitoba Book Publishing Tax Credit.

FSC
www.fsc.org
MIX
Paper from
responsible sources
FSC® C016245

Contents

Illustrations

Elder Brother and
the Law of the People

Introduction

In the winter of 1998, I visited Cowessess First Nation to interview Edwin Pelletier, among others, for my master's research on Saskatchewan Aboriginal veterans. My maternal grandfather, Samson Pelletier, and Edwin were first cousins. Mosom[1] Edwin told me that he and my grandfather grew up in the same house. During the 1930s, they were old enough to earn a living, but worked as farm labourers for non-Native farmers because there was little work available on the reserve for the men during the Depression. As young men, Mosom Samson and Mosom Edwin traveled from farm to farm, hopping freight trains. When war broke out in Europe, many Cowessess men enlisted. According to James Lavallee, another Cowessess band member and Second World War veteran, Samson was the first from the reserve to enlist. Mosom Edwin also enlisted, but did not have an opportunity to see my grandfather before he (Samson) left for the war. When Edwin returned to the reserve after the war, Samson had already come back from Europe, but left the reserve. My grandfather never again lived on the reserve. Until I met with him in 1998, Mosom Edwin never knew what had become of my grandfather.

In 1933, Samson's wife, Elizabeth Pelletier, died of tuberculosis. At the time, my mother, Muriel Pelletier, was not yet one year old, and her sister, Rosemary Pelletier, was almost three years old. While my grandfather worked as a farm labourer, my mother and aunt lived with various relatives over the next three years. In 1936, life was difficult for those living on the reserve, and my relatives could no longer afford to take care of two extra children. My grandfather placed my mother and aunt in the residential school on

Cowessess for the next three years. In 1939, my grandfather married Rose Agathe Pelletier, who was from the neighbouring Métis community of Marievale. Soon afterward, my grandfather enlisted in the military service and was shipped to Europe. My mother and aunt lived with Rose Agathe and her daughter, Margaret, in Biggar, a small town just north of the reserve, for the next six years until the war was over.

My grandfather was thirty-five years old when he returned from the war, but he looked thirty years older than that because he walked with a cane and had grey hair. He had been given six months to live due to a war injury. However, he recuperated for a few years, and then, in the late 1940s, the family moved to La Ronge, in northern Saskatchewan, where my grandfather took a job as foreman of a fish factory. According to one band member, my grandfather was forced to enfranchise (i.e., give up his legal status as a federally recognized Indian) by an Indian agent named Kurley because he (Samson) was agitating for change on the reserve. Meanwhile, my mother became old enough to work as a nurse's aide in La Ronge. A few years later, she transferred to North Battleford, Saskatchewan, then to Prince Rupert, British Columbia, and finally, in the late 1950s, she moved to Vancouver, where she met my father, James Innes. When my parents divorced, my mother decided that she, my older brother, Brian, and I would live with my grandparents, who had by that time relocated to Winnipeg, Manitoba. In April 1968, my younger brother was born, whom Samson named Anthony Paul Innes. Anthony was Mosom Samson's brother, who died at the age of ten, and Paul was the name of Samson's first wife's father. In October of that year, my grandfather passed away at the age of fifty-eight.

My aunt, Rosemary, led an arduous life. No doubt affected by difficult experiences in the residential school, and with an unkind stepmother, my aunt became alcoholic, mentally unstable, and homeless in Edmonton. In the early 1990s, she returned to her birthplace, Crooked Lake, living along its shores for a few days until a woman from Broadview befriended her and took her to town. In Broadview, Social Services obtained for her a small house, and she settled into the community. Because she still dressed as a homeless person, wearing a toque and heavy coat in all seasons, and walked around the small prairie town pushing a bundle buggy or pulling a little wagon, people in the area were initially apprehensive of her. In a short time, however, Rosemary's perky personality and ability always to remember peoples' names disarmed their fears, and she became known affectionately as the "Bag Lady." Most people did not know that she had been born on Cowessess, as she had been very young when she left the region. Nevertheless, everyone, white and Indian, accepted her as part of the Broadview community.

In 1989, I applied for and received my Indian status from the Department of Indian Affairs. My mother had applied to have her status reinstated a few years earlier, after the passage of Bill C-31 amended the membership code of the Indian Act in 1985. Membership in a band had to be applied for separately, and in 1990 Cowessess accepted me as a band member, even though I had neither visited nor knew anyone from there. In 1994, I met Terrence Pelletier and Herbert Gunn in Toronto. They were representatives of Cowessess First Nation, there to explain to band members living in Toronto the significance of the Treaty Land Entitlement agreement that Cowessess First Nation had recently signed with the federal government. Most of those at the meeting had never been to Cowessess. Both men encouraged these band members to visit. The next summer, my older brother and his son took our mother, who was still living in Winnipeg, to Cowessess for their first visit. A few weeks later, my wife and I visited Cowessess for the first time. While we were there, Terrence introduced us to many people. Like Terrence, all the band members we met expressed pleasure at meeting and becoming better acquainted with band members who had never been to the reserve. This struck me as contrary to how people on other reserves had been reported to treat their C-31 members. I was even asked a few times whether I had considered moving to the reserve to live. The following year, my wife and I moved to Saskatoon and enrolled in graduate school at the University of Saskatchewan. In Saskatchewan, I continued to meet more Cowessess people, most of whom showed the same level of interest towards other band members.

As mentioned earlier, the seeds for this research came while I conducted research for my master's thesis. That research included interviewing Edwin Pelletier, James Lavallee, Robert Stevenson, Mr. Redwood, and Joe Ewack, who were all Second World War veterans and Cowessess band members, except for Ewack, whose wife Rose had been born on Cowessess. During these interviews, they told me stories of my grandparents, giving me a sense of connection to them and to Cowessess. When I interviewed Mosom Edwin, one of his daughters, Shirley Pelletier, was present with her son during the interview. Although Shirley and my mother and Aunt Rosemary were second cousins, they had never met when they were children because my family had left the reserve at so early an age. I told them that Rosemary had moved to neighbouring Broadview and was known as the Bag Lady. When Shirley realized that Rosemary was her second cousin, she turned to her son and said to him, "The next time you see her, you make sure you shake her hand because she is your relative." I was struck that Shirley Pelletier instructed her son to treat my aunt, heretofore mostly a stranger, as a relative. Though I had grown up with many Native people and had witnessed the strong kinship ties, this was the first time I had experienced kinship practice from someone not from my immediate family. I further thought about how other Cowessess band members had reacted to me and other members who had never lived on the reserve, and wondered what led band members to respond in such a welcoming manner. I soon realized that I had the beginning of a potentially intriguing research question that would allow me to explore the history of Cowessess.

Raymond DeMallie has argued that kinship studies are a significant but often ignored area of research within Native Studies, further suggesting that Native Studies scholars' aversion to kinship research has been due to its close association with anthropology.[2] According to DeMallie, kinship studies, with their evolutionary and cultural relativist theories, abstract taxonomies, and endless charts, seem far removed from and irrelevant to Native Studies scholars and Native communities. Yet, in pointing to examples of the negative impact of kinship breakdown on the Grassy Narrows Ojibwe, and the possibility for positive change with the revitalization of the Pine Ridge Lakota kinship unit (*tiyoshpaye*), DeMallie stated that kinship is "fundamental to every aspect of Native American Studies." Accordingly, he challenged Native Studies scholars "to explore the richness of the Native American social heritage and find creative ways to build on it for the future."[3]

As a Native Studies scholar, my research is an attempt to take up Demallie's challenge by examining the importance of kinship relations in the maintenance and affirmation of individual and collective identity for members of Cowessess First Nation, located in southern Saskatchewan. Specifically, this book examines how Cowessess has undermined the imposition of the Indian Act's definitions of Indian by acknowledging kinship relations to band members who either had not been federally recognized as Indians prior to 1985, or were urban members disconnected from the reserve. This acknowledgement defies the general perception that First Nations people have internalized the legal definition of Indian, and in the process rendered traditional kinship meaningless. It also questions the accepted idea that conflict is the only possible outcome of any relationship between "old" members and "newly recognized" Indians. The importance of kinship to Cowessess band members blurs the boundaries (as defined by the Indian Act) between status Indians, Métis, and non-status Indians, illustrating the artificiality of those boundaries.

The attitude of older Cowessess band members toward new members, I argue, stems from understandings and social practices that are historically rooted in cultural kinship practices conveyed in the Law of the People through stories of Elder Brother that predate the reserve era and have persisted into the twenty-first century. In the pre-reserve era, Aboriginal bands on the northern plains were relatively small, kin-based communities that relied on the unity of their members for survival. Band membership was fluid, flexible, and inclusive. There were a variety of ways that individuals or groups of people could become members of a band, but what was of particular importance was that these new members assumed some sort of kinship role with its associated responsibilities. Band membership, then, served to strengthen social, economic, and military alliances with other bands of similar cultural origins. However, many bands in the northern plains were multicultural in nature, so the creation and maintenance of alliances cut across cultural and linguistic lines. Cowessess First Nation is an example of a multicultural band, as its pre-reserve composition comprised five major cultural groups—Plains Cree, Saulteaux, Assiniboine, Métis, and Halfbreed people—as well as other cultural groups.[4] This book describes how kinship for contemporary members of Cowessess First Nation persists to define community identity and interaction in spite of the historical, scholarly, and legal classifications of Aboriginal peoples created and imposed by Euro-Canadian outsiders. Classifying Aboriginal people has had profound impacts on the ways that non-Aboriginal people view them, and on how Aboriginal people view themselves. Cowessess members' interpretations, then, take on great significance.

Basil Johnston writes that if Aboriginal people and their cultures are to be understood, "their beliefs, insights, concepts, ideals, values, attitudes, and codes must be studied." For him, to comprehend Aboriginal world views requires "examining native ceremonies, rituals, songs, dances, prayers, and stories." He explains, it is through these forms of communication that Aboriginal people's beliefs of "life, being, existence, and relationships are symbolically expressed and articulated."[5] From this perspective, to understand the way in which Cowessess First Nation band members practice kinship in the contemporary context, it is necessary to understand the values that guided their practices historically. For Cowessess people, these values are embedded in the stories of Elder Brother. Wîsahêcâchk and Nanubush, in Cree and Ojibwe/Saulteaux oral stories respectively, are also known by the kinship term Elder Brother. The Elder Brother stories as well as others were told in the wintertime by skilled storytellers. Storytellers were valued by the way they delivered a story and how they were able to adapt or provide a twist and still maintain the story's integrity. Elder Brother stories contain spiritual beings, and though there is some debate among scholars about whether Elder Brother is a spirit being, as will be discussed in Chapter 1, this is not of great concern to Cree or Ojibwe people. These stories fall within two main categories—*âtayôhkêwina* and *âcimowina*—which contain many stories of different spirit beings. This book focuses on Elder Brother, as he is the central character in Cree and Ojibwe mythology. The Elder Brother stories, along with the other stories, form the basis for the Law of the People that guided the people's social interaction with all of creation, including kinship practices. Understanding these stories, then, can provide a tool, a framework to help explain contemporary Cowessess kinship practices.

Legal definitions of urban members have not adversely affected the reception that they received from on-reserve members. Although reserve residents occasionally ask urban members whether they are C-31s, the predominant question is, "Who is your *mosom/kohkum*?" Once kinship is established, reserve residents explain how they are related to the urban members, or how they know their relatives. Many reserve members ask if the urban members have considered moving to the reserve. Most reserve residents are interested to know about the urban band members' lives and experiences. They relate the accomplishments of other urban band members, and point out the many urban and reserve band members whom the Cowessess band has funded to attend university. This welcoming reaction of reserve residents to their urban counterparts is a stark contrast to media-generated images of the tensions between reserve residents and C-31s. The contention, here, is that the persistent adherence to the values in the Law of People by Cowessess members, even by those who have not actually heard the stories, sheds light on this phenomena and their other kinship patterns.

This suggests a number of questions addressed in this research:

1. How do people define and live out kinship? Are there variations on reserve, with off-reserve members who come to the reserve, or in off-reserve locales?

2. What factors have led to Cowessess reserve-based band members' inclusion of new or previously disconnected members?

3. Is the contemporary practice of inclusion based on notions of traditional practices of inclusion, or is it a contemporary development?

4. How does this inclusion affect the individual and collective identity of Cowessess' band members?

5. Has the Indian Act's definition of "Indian" influenced Cowessess members' reactions to the Bill C-31 amendment to the Indian Act? In what ways have Cowessess members responded to new band members?

6. In what ways have band members responded to the inclusion of new band members in the ratification of the Cowessess Treaty Land Entitlement (TLE) agreement? Did the Indian Act's definition of "Indian" impact their responses?

Classifications of Aboriginal people in the Canadian subarctic and northern plains were coined and applied by fur traders and missionaries from the seventeenth to the nineteenth century. Group designations employed in primary sources and secondary literature differed greatly from current tribal labels. The difference has caused much confusion and debate between twentieth and twenty-first century scholars attempting to link seventeenth century groups with contemporary peoples.[6] In the nineteenth century, British colonial and then early Canadian state governments created legal definitions for what constituted an "Indian." This legal definition subsequently underwent numerous changes, but the underlying goals of assimilation and protection within the fiscal constraints of the government never altered. These legal classifications have tended to move from the specific to the general. In other words, early observers often described Aboriginal people (albeit inaccurately) at the band level, while later commentators described them at the tribal level.[7] Even more generic terms, such as "Indian," "native," and "savage," were applied not only to tribal groups but also to individual bands. Of course, there were those who used all three levels of description simultaneously. Furthermore, there was a tendency to move away from the band designation to either tribal or generic labels.

Meanwhile, scholars have, for the most part, used tribal names to describe Aboriginal groups. This is reflective of the historical documents available to them. As a result, there are many historic and ethnographic studies that emphasize distinct boundaries between Aboriginal groups. Although scholars acknowledge intra-Aboriginal interactions, they differentiate groups from one another (e.g., Plains Cree are distinguished from Assiniboine or Saulteaux).[8] Cultural and social historical differences have been regularly emphasized despite the long-term practice of intermarriage between these groups. In addition, the history and culture of the Métis are presented as being significantly different from that of First Nations. Early twentieth century scholars, with a highly racialized view of the world, constructed the Métis and First Nations as culturally distinct.

Race as a conceptual category has been delineated by the work of nineteenth century social theorists.[9] These theorists sought to document the social evolution of human civilization, from savagery to barbarism to modern civilization. One preoccupation was to rank various human groups based on perceived racial characteristics. Within this framework, Europeans represented the height of human evolution, followed by Asians and then Africans. Indigenous peoples, when included, usually ranked at the bottom of the human evolutionary ladder (though occasionally placed above Africans).

As products of First Nation and European parents, the Métis and English Halfbreeds drew attention from ethnologists such as Henry Lewis Morgan, who were interested in the impact of racial intermarriage on the children. University of Toronto anthropologist Daniel Wilson believed that the mixed-blood offspring inherited the best racial qualities of both parents, which would help them find a significant place within an industrial society. Early to mid-twentieth century writers, such as Marcel Giraud, George F. G. Stanley, and W. L. Morton, believed the Métis "race" to be morally, physically, and intellectually deficient because they inherited not the best but the worst racial qualities of their parents, and would therefore be confined to lower strata of the social hierarchy.[10] The focus on racial characteristics not only justified the socio-economic position of the Métis but also perpetuated the notion that they were racially different from Europeans and First Nations.

More recently, scholars, having recognized that race as a "natural human division in human populations has been widely discredited by science,"[11] have focused their attention on Métis cultural expression rather than race as the source of difference. Nevertheless, race is still an implied factor in many scholars' discussion of, for example, the ethnogenesis of the Métis.

The result of this emphasis on the cultural differences between, say, the Plains Cree, Saulteaux, Assiniboine, and Métis is a lack of acknowledgement of the cultural similarities among these groups. This book will highlight their historical cultural similarities, arguing that such similarities were facilitated by the role that kinship played in the relationships between these groups, and that these similarities impact the way that contemporary Cowessess members interact with each other.

In order to demonstrate the lasting cultural notions of kinship, this book will examine the responses of Cowessess members to Bill C-31 and the Treaty Land Entitlement (TLE) agreement. Bill C-31 amended the Indian Act ostensibly to eliminate gender discrimination found within the legislation. From its inception in 1876 through to 1985, the Indian Act has defined Indian status as a legal category via the male line. It is important to remember that the legal status of "Indian" has not necessarily matched up with a person's "biological" status of relatedness to Native or non-Native families/communities; hence many of the difficulties with the term. Prior to the 1985 amendment, if a status Indian woman married a man who lacked status—i.e., non-status Indian, Métis, or non-Indian—she lost her status as an Indian and was no longer considered the responsibility of the federal government. Conversely, upon marrying a status Indian man, women who were initially not status Indians, Aboriginal or not, gained federal recognition as status Indians.

In 1985, the Canadian government, under pressure from Aboriginal women, their feminist allies, and the United Nations, passed Bill C-31, which amended the membership code of the Indian Act to allow First Nations women to regain federal recognition as status Indians.[12] These women's children were also eligible to gain status, although those children were not allowed to pass their status on to their own children. These "new" status Indians are popularly known as "C-31s." Women who gained status through intermarriage were not required to relinquish their status. Comeau and Santin note that "senior bureaucrats had given the politicians two scenarios of Bill C-31's impact: either a 10 percent or a 20 percent increase in registered Indian population."[13] The government chose the lower number when adjusting the Department of Indian Affairs' budget. The actual number who applied for reinstatement far exceeded the highest projected figure. This resulted in individual First Nations' budgets being stretched to the limits and beyond, and generating hostile feelings toward the C-31s among status Indians.[14] Nevertheless, the C-31s, as well as urban band members, played a significant role in a landmark land claims settlement reached between the Canadian government and twenty-five Saskatchewan First Nations in 1992.

In the early 1990s, the federal and Saskatchewan provincial governments and twenty-five Saskatchewan First Nations entered into Treaty Land Entitlement negotiations. The TLE was a process by which the federal government compensated individual First Nations for their land shortfall, which dated from the treaty-making era. At the time of treaty making, lands for each reserve were calculated based on an equation of 640 acres per family of five, or 128 acres per person.[15] However, the official government census of many bands did not accurately reflect population size, leaving many reserves with a shortfall in legally entitled land. Any TLE agreement required approval from fifty percent plus one of all band members in a referendum. By the 1990s, urban band members comprised nearly half of all status Indians in Saskatchewan, but for Cowessess First Nation the urban band membership was much higher—nearly 80 percent—with a significant number of these being C-31s. It was therefore incumbent on the TLE First Nations, especially Cowessess, to reach out to those urban and Bill C-31 members.

The number of researchers pursuing kinship studies of Native North Americans has declined greatly since the 1970s. Instead, researchers have focused on international Indigenous people and applied unique approaches to kinship studies. A brief review of the innovative approaches to kinship research of Indigenous people worldwide provides Native Studies scholars with exciting possibilities for undertaking similar research on Aboriginal people. These studies further point to a need to answer DeMallie's call for more kinship studies in a Native North American context. They also demonstrate that studies that attempt to explore to what degree cultural values that guided historical kinship practices persist into contemporary times are few.

One approach has been to examine the relationship between gender and kinship. Thomas Hakansson, for example, argued that, among the Gusiis and Luyia in Kenya, changes in the gender and family relationship are not only caused by political-economic factors but also depend on changes in women's relations with biological kin and on the role of marriage, which defines women's social identities.[16] Kevin Birth examined how ideas of kinship and race interact to create claims of similarities and differences within an eastern Trinidadian community with a high number of interracial marriages.[17] Cornelia Ann Kammerer analyzed the local construction of gender of the Akha in Burma to argue that an "asymmetric alliance is not only compatible with egalitarian organization but can also be constitutive of it."[18] Edward Lowe, in his study of the people of Chuuk Lagoon of the Federated States of Micronesia, argued that human beings share idealized models of attachment where specific kinds of kinship relations fulfill specific needs based on relational histories of reciprocity during various stages of a person's life.[19] These idealized models also form the continual construction and legitimization of kin relationships.

Other anthropologists have explored the link between economics and kinship. Soo Ho Choi demonstrated how rapid capitalist development in a South Korean village has impacted kinship relationship.[20] Doug Jones studied the link between group nepotism and human kinship, and argued that human groups have "psychological adaptations not only for individual nepotism but also for group nepotism—adaptations leading them to construct sodality groups enforcing an ethic of unidirectional altruism toward kin."[21] Diane Austin-Broos, in her study of the Arrente people of central Australia, linked issues of welfare and economics to kinship, arguing that the Arrente have "come to objectify kin relations more in terms of commodities and cash and less in detailed knowledge of country."[22] These distinctive ways of approaching kinship studies have been all but absent in studies of Native Americans.

Recent studies of Native American identity construction serve to demonstrate the importance of community self-identification.[23] These authors examined the persistence of distinct cultural identity within contemporary Native American communities. Fowler examined the impact on Gros Ventre and Assiniboine identity of sharing the same residence on the Fort Belknap reservation in Montana since 1888. Meanwhile, Harmon studied how the identities of Native Americans in the Puget Sound region of Washington State have been influenced by prolonged contact with non-Native Americans. Knack pointed out that anthropologists had incorrectly predicted an end to Southern Paiute identity and culture in the face of an expansion by a more aggressive, modern, and progressive American civilization. Berndt challenges the notion that the Fort Robinson Massacre of 1878 led to the creation of a reservation for the Northern Cheyenne and demonstrates that a complex set of interactions was at play and that the Northern Cheyenne were more active in the obtaining of their reservation. She argues, in fact, that their kinship practices were utilized as a "strategic political action in their negotiations with the United States government."[24] Yet, in all cases, Native Americans have maintained distinct identities from both non-Natives and other Native American neighbours. These studies suggest that ethnic identity is a fluid, not a static, process. A few scholars have examined Aboriginal kinship. Two notable studies completed recently were conducted by Nicole St-Onge, who explored marriage patterns between the Saulteaux and Métis, and Brenda Macdougall, who traced the genealogies of the Métis in northwestern Saskatchewan.[25] No Canadian studies have linked traditional kinship practices to the way in which contemporary people interact with each other. How members of Cowessess First Nation have constructed their identities over time, and the link between their contemporary identities and their notion of kinship, are of prime importance to this book.

In selecting participants, I relied heavily on individual band members to supply the names of people who might agree to participate. In many cases, band employees, such as Pat Criddle, executive secretary to the chief, and Dwayne Delorme, the Cowessess Urban Office manager in Regina, were helpful in locating participants. In total, I conducted twenty-two individual interviews and one group interview. The group interview consisted of seven elders who resided on Cowessess First Nation. Of the twenty-two individuals interviewed, half resided on the reserve, ten lived in Regina, and one lived in Saskatoon. I initially offered participants a $20 stipend for their involvement. In many cases, however, participants declined the offer, though some agreed to allow me to buy them a meal.

The interview schedule that I employed supplied the framework for the kind of information to be obtained. For the group interview, the first question on the interview schedule invited elders to introduce themselves and then talk about their thoughts about kinship. The initial idea for the introductions was that I believed that some band members, especially urban members, might not have known one another. This approach did not provide the expected result. The elders, all of whom lived on the reserve, of course knew one another quite well. They did not, however, know me. As a result, I was the one who had to introduce myself to them. They all wanted to know to which family I belonged.

In each interview setting, both group and individual, there was a diverse discourse style, which required me to be flexible in following the interview schedule. Some participants spoke in great detail, while others did not say as much. Some took their time in responding and provided lengthy answers, while others responded quickly with short answers. The onus was therefore on me to follow exactly what was being said and carefully allow discussion to flow without interjecting prepared questions that may not have corresponded with the discussion. This approach allowed participants to address those topics that they perceived as most important. As I have observed, many Aboriginal informants do not respond well to the standard question-and-answer interview: "Aboriginal respondents provide answers that are more like stories. These stories may contain the answers to numerous questions.... Native Studies methodologies require that the informant be allowed to speak in the manner to which s/he is accustomed, such as storytelling or conventional style. The less obtrusive the interview, the more the researcher gains information and respect from the informant."[26] Furthermore, when interviewing Aboriginal people, researchers should note that many might not be accustomed to the barrage of questions typical of an interview schedule. It becomes incumbent on the interviewer to be patient, to give them leeway to complete their answers, especially if the answers are in the form of a story (many elders prefer to tell their stories without interruption).[27]

Being a Cowessess band member did not mean I gained instant access to community members or some kind of insider privilege. In certain respects, I was very much an outsider, because I had not grown up on the reserve. Prior to the research, I did not know a great majority of the research participants, meeting many for the first time at the actual interview. In addition, being a researcher inherently situated me as an outsider. My outsider status was tempered, however, by the fact that I am a Cowessess member and a relative to some of the participants, even though I did not know these relatives before conducting the research. Additionally, and perhaps unlike other First Nations, being an urban member did not automatically confine me to outsider status, as 80 percent of Cowessess members live in urban areas. Indeed, more than 1,000 people out of a total band membership of just over 4,000 live in Regina, an hour-and-a-half journey west of the reserve. It is significant that while my insider status was somewhat tenuous, it was enough for the research participants to overlook the factors that made me an outsider. The significance lies in the fact that the basis of my research was to examine contemporary Cowessess members' inclusive kinship practices. Nonetheless,

Map 1. Western Canada. Cowessess First Nation is located in southeastern Saskatchewan.

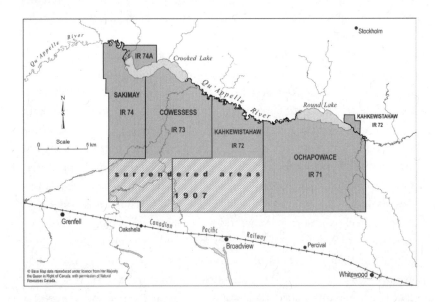

Map 2. Cowessess and its neighbouring First Nations, Sakimay, Kakewistahaw, and Ochapowace.

like many insider researchers, I still had to undergo a period of outsider/ insider reconciliation, during which I had to earn a certain level of trust and credibility with the participants.[28]

I made several trips to Cowessess in the course of this research and had many opportunities to talk informally with many band members. I was also fortunate to be a part of a residential school survivor program designed for people who had either attended residential school or had parents who had attended. The objective was to provide coping skills to combat the negative effects and address the intergenerational impacts of residential schools. I was hired to speak on the history of Saskatchewan First Nations, and spent my two weeks with the program getting to know the participants well. Many participants freely shared their experiences. I also attended a number of band functions, including an education meeting, a pow-wow, and elections. All these experiences allowed me to gain greater insight into many band members' understandings of family.

Undoubtedly, many of those who participated in the research, including the elders and members of the residential school program, would have participated even if I had been a complete outsider. However, the participants related to me as more than just a researcher, but as a Cowessess member and as a relative. Once satisfied with my insider status, the demeanor of many participants changed, and they became a little more willing to discuss issues that we had in common. It appeared that the participants' vested interest in the research increased when they talked with an insider researcher. This was underscored by a number of participants who mentioned to me in an inclusive manner the importance of writing "our" history about "our" people and "our" community, and by the fact that some participants, who were at first reluctant to participate, did so eventually after becoming aware of my insider status. My outsider status did not undermine my insider status. Given the composition of Cowessess, in some ways my outsiderness—being a Bill C-31 and urban member—was indicative of my insiderness. Thus, once I had negotiated my research relationship, it did not impinge greatly on my credibility and my ability to gain the trust of and access to the research participants.[29]

. . .

Cowessess First Nation is located in southeastern Saskatchewan on Crooked Lake in the Qu'Appelle Valley, neighbouring the Sakimay, Kahkewistehaw, and Ochapowace First Nations (see Maps 1 and 2). As of July 2013, Cowessess band membership was 4,019 persons, of whom 853 live on the reserve, 63 live on other reserves, and 3,103 live off reserve (see Table 1). This represents the third-largest of seventy-five First Nations in Saskatchewan, and the largest in southern Saskatchewan.

Table 1. *Population of Cowessess First Nation, July 2013*

Residency	# of People
Males on own reserve	440
Females on own reserve	413
Males on other reserve	32
Females on other reserve	31
Total on reserve	916
Males off reserve	1424
Females off reserve	1677
Males living elsewhere	0
Females living elsewhere	2
Total off reserve	3103
Total males	1896
Total females	2123
Total Population	4,019

Source: Department of Indian Affairs and Northern Development (http://pse5-esd5.ainc-inac.gc.ca/fnp/Main/Search/FNRegPopulation. aspx?BAND_NUMBER=361&lang=eng).

Approximately one thousand band members reside in Regina, Saskatchewan's capital, about one-and-a-half hours drive west of Cowessess; another estimated three hundred live in Saskatoon, a four-hour drive northwest of the reserve. Band members live throughout the province and in every province and territory in the country, particularly in major urban centres like Winnipeg, Calgary, Edmonton, Vancouver, Toronto, and Ottawa. Band members have also relocated to several foreign countries. Many of these off-reserve members were men and their wives and descendants, who first left the reserve in the 1950s. A significant number were also C-31s—that is, women who left the reserve to find employment and/or married non-status Indians and thus lost their status—who regained their status and had their children's status reinstated.

• • •

This book is organized into seven chapters. The first chapter outlines the roles and function of "trickster" stories. The chapter's first section discusses the way in which scholars have analyzed Trickster from the academic perspective. It also discusses scholars' disparate views of tricksters as a means of gaining insight into the significance of Elder Brother, a figure who is central to the Cree and Ojibwe/Saulteaux, and more specifically to Cowessess. The chapter's second section outlines the two main categories of traditional stories—*âtayôhkêwina* and *âcimowina*—that place Elder Brother stories in their cultural context. Elder Brother stories fit within these two categories, along with a multitude of other stories. These stories are not just ways Aboriginal people made sense of the world historically, but, as this section suggests, can be used to help understand contemporary Aboriginal people. After the more general discussions of the first two sections, the third focuses specifically on Elder Brother as the cultural hero of the Plains Cree and Saulteaux, highlighting how Elder Brother stories of both groups share similar structure, form, and purpose. The last section links Aboriginal legal traditions to Aboriginal stories in general, and assert that Elder Brother stories informed the legal tradition of Cowessess First Nation. It presents examples of Elder Brother stories collected by anthropologist Alanson Skinner in the early part of the twentieth century to demonstrate that they contain the Law of the People. The aim of this chapter, then, is to establish the central role stories played historically. This will provide the framework for the rest of the book, which in turn will show that the Law of the People has been kept alive by Cowessess people's social interactions.

Chapter 2 places the research into proper context by reviewing how researchers have discussed the emergence on the plains of the Plains Cree, Saulteaux, Assiniboine, and Métis, and provides a history of these four groups up to 1885. Scholarly research has focused on the differences between these groups; and to illustrate such differences, researchers have extrapolated examples of inter-band interaction and presented them as examples of inter-tribal relations. This perspective distorts the historic realities of Saskatchewan Aboriginal relations, as the similarities between these groups have not been

afforded proper recognition. The close social, economic, and political ties of
the Cree, Saulteaux, Assiniboine, and Métis led to a high degree of cultural
similarities between them.

Chapter 3 provides a critique of the use of the term "tribe" as put forth
by scholars as a means to categorize and discuss Aboriginal history in the
northern plains as tribal specific. Constructing tribal histories does not take
into account the role of bands as the primary political and social units, the
way northern plains people organized themselves historically, and the way
in which most contemporary Aboriginal groups are viewed. The chapter
also examines the ways in which scholars explain Métis as being culturally and racially distinct from First Nations groups so as to erase the actual
close relations that existed between the Métis and Plains Cree, Assiniboine,
and Saulteaux. These close relations help us to understand how it was that
pre-treaty First Nations bands also included a significant number of Metis
people. Therefore, this chapter demonstrates that the cultural boundaries
drawn between Aboriginal groups through the tribal history approach is a
fiction that has served scholars and government officials well, but has little
direct relevance to the actual lives of the people. This chapter provides the
context to explore the multicultural composition of Cowessess First Nation.

Chapter 4 provides a history of Cowessess First Nation from 1870 to
2000, illustrating the degree to which scholars have misinterpreted ethnic
identities of Saskatchewan Aboriginal people. This history demonstrates the
flexibility and inclusiveness of the Cree, Saulteaux, Assiniboine, and Métis
groups generally and Cowessess First Nation specifically. Band membership was based not so much along ethnic lines but on kinship relations, real
or fictive. After 1885, First Nations were faced with pressure to assimilate,
as the federal government implemented repressive policies with the aim of
eliminating First Nations' cultural practices. Though Cowessess members
resisted many demands to replace aspects of their traditional cultural ways
with Canadian cultural practices, in many ways they adapted relatively well
to the demands. One aspect of the band members' pre-reserve culture that
did not change, however, was the continued use of their traditional form of
kinship, which allowed the band to maintain its mixed ancestry composition
well into the twentieth century.

Chapter 5 discusses a number of themes identified from interviews of
Cowessess band members that outline the ways in which family obligations
have both changed and persisted. Factors that have led to changes include

the existence of social dysfunction on the reserve and economic opportunities offered in urban areas resulting in members leaving the reserve. In addition, many interviewees mentioned the impact that assimilation policies and contemporary circumstances have had on marriage practices, the maintenance of language, and traditional family roles and responsibilities. Even with these demands, Cowessess people have managed to preserve a strong belief in the importance of traditional family obligations. The formal and informal interviews, together with participant observation, provides a glimpse of how Cowessess people put into practice their belief in the importance of family. Central practices that act to maintain family connections as identified by Cowessess people include the ways that family responsibilities are carried out; the roles of elders as agents of socialization; how important links between the past, present, and future are sustained through family and community gatherings; how some members define family to act as a means of challenging imposed legal or racial classification of Indians; and the strategies adopted by members living in the urban context. This chapter illustrates, that even though kinship patterns have changed due to outside forces and contemporary realities, kinship continues to be an important mechanism that defines community and individual identity for many Cowessess First Nation members and acts to guide social interactions.

Chapter 6 explains the processes that led to the development of and reaction to the 1985 Bill C-31 amendment to the Indian Act. It outlines the imposition of external definitions of "Indian," by the Canadian government. The Canadian definition for "Indian" was established nationally through the Indian Act of 1876, but underwent numerous changes up until 1985. These definitions suited the purposes of the government while interfering with First Nations' cultural kinship practices. These definitions also influenced both how Canadians viewed people defined as Indians, and how First Nations people viewed themselves. In the 1970s and 1980s, a number of First Nations women who believed that the membership code of the Indian Act discriminated against them as women launched a court challenge that engendered a national debate among Aboriginal people. The debate, which was documented in newspaper articles and Senate Committee hearings, centered on notions of tradition, culture, self-government, and colonial oppression. These debates underscore the level of acceptance of the imposed definition of Indian by many First Nations leaders and people.

Chapter 7 situates the Treaty Land Entitlement negotiations within the larger discussion of the Aboriginal rights movement. First, a review of the important Supreme Court decisions in the Calder (1973), Guerin (1984), and Sparrow (1990) cases will be presented. These cases are significant, not only for their content but also for the impact they had on government-First Nations relations. The Supreme Court's decisions were major contributing factors that compelled governments to continue to negotiate TLE agreements with Saskatchewan First Nations. Next, an examination of the initial TLE negotiations between 1975 and the late 1980s shows how tensions between the federal and provincial governments were a major stumbling block to reaching an agreement. Finally, this chapter discusses Cowessess First Nation's TLE negotiations, which took place after the majority of Saskatchewan First Nations had signed their agreements with Canada. Cowessess was able to utilize arguments not used by the other First Nations and thereby eventually garner better terms. One significant difference of the Cowessess agreement was that its compensation was based on a negotiated figure of their original band list. The band also went to great lengths to provide assistance to any person who was eligible to be registered as a status Indian.

Elder Brother as Cultural Hero:
The Law of the People and Contemporary
Customary Kinship

At a 2011 conference, I was invited to sit on a panel with five senior scholars to discuss the Tri-Council ethics requirements to conduct research
with Indigenous communities. At one point, an Aboriginal scholar told a
traditional story to place the issue of research ethics within an Aboriginal
perspective. One particular scholar, who had serious concerns about the ethics
requirements—even though there was little evidence that she had conducted
any recent research in Indigenous communities—questioned the legitimacy
of traditional stories. She stated that there is no way to prove that the events
that were said to have taken place in any of the stories actually happened,
which meant that the stories do not actually contain knowledge. As she stated
before a shocked audience, "knowledge is only knowledge if it is right." For
this person, therefore, any scholarship that is based on traditional stories is
inherently faulty.

Of course, since she was more concerned with whether or not the events
in the stories actually occurred, she failed to consider the real importance of
the stories. There are stories about historical events, in which facts are carefully recounted to detail certain events and people accurately. Spiritually or
supernaturally based stories (or *âtayôhkêwina* and *âcimowina* in Cree), such
as the Elder Brother stories, express certain values central to the culture in a
way that differs considerably from historically based traditional stories. The
values embedded in these spiritual stories are more important than their
historical accuracy. By viewing all stories as historical accounts, rather than
acknowledging that there are categories of traditional Indigenous stories that

operate differently from one another, allows some scholars to dismiss them all as fabrications. Whether the events in the spiritually based stories actually took place is a matter of conjecture for some. What is certain, however, is that these stories did and continue to exist in oral and written form, and thus continue to guide Aboriginal peoples' interactions. In addition, the stories can assist scholars to understand these interactions and to demonstrate cultural persistence, revitalization, and resistance to colonization.

In recent years, Native Studies scholars have employed traditional stories as a means to help gain a better understanding of Aboriginal people's perspectives.[1] These scholars present compelling evidence of the central role of Aboriginal stories to Native Studies, outlining Aboriginal communities' various efforts to preserve their cultures and explaining how Aboriginal cultural values and principles inform Aboriginal peoples' actions. What becomes apparent from these authors is that, in order to come to grips with Aboriginal cultural understandings, it is crucial to become familiar with certain central Aboriginal cultural concepts. As most of these recent authors show, maintaining kinship roles and responsibilities is an important cultural concept for Aboriginal people.

This chapter explores the connection between Aboriginal peoples' beliefs, insights, concepts, ideals, values, attitudes, and codes found in traditional stories and expressed in their cultural kinship practices. The basis of this chapter is the notion that, historically, traditional stories, such as stories of Elder Brother, governed peoples' interactions. Understanding how stories functioned historically will help to elucidate how the stories continue to direct contemporary kinship among Cowessess people. The contention, here, is that the Elder Brother stories are the basis for the way in which contemporary people from Cowessess First Nation guide their kinship. Working toward this understanding begins with an examination of how stories worked in traditional societies.

Tricksters

The Trickster figure is familiar to readers of Native literature, but it should be understood to be more complex than the simplified and essentialized element to which it is commonly reduced in Native literary criticism. Tricksters have garnered much attention in scholarly work. In her article, "What's the Trouble with the Trickster?", Kristina Fagan points out that in the late 1980s and

1990s, trickster characters came into prominence in Native literature in North America through the work of writers such as Tomson Highway, Beth Brandt, and others.[2] For Fagan, the trouble with the trickster is not the way Aboriginal writers creatively include it in their works, but the way literary critics use the trickster as a means to further an agenda of highlighting Indigenous difference. According to Fagan, the literary critics view trickster characters in such a generalized manner that it ignores cultural and geographical specificity. "From this perspective," she states, "we can see that the pan-tribal trickster archetype offered a way to manage the issue of Indigenous 'difference' without requiring extensive research into the complexity of particular Indigenous peoples … stripped of the burden of belonging to any particular time or place, the trickster was then free to represent the critics' ideals."[3]

First, however, it must be acknowledged that the narrowness of the term "trickster" has been questioned. Neal McLeod, in particular, has taken exception to the term because it "suggests to some that this sacred being is a little more than a buffoon." He states that the "term 'trickster' is part of this same trickery, making Indigenous narratives conceptually empty and potentially devoid of truth."[4] Nonetheless, when a being burns its own buttocks as punishment for making too much farting noise, there is a certain level of buffoonery.[5] Such actions are meant to be funny and to contribute to the entertainment value of these stories. Also, in various Indigenous cultural stories, tricksters are able to persuade others to do things against their character or better judgment, with the result almost always benefitting only the tricksters. So, to the degree that tricksters perform a high rate of trickery, they are associated with the label "trickster." Beyond that, as McLeod correctly points out, the term "trickster" and its representations have been essentialized both by outsiders and by some insiders. Tricksters have been interpreted largely through a Western lens, with partial or no sensitivity to the possible meanings from Indigenous perspectives. Using the term "trickster" focuses on qualities like foolishness and self-serving deceit, but blurs the fact that these beings also have other characteristics. This is why many people also refer to them as Cultural Hero, Deceiver, Transformer, or other such terms. As a Cree person who studies Cree oral tradition, McLeod's solution is to use the Cree term *Wîsahkêcâhk* as a matter of Indigenous linguistic sovereignty, invoking the nuance of Cree semantics. In this first section, however, the academic treatment of tricksters is the focus—in particular the narrow and specific use of the term.

Paul Radin's 1956 book *The Trickster: A Study in American Mythology* is a seminal work on the topic.[6] Radin focuses on the Winnebago (Ho-Chunk) trickster figure, Wakdjunkaga, and provides a brief discussion on the trickster figures of the Assiniboine (Iktomi) and the Tlingit (Raven). Radin's description of tricksters has been widely accepted and cited by scholars.[7] According to Radin, the trickster figure in Aboriginal stories is full of contradictions: he creates but also destroys, gives but also steals, and tricks people to get what he wants, though in many cases his tricks backfire such that he often ends up with less than he started with. Radin continues, "He wills nothing consciously. At all times he is constrained to behave as he does from impulses over which he has no control. He knows neither good nor evil, yet he is responsible for both. He possesses no values, moral or social, is at the mercy of his passions and appetites, yet through his actions all values come into being."[8] In various Aboriginal myths, tricksters possess spiritual powers; they are responsible for creating or recreating the world or certain aspects of the physical environment; and they are almost always hungry, wandering, and oversexed.[9] A significant aspect of tricksters is humour, as Radin explains: "Laughter, humour and irony permeate everything Trickster does. The reaction of the audience in aboriginal societies to both him and his exploits is prevailingly one of laughter tempered by awe … it is difficult to say whether the audience is laughing at him, at the tricks he plays on others, or at the implications his behaviour and activities have for them."[10] Radin's work has had a lasting impact on trickster analysis.

Though Radin's descriptions of tricksters are echoed in other writers' descriptions, his observations hint that he may not fully comprehend Aboriginal world views. One reason that Radin and others have difficulty in grasping the essence of tricksters is due to the figures' multiple roles and characteristics. To the uninitiated, these roles could appear almost fragmented or opposing. For example, Mac Linscott Ricketts identifies three main qualities associated with tricksters:

> he is a trickster, a worldly being of uncertain origin who lives by his wits and is often injured or embarrassed by his foolish imitations and pranks, yet who never takes himself too seriously or admits defeats; b) he is a transformer, a being of myth times who goes about doing things that set the pattern and form of the world for all time, acting customarily without apparent plan

or forethought, and leaving the world as it is today, having thus prepared it for mankind, his "children"; and c) he is a culture hero, who, unassisted, risks his life and limb in daring entanglements with supernatural powers in order that the world may be a better place for those who are to come.[11]

Radin's Western interpretation of the Indigenous cultural icon is revealed in his discussion of whether the apparent contradictions found within tricksters relegate them to something less than divine. Radin states that, "in all these tribes we find the same break between Trickster conceived of as a divine being and as a buffoon."[12] How is it that tricksters could possess divine powers to create or recreate the world, change the physical appearance of a region's animals and geography, while at the same time possess the ability to act cruelly, selfishly, and buffoonishly? For Radin, the tricksters were not divine, though he points out that many cultural groups attempt to elevate their trickster figures to the level of deities. He asserts that these attempts fail in most cases, as the trickster is either defeated or displaced by a "real deity." In the end, he concludes that, "Tricksters' divinity is always secondary and that it is largely a construction of the priest-thinker, of a remodeler."[13]

Radin's inability to reconcile these qualities has led recent scholars to point out his Euro-centric perspective and academic objectives. For instance, Niigaanwewidam James Sinclair acknowledges that Radin's work "is an activist text, interested in presenting aspects of Native American cultures, histories, and 'authentic' versions of their myths to a broader, academic, mainstream audience and suggest their inclusion in a larger evolutionary chain of human development."[14] Sinclair places Radin's study in the historical context it was written in to demonstrate that it was heavily influenced by 1950s popular thinking about Aboriginal people. Sinclair notes that Radin accomplishes his goal in a way that reduces "Indian cultures and stories into a singular, monolithic version and explains them in such a way as to serve Amer-European needs and perspectives." Ballinger makes it more explicit, stating that, "Most [of what] Radin says is true enough, yet his point of view as a whole is askew because it is too governed by Euro-American categorization, too reliant on Western dualistic perception to present a really accurate image of American Indian tricksters."[15] So, while Ballinger states that Nanabush "created the world, to be sure, which makes him a higher being than humans, but he is still less than the *manitou* (the spirits that inhabit all living things). And so, it would appear he is a mediator between humans and the gods." She is able to move beyond Radin's either/or binary.[16] She points out that, "If we can conceive of divinity as a being or force of multifarious creative energy, perhaps many creative-transforming tricksters are as sacred as other more obvious gods of American Indians. Unfortunately, many in the dominant culture have not advanced beyond their misconceptions about American Indian 'idolatry' and 'pantheistic nature worship.' Our mistaken beliefs notwithstanding, tribal religions are anything but simple and primitive."[17] The perception of the simplicity of Trickster's stories leads many to brand them children's stories. As Basil Johnston states, "Primitive and pagan and illiterate to boot, 'Indians' could not possibly address or articulate abstract ideas or themes; neither their minds nor their languages could possibly express any idea more complex than taboos, superstitions, and bodily needs."[18] For Sinclair, the result is clear:

> [With Radin] we get a thoroughly selective analysis that privileges structuralist parts of trickster stories (orality, characterization, and humanism) over specific local, political, and historical contexts of the literatures ... it is blatantly obvious that these editorial choices register colonial interests in their discursive and political implications.... Radin streamlines these literatures into widely understood categorical themes and patterns—reflecting his interest in how they can prove all-encompassing relativistic theories. And, even though the stories do document some parts of his informants' epistemologies, experiences, and politics, Radin engages in the process of Native dispossession by denying aspects of their specific locations, histories, and subjectivities.[19]

The main point here is not simply to launch another attack on a non-Aboriginal anthropologist for failing to understand Aboriginal perspectives. After all, as Sinclair and Ballinger point out, Radin did make a number of correct observations. The main point is that to truly grasp Aboriginal perspective(s) of Trickster requires a deeper understanding of Aboriginal world view(s). This was Radin's shortcoming.

To begin to understand the world views that inform Aboriginal sacred stories, the levels of complexities of these stories need to be acknowledged. As Johnston points out, there are different levels at which one may understand stories. At one level, the trickster stories were a form of entertainment. However, as Ballinger points out, "even while they entertain, they instruct and act as societal control by dramatizing community values and behavioral limits."[20] This is the underlying role of all trickster stories in North America. Sean Teuton states, "Whether as Coyote, Rabbit, Raven, or Nanabozho, the trickster in the traditional tribal narrative, however, most often serves as a negative example to remind tribal people to regulate tribal values....That oral traditional trickster reminds us through his hasty and unself-aware behavior that we should reflect before diving in for our desires, for what we truly need might be right in front of us."[21] The trickster stories, then, provide guidance to the people. Ballinger identifies three foci of trickster stories that provide the framework within which the stories can accomplish their guiding task:

> 1. Enlargement of social boundaries in expanding the limits to what is possible and allowable, as well as defining (as in limiting) the boundaries of the acceptable.

> 2. Defying and confusing social rules and expectations, such as the rules of hospitality or socially determined expectations about activities like rituals.

> 3. Dramatization of the contradictions inherent in social life, as well as the internal clashes attending confrontation between instinct and reason, emotion and thought.[22]

Though most trickster stories adhere to Teuton and Ballinger's assertions that tricksters teach through negative examples, this is not always the case. Johnston, for example, discusses significant philosophical meanings embedded in the Nanabush stories that do not entirely conform to Teuton and Ballinger's view.[23] By demonstrating that the stories operate on three levels, Johnston states that the term *Anishinaabe* (his spelling is *Anishinaubae*) derives its meaning from two words: *onishishih*, which means good, fine, beautiful, and excellent, and *naubae*, which means man/human. He asserts that only by examining the stories of Nanabush does the meaning of the term *Anishinaubae* become clear. Since, as he states, "Nanabush was always full of good intentions," the people perceived themselves as people with good intentions. Therefore, "From this perception they drew a strong sense of pride as well as firm sense of place in the community. This influenced their notion of independence." As will be seen in the examples below, certain Elder Brother stories taught Cowessess people through positive examples. Even those stories with positive examples follow the criteria outlined by Ballinger.

In many of the stories, tricksters wander the earth in a sort of exile outside the social group as a consequence of their socially unacceptable transgressions, insatiable hunger, and/or sexual appetite. However, there is evidence to suggest that this interpretation is too narrow. For example, Johnston notes that one of the long journeys Nanabush took was to find his father and exact revenge.[24] In some recorded stories of Wîsahkêcâhk, his little brother turns into a wolf after they have become separated, and, though it is never stated explicitly, his subsequent journeys could be seen as Wîsahkêcâhk's attempt to find his younger brother.[25] Ballinger questions the idea that tricksters were simply "marauding outsiders" lingering on the social fringes of communities. She posits that from Aboriginal perspectives, "it may be that American Indian storytellers and audiences have traditionally perceived the trickster as an insider gone awry."[26] According to her, it is a mistake to consider the tricksters' journeys without also considering the implied social contexts in which they occur, for these circumstances are a significant part of "tricksters' didactic function … most of their shenanigans do indeed occur in one way or another within social boundaries." Ballinger further asserts that the tricksters "cannot escape the bounded community."[27] From this perspective, through their travels, tricksters not only demonstrate the social boundaries of their groups, but they do this from within the boundaries of their group's cultural knowledge. The cultural boundaries of the group, and therefore of the trickster stories, are framed from an understanding of the way in which kinship works.

Thus, in many ways kinship roles and responsibilities are at the heart of trickster stories. Not only do the tricksters' adventures and misadventures provide relational guidance for the way humans should interact with each other, the stories also outline how humans should relate to nonhumans, be they animals, land, or spirits. Therefore, in most stories, humans and nonhumans are referred to in kinship terms, using these terms whether or not they are related to the ones they are interacting with. As Ballinger notes, "because kinship implies obligations of support, tricksters often address others in kinship terms even when there is in fact no kinship, thereby hoping to benefit from the ostensible relationship."[28] Traditionally, listeners would have understood that the particular kinship terms used carried with them the associated familial expectations. There would have been an understanding, for most Indigenous groups, that cultural protocol required that a kinship relationship be established between strangers for any sort of social, economic, or political dealing to occur. In the stories, the tricksters use these expectations to place themselves in a supraordinate (calling someone my little sister/brother or nephew/niece), subordinate (calling someone mother/father, or grandfather/grandmother), or equal (calling someone sister/brother) position with the characters they are interacting with, depending on the context of the situation. Many times, the tricksters employ kinship terms as a means to place the other person at ease in order to obtain something through deception. At other times, however, the tricksters use these terms in positive, culturally appropriate ways. Examples of both uses of the kinship terms will be presented below.

The misconceptions found within trickster analysis prompted Deanna Reder and Linda M. Morra to publish a collection of essays, *Troubling Tricksters: Revisioning Critical Conversation.* Morra notes, in the preface, that images of tricksters have been appropriated in literary criticism and have become "emblematic of a postmodern consciousness rather than as part of specific Indigenous cultures, histories, storytelling; and since tricksters have often been used in the service of a predominantly white and colonial culture that characterized this figure as exotic, tricksters need to be relocated within specific Indigenous socio-historical contexts, and understood properly within those contexts."[29] Radin's and others' views of Trickster have, according to Sinclair, left a legacy of "trickster criticism," which perceives the stories as reflecting "archaic" and diminishing thought processes that teach Aboriginal peoples that their cultural expressions are "'fictions' and sole expressions of 'liminality,' and don't privilege deeply held concerns and interests in defining and locating specific subjectivities, politics, and histories."[30] Reder and Morra's book is significant for not only contributing to the necessary deconstruction of the trickster image in literary criticism, but also providing new, culturally specific examples of trickster criticism that have cultural authenticity, preservation, and revitalization at their core.

Âtayôhkêwina and *Âcimowina*

In Cree, the two main categories of stories are *âtayôhkêwina* and *âcimowina*. *Âtayôhkêwina* refers to the ancient stories, while *âcimowina* are the stories of more recent times. The stories have been understood by some scholars to progress in a somewhat linear fashion, from the very old stories to the more recent. As Brightman states in discussing the Rock Cree of northern Manitoba, "events in *âcaoohkiwina* are understood as temporally antecedent to those in *âcimowina* and comprise most of what is conventionally labeled as 'myth.'"[31] Linklater explains that, for the Nelson House Cree, the stories within *âtayôhkêwina* are further divided into four subcategories: the beginning of time (*Mimoci Kiyahs*), ancient time (*Mawac Kiyahs*), long ago (*Kiyahs*), and more recent time (*Anohciki*). She states that the "Cree notion of *kayahs*, a long time ago, is without calendrical years; it is a single time beyond living memory. It is a mythic time in which the creation story and subsequent history were acted on the landscape of north central Manitoba.... These stories are validated by our elders and they are witnessed on the land."[32] Linklater explains:

> It is said that in *Kiyahs*, that there were many beings that are different from today. The *Mimikwisihwahk* were the water people who could go through rock. Their house and canoe was located at *Wahskahihkahn awka Cimahn* and here they continue to reside. There was *Mihsihpihsew*, the water lynx and *Wasahkacahk*, the transformer. A conflict between these two beings resulted in a great flood over the land. Muskrat then brought *Wasahkacahk* a dab of dirt on his paw, and from this he recreated the earth and made it livable for Cree people. In gratitude, *Wasahkacahk* gave muskrat a special place to live, a river (*Wahcasko-sipih*) and a lake (*Wahcasko-sahkahikahn*). Muskrat's relatives continued to be found here in great numbers until inundation by Churchill River diversion. *Wasacahkacahk* then began his travels, changing the animals and the land into what they are today. In his journey, he was always hungry and continually tricked other animals into becoming his meal.... Most importantly, however, as *Wasacahka-cahk* continued his travels through the land, he left behind marks of his passing so future people would know of his presence ... at *Otitiskiwihnihk* he left his footprints in the cliff, giving rise to *Otitiskihwin-sahkahihkahnihk*, the Lake of the Footprints. It is on Footprint Lake that the Nelson House people have now chosen to reside."[33]

She adds, "That many of these sites continue to be remembered at all, in spite of their current situation beneath several feet of water, emphasized their importance to sense of place and sense of identity for the Nelson House people."[34]

However, there was overlap between the two categories of stories. Brightman, for example, states that *âcimowina* "focus on human characters, but this is not their defining feature since humans figure also in *âcaoohkiwina*."[35] That is, *âtayôhkêwina* and *âcimowina* are not completely distinct from one another, as they "are temporally situated in a kind of 'historical' time possessing continuity with the situation and narration." As Winona Wheeler points out, echoing Linklater, "*âtayôhkêwina* are sacred stories of the mystical past when the earth was shaped, animal peoples conversed, and Wisakejac transformed the world."[36] However, *âcimona* also include mythical elements.[37] Wheeler explains that, "*âcimowina* are stories of events that have come to pass since Wisakejac's corporeal beingness transformed into spirit presence, that there are many different kinds of overlapping and related *kayâs âcimowina*, stories about long ago, that are often infused with the sacred."[38] Brightman says that *âcimowina* stories can relate true events that can be old or contemporary, funny or serious, but also notes that they may not all be factual and could contain supernatural characters. According to Brightman, *kayâs âcimowina* "refers to stories which are temporally remote from the situation of narration."[39] Therefore, *âtayôhkêwina* has influenced the way in which *âcimowina* can be told, because it allows for the inclusion of spiritual components into stories of relatively recent times.

Âtayôhkêwina contains many characters known as *âtahôhkanak*, the mythical beings that helped shaped the earth and its people. Neal McLeod explains that, "*âtayôhkanak*, which means 'spiritual helpers,' spiritual grandfathers and grandmothers [*Âtayôhkêwina*] are essential because they give insight into the way in which Cree people related to their ecology and the environment, and with other beings."[40] According to elder Stan Cuthand, *âtahôhkanak* include Pine Root and Beaded Head, who "were the original beings of the earth" who changed themselves into various entities such as the stars, plants, and animals. Also, there were the gentle and comical little people, *mêmêkwêsiwak*, that occupied "coulees and river banks in the prairies they are harmless little people and friendly to humans but they can play tricks on some people who are non-believers."[41] Other important *âtahôhkanak* include beings such as the Thunderbird, the Great Serpent/Lynx, which caused the great flood; the Wîhtikôw, a cannibal that preys on human flesh; and the *Pâhahk*, "the skeleton being that reinforces the value of sharing of food and material goods."[42] According to Nathan Carlson's oral historical research of Cree and Métis in northern Alberta, Wîhtikôw is one character that has crossed the boundary from *âtayôhkêwina* to *kiyâs âcimowina*.[43] This opens the possibility of thinking about other *âtahôhkanak*, such as Elder Brother, who may also have made that journey. For example, McLeod notes that,

> The narratives of *wîsahkêcâhk* should be seen as part of the *genre* of sacred stories, *âtayôhkêwina*. The term *âtayôhkêwina* denotes stories of *wîsahkêcâhk* (and, indeed, other beings). When we shift the paradigm to think of *âtayôhkêwina* as "spiritual narratives," we can see them as core to Cree culture and beliefs. They are key to the construction of what is meant by Cree narrative memory, and also Cree narrative imagination, which is essentially the process of expanding our narrative memory in light of new experiences. These narratives re-imagine the landscape of Cree territory, noting the place names of *wîsahkêcâhk*'s travels. The narratives also point to relationships between humans and other beings, and to the possibility of radically re-imagining constructed social spaces.[44]

McLeod's notion of Cree narrative memory can be of assistance in applying concepts found within *âtayôhkêwina*, and indeed *âcimowina*, to a contemporary context.

Elder Brother as Cultural Hero

As the most important character in Cree/Ojibwe stories, Elder Brother is more than just a trickster; he is really the Cree/Ojibwe cultural hero. Though some Cree and Ojibwe traditional stories have some significant differences, they are very similar in structure, form, and purpose. For example, Cree and Ojibwe share many of the same mythical beings. The Ojibwe mythical beings are known as *atiso'kanak* (variously spelled) as opposed to the Cree *âtahôhkanak*. According to A. Irving Hallowell, *atiso'kanak* "refers to what we would call the characters in these stories; to the Ojibwa, they are living persons of an other-than-human class.... A synonym for this class of persons is 'our grandfathers.'"[45] Many of the *âtahôhkanak* found in Cree stories, like the Thunderbird, the great Lynx, and others, are also Ojibwe *atiso'kanak*. The stories of the spirit beings have a direct relationship to how Ojibwe and Cree society operate as they serve to reinforce socially beneficial behaviour. Theresa S. Smith provides examples from a series of Thunderbird stories to illustrate the importance *atiso'kanak* played in Ojibwe society. In these stories we learn, among other things, that the Thunderbirds live in communal groups with a heavy emphasis on sharing; and that the young Thunderbirds, due to their immaturity and their inexperience with lightning strikes, cause havoc to the environment and to humans. We also learn that it is the responsibility of the older Thunderbirds to teach the young how to act properly, but that they need to exercise patience, as the young are reluctant to listen to their elders.[46] Whether Ojibwe *atiso'kanak* or Cree *âtahôhkanak*, the stories of these spirit beings were central to their societies. As Wheeler states, "*Âtayôhkewina* are the foundations of Cree spirituality/religion, philosophy, and world view, and contain the laws given to the people to live by."[47] The same is true for the Ojibwe.

The similarities between Ojibwe and Cree stories are relevant to the Cowessess situation, as the principles found in both people's stories are evident in *âtayôhkêwina* collected by Alanson Skinner when he visited Cowessess in the early twentieth century. This is not surprising for a number of reasons, which will be expanded upon later in this and upcoming chapters. Suffice it to say for now that the cultural similarities and the social, economic, and political relationships between the Saulteaux (Plains Ojibwe) and Plains Cree are evident on Cowessess and continue to impact contemporary members as the composition of Cowessess is comprised of both of these groups (together with some from other cultural groups, significantly the Assiniboine and Métis). Understanding how the *âtayôhkêwina* work not only gives us insight into how Cree and Ojibwe societies operate, but can also provide us with a theoretical framework through which to approach contemporary Aboriginal kinship in general and Cowessess kinship in particular. This is exactly what Neal McLeod advocates, as he states, "the use of *âtayôhkêwina*—sacred stories or spiritual history, as one elder has described it—is one source of conceiving of a Cree critical theory; a narrative embodiment that creatively reflects on the situation and the world in which we find ourselves."[48] Given the culturally mixed composition of Cowessess, McLeod's idea of a Cree critical theory may not quite apply seamlessly in this study. Nonetheless, the notion of utilizing the values and principles embedded in the ancient stories of Elder Brother to assist in explaining contemporary peoples is appealing. A central being within *âtayôhkêwina* is Elder Brother, who has been identified as belonging to what many scholars call the trickster category, but he is probably more accurately described as a cultural hero.

According to Brightman, Wîsahkêcâhk was the cultural hero for Cree people from Ontario westward, while Nanabush (variously spelled) was the cultural hero of the Ojibwe. He notes that although these two characters are different in many ways, there are some important similarities. For example,

Smith notes that, like the Cree, at least some Ojibwe refer to Nanabush by the kinship term "Elder Brother."[49] More interesting is the fact that "many attributes of the characters are similar and many stories are common to both" the Cree and Ojibwe.[50] In fact, in Brightman's search of the historical record, he found the first reference to Wîsahkêcâhk was attributed to the Ojibwe and Odawa of the Mackinac region in 1669, in which a fur trader recorded the worded "Ouisaketchak" as referring to "the great hare." Many commonly refer to Nanabush as the Great Hare.[51] According to Brightman, numerous fur traders and anthropologists have noted that some Ojibwe used the term Wîsahkêcâhk instead of Nanabush, and that some Cree and Ojibwe used the term interchangeably. For example, Edward Ahenakew relates a Plains Cree story of "Wesakaychak and the 'Startlers,'" which seems to correspond to these observations:

> As he went along he came upon a nest of young prairie chickens. "Little prairie chickens," asked he, "pray, what is your name?" "That is our name you call us by," they replied. "Everything that breathes has two names," said Wesakaychak. "I myself have three: Wesakaychak, Nanaposo, and Mutchekewis. Do not tell me you have only one name." "Well, then," replied the little birds, "we are sometimes called startlers."[52]

That Elder Brother is known by more than one name could help to explain why some people in the past had multiple names and why the use of nick-names in contemporary times is common.

In some cases, Wîsahkêcâhk and Nanabush are differentiated, and appear in stories of each group as secondary characters. There is evidence that the two heroes are not the same. As Brightman notes, "Despite derivation from a shared Algonquian literary stratum and evident reciprocal borrowing of plot and motif, the Wisahkicâhk and Nênapos cycles are distinguished by many features including details of the transformer's parentage and the incorporation of Midewiwin origin stories in the Ojibwa cycle."[53] In the end, Brightman asserts that the similarity between the Cree and Ojibwe cultural hero relates to the proximity of the two groups prior to contact with Europeans. Ojibwe/Saulteaux, who resided in the northern boreal region prior to contact, have no cultural influence with the Cree, while those Ojibwe/Saulteaux who moved into the region after the contact period were impacted by Cree cultural influences.[54]

Elder Brother Stories as Law of the People

The legal systems of pre-contact Aboriginal peoples, as James Zion points out, "were based upon the idea of maintaining harmony in the family, the camp, and the community."[55] The failure to follow prescribed regulations could, according to what happens to Elder Brother in the stories, result in severe negative consequences. Conversely, adhering to the positive behaviour that Elder Brother displays was seen as the ideal that all should strive to attain. An understanding of the stories facilitates an understanding of the incorporation of members into the Cowessess band in the pre- and post-reserve periods, a process that will be explained in later chapters. The stories are also helpful in gaining insight into contemporary peoples' ability to maintain certain aspects of their kinship roles and responsibilities.

Traditionally, stories acted to impart the philosophical ideals upon which Aboriginal societies should function. As Robert Williams Jr. notes, "The stories socialized children and reminded adults of their roles and place within the universe…. Indians have long practiced the belief that stories have the power to sustain the many important connections of tribal life."[56] The telling of stories, such as those of Elder Brother, was a means by which to convey Aboriginal philosophical meanings to the people. As has been noted, he can be generous and kind, yet also selfish and cruel. In the stories, when he is kind, he usually meets with success; when he is cruel, he often meets a disastrous and sometimes humorous end. His adventures and misadventures acted to guide the peoples' social interactions, and because of this, he is highly regarded. As Basil Johnston states about the esteem the Ojibwe have for Nanabush, "For his attributes, strong and weak, the Anishnabeg came to love and understand Nanabush. They saw in him themselves. In his conduct were reflected the characters of men and women, young and old. From Nanabush, although he was a paradox, physical and spirit being, doing good and unable to attain it, the Anishnabeg learned."[57] As Sinclair states,

> Now, as before, stories reflect the experiences, thoughts, and knowledge important to Anishinaabeg, and collectively map the creative and critical relationships, and philosophies and histories of kin. Among other reasons, stories create, define, and maintain our relations with each other and the world around us, and when shared, cause us to reflect, to learn, to grow, as families, communities, and a People. Stories also indicate where we are in the

universe, how we got here/there, and often indicate where we
need to go.... Anishinaabeg storytelling, therefore, is not a simple
one-dimensional act but a complex historical, social, and political
process embedded in the continuance of our collective presence,
knowledge, and peoplehood.[58]

Elder Brother stories conveyed Cowessess traditional law to the people;
and thus functioned as a legal institution. While this institution was unlike
those in other parts of the world, it functioned in the same way. As Zion and
Robert Yazzie explain, "When a legal institution articulates a norm or vali-
dates a custom, that is 'law.'"[59] The Elder Brother stories explained the rules
and expectations for normative behaviour. These ideals were enshrined in the
peoples' notion of themselves, with each retelling of Elder Brother stories and
with each act that could be attributed to these stories.

A number of legal scholars have linked traditional narratives of Aboriginal
peoples, whether stories, songs, or prayers, to their traditional legal systems.[60]
For example, Williams points out that, "stories are told in tribal life to edu-
cate and direct young ones, to maintain the cohesiveness of the group, and
to pass on traditional knowledge about the Creator, the seasons, the earth,
plants, life, death, and every other subject that is important to the perpetua-
tion of the tribe."[61] John Borrows states that the traditional tribal customary
principles "are enunciated in the rich stories, ceremonies, and traditions
within First Nations. Stories express the law in Aboriginal communities,
since they represent the accumulated wisdom and experience of First Nations
conflict resolution."[62] Donald Auger asserts that, "the knowledge gained by
individuals from story-telling was that of relationships and the importance
of maintaining balance and harmony."[63] Stories act to connect our "normative system to our social constructions of reality and to our vision of what the
world might be."[64] Robert Cover explains further the connection between
narratives and law: "No set of legal institutions or prescriptions exists apart
from the narratives that locate it and give it meaning. For every constitution
there is an epic, for each Decalogue a scripture. Once understood in the context of the narratives that give it meaning, law becomes not merely a system
of rules to be observed, but a world in which we live ... in this normative
world, law and narrative are inseparably related ... every narrative is insistent
in its demand for its prescriptive point, its moral."[65] The Elder Brother stories
reflect the moral normative behaviours that Cowessess band members were

expected to follow. Through these stories, as Johnston notes, "their sense of justice and fairness" were prompted.[66]

In 1913, anthropologist Alanson Skinner collected Elder Brother stories from a number of Cowessess elders that set the parameters by which Cowessess people were expected to act. The following is a condensed excerpt from a story of Elder Brother and a group of wolves. In the story, Elder Brother is adopted by the wolves and then assumes the accepted kinship roles and responsibilities:

> One night some wolves heard Elder Brother singing. The oldest says "I believe that is my eldest brother. He has a good song … watch for him, and run and say to him, 'My uncle, what are you saying?'" When the wolves met up with Elder Brother, they told him that their father wanted to meet him. The father asked his elder brother what his song meant. Elder Brother told him and then decided that he would stay with the wolves for a while. Some time later, Elder Brother decided he wanted to leave, but he wanted one of his nephews to go with him. The old wolf allowed his youngest son to leave.
>
> After a dream, Elder Brother addressed the young wolf, "My nephew, never go along the lake-shore. Do not run on the beach." Later, the young wolf was thirsty. Forgetting Elder Brother's instructions, he went to the lake and drank some water. He suddenly became crazy. Elder Brother realized his nephew had gone missing and knew that the White-Lynx had taken him. He tracked White-Lynx and, listening to the Sun, shot at his shadow. He was successful on the attempt, but he did not kill him. The White one, though injured, escaped. Elder Brother met up with old toad, who was on her way with her medicines to heal White-Lynx. Elder Brother killed and skinned her and put on her skin. He went to White-Lynx, now as the old toad. When he arrived, the people said, "Oh, our old grandma is coming again." As the toad, Elder Brother entered the White-Lynx's lodge. Upon entering, he saw the skin of his nephew hanging on a pole. He then saw White-Lynx with an arrow in his side. He had a pipe filled and then asked everyone to leave. "Now, shut the door. I shall smoke and take out the arrow now, but don't let any one look in." When

this was done, Elder Brother walked up to White-Lynx and grabbed the arrow in his hand and pushed it into the Lynx's heart as hard as he could. He then grabbed his nephew's skin and fled, tearing off the toad skin. Once Elder Brother had ensured that he had lost his pursuers, he brought him back to life.[67]

The story outlines a number of prescribed behaviours required in the maintenance of respectful kinship relations with Cowessess people. It shows Elder Brother demonstrating positive qualities to which people should aspire. The story highlights the value of inclusion by certain facts: although Elder Brother was not related to the wolves, he was adopted into the pack and considered a relative; the younger wolves were expected to address and treat him as an older relative; and he assumed the roles and responsibilities expected of a relative. In the same way he was adopted by the wolves, Elder Brother is permitted to adopt a younger wolf that Elder Brother calls nephew. However, it is when Elder Brother and the young wolf were on their travels that the kinship roles and responsibilities become more explicit. Elder Brother is responsible for the well-being of the young wolf. When the young wolf goes to the water against the instructions of Elder Brother, the listeners learn that there are negative consequences for not heeding the words of elders. In searching for and rescuing his nephew, Elder Brother fulfilled his responsibility, not only to the young wolf but also to his other relative, the old wolf. By entering the White-Lynx's village, Elder Brother exhibits characteristics like bravery, daring, and ingenuity, which are important for young males to internalize. These qualities were central tenets of the warrior societies, whose primary duty was to protect and provide for the people. In this story, Elder Brother exhibits positive characteristics with a positive outcome.

In the following story, Elder Brother's sexual appetite and deception are the central components:

> Elder Brother travelled on. He came to a tent filled with women, and cried, "I have news, people are dying!" One of the women begged to know what she could do to escape death. Elder Brother told her to accept him as her lover. He had children by all of them, and went on, leaving a son and a daughter. He told the women, "I shall become sick and die. Marry our daughter to the first person who comes along. Bury me anywhere, break camp, and when you come back you will only find my bones." But he deceived them

and only went into hiding. The people came back, and found bones, but he was alive. After a while a stranger came to camp; and the mother, remembering her husband's command, gave him her daughter. It was Elder Brother who married his own daughter. He went off to hunt with his own son, calling him brother-in-law. His wife, when hunting lice on his head, saw a mark by which she recognized her own father. Then he was driven away. He went south, where he heard children laughing, and asked, "What is the news that amuses you?" "Oh, haven't you heard? Elder Brother married his own daughter." So he went on south, where he is still living.[68]

This story shows how Elder Brother's negative behaviour also reinforces societal norms and expectations. The story implies that Elder Brother may have understood that incest was not tolerated; certainly the teller and listeners would have known. He may not have control over his impulses, but he does seem to be conscious of his actions. He exerts much effort in devising and executing his plan to take his daughter as his lover. Would he have gone to such lengths had he not thought it was wrong to take his daughter as his wife? Deception, as evidenced in the previous story, is not always seen as a negative attribute. Here, however, his deception combined with his self-centredness, and his overindulgence for his own gratification is clearly viewed negatively. Not only is incest considered an extreme violation of social norms, but so, too, is putting your own needs ahead of the group's. His punishment for failing to abide by the Law of the People is ridicule and banishment from the social group. From these and other Elder Brother stories, the kinship obligations for Cowessess people were made clear. The people understood that, for the society to be self-perpetuating and for the people to attain a good life, it was incumbent upon members to adhere to the principles of Elder Brother stories.

In the story above, whether Elder Brother actually married his daughter is not as important as the repercussions he faced for doing so. In plains cultures, strict laws were in place that restricted the interaction between male and female relatives, especially between son-in-law and mother-in-law, and between siblings.[69] These laws were in place to ensure sexual relationships did not occur, acts that would have been considered incest. Though Mandelbaum is silent on the issue of parent-child incest, the Elder Brother stories are not. The cultural value is clear; incest was not tolerated. Fathers who committed incest faced banishment and ridicule. In a society that depended on the group for individual survival, banishment was akin to a death sentence. Ridicule of the perpetrator after he was banished helped to ensure that others in the band understood the seriousness of the crime and thus acted as a deterrent and a reminder of the fate of those who commit an act considered to be an atrocity. The above story helps to explain, in part, the strong aversion of many Cowessess people to sexual relations between relatives.

Traditional stories help us understand how Aboriginal people view and practice their kinship relations, and this is perceived by many as being what differentiates them from mainstream Canadians. It is of little wonder, then, that DeMallie has implored Native Studies scholars to be creative in their approach to recognize and gain a better understanding of the importance of Native kinship patterns. Kinship patterns do not exist in a vacuum; they interact with the social environment that surrounds the people who exercise them. Like other cultural aspects of the band, kinship practices on Cowessess have changed considerably since members first settled on the reserve. Some of these changes were forcibly imposed on them, while others were adapted by members to meet the challenges of a new era. What may be surprising to many is the degree to which contemporary kinship practices—whether customary or new adaptations—still observe the principles found within the Law of the People.

Elder Brother stories help to explain traditional kinship practices of the pre-reserve and early reserve periods, when Cowessess people easily incorporated others into their band, including the adoption of white children. The Canadian government's assimilation policies, however, sought to undermine the Law of the People, including regulations guiding kinship practices. These attempts were in many respects successful. Yet, for many Cowessess people, the notions of kinship as epitomized in Elder Brother's behaviour continue to obtain, demonstrating that the ideals of the traditional Law of the People remain implicitly central principles guiding band members' social interactions. The extent to which current Cowessess band members tell Elder Brother stories or even know about them is not certain. What is apparent, however, is that the values encoded in these stories have persisted from the pre-reserve and early reserve periods to the present. Unfortunately, scholars have not taken Elder Brother stories into account when describing historic northern plains Aboriginal societies.

2

A Historical View of the Iron Alliance

Cowessess First Nation's history is interwoven with the creation of an economic, social, and military alliance among the Plains Cree, Assiniboine, Saulteaux, and Métis peoples outlined in the Elder Brother stories. These four peoples entered into various alignments with each other, the Blackfoot Confederacy, Gros Ventre, Shoshone, Mandan, Hidatsa, and other plains peoples, as well as English and French fur traders. Studies by historians and anthropologists, however, have not emphasized these interconnected relationships. Few have explored the basis of these relationships in any great detail. Authors have noted their social, economic, and political motivations, but not the cultural values that guided and regulated these relationships. Instead, scholarship has been preoccupied with linking band societies within larger tribal contexts. This perspective of Saskatchewan Aboriginal prairie peoples' history has confused and distorted contemporary realities of Saskatchewan Aboriginal relations. Though these groups' cultures, beliefs, histories, and languages were different from one another, they also shared considerable similarities and overlap. In later chapters, I will outline the cultural similarities between these groups in contrast to dominant views. To provide the context for my contention that the social, political, economic, and especially cultural similarities of these groups have been ignored or downplayed by most scholars, this chapter demonstrates the ways in which historians, anthropologists, and archaeologists have portrayed Aboriginal people in southern Saskatchewan. It is important to conduct such a review, since members of these groups were a part of the pre-reserve Cowessess band.

This chapter is divided into three sections. The first, divided into four subsections, examines the historical, anthropological, and archaeological treatment of the emergences of Aboriginal people in southern Saskatchewan. The second section explores the political, military, and economic alliances among bands in order to highlight the interconnectedness of Plains Cree, Assiniboine, Métis, and Saulteaux. The final section discusses the importance of kinship during the treaty and post-treaty negotiation periods. The purpose of the chapter is to outline the scholarly literature on plains groups to highlight the shortcomings of the distinctly tribal historical perspective. A critique of this perspective will be expounded upon in the following chapter. In addition, a review of the tribal history of southern Saskatchewan Aboriginal groups provides the historical backdrop to help understand contemporary Cowessess people.

Emergence of the Iron Alliance

Western Expansion, the Fur Trade, and the Plains Cree

From the early 1800s, it was accepted that the Plains Cree and the Assiniboine migrated to the northern plains of Saskatchewan after European contact. It has been argued that their westward movement was motivated by their participation in the fur trade, which provided them access to guns and led to the over-trapping of beaver and over-hunting of game in their northern Ontario homeland.[1] With some notable exceptions, historians and anthropologists supported this post-contact migration theory well into the 1990s. Beginning in the 1980s, however, archaeological studies had provided a more complex understanding of Plains Cree and Assiniboine history that countered the accepted historical and anthropological view.

Scholars have relied heavily on Sir Alexander Mackenzie's accounts to solidify their views of a post-contact Plains Cree migration westward. Mackenzie, a fur trader/explorer with the Northwest Company, who in 1793 became the first European to reach the Pacific by way of an inland route, was the first to present the notion of a westward Cree migration linked to the fur trade. The journals of his travels through Cree and Dene territories, published in London in 1801 and Philadelphia the following year, were widely read and influential. Mackenzie is regularly cited in historians' assertion of the invasion of the Cree: "When this country was formerly invaded by the Knisteneaux [Cree] they found Beaver Indians [Dene-tha] inhabiting the land about Portage la Loche; and the adjoining tribes were those they called slaves. They drove both these tribes before them."[2] As the only written account of the subarctic environment, Mackenzie's journal was regarded as authoritative. All subsequent explorers—Sir John Franklin (1819–1822), Richard King and Sir George Black (1825–1827), Sir John Richardson (1848), and particularly explorers of the Canadian prairies, such as Captain John Palliser, (1857–1860), Henry Youle Hind (1857–1858), and Sir William Samuel Butler (1870)—concurred with Mackenzie's view of Cree migration. By the end of the nineteenth century, Mackenzie's interpretation was entrenched as fact.[3]

Early twentieth century historians and anthropologists continued to employ this post-contact theory, emphasizing Cree and other groups' tribal boundaries while downplaying their intimate relations.[4] While a doctoral student at the University of Chicago, David Mandelbaum made two visits to Saskatchewan in 1934 and 1935, and conducted the most in-depth ethnological study of the Plains Cree, which he published in the United States in 1940. Mandelbaum noted four distinct periods to Plains Cree migration. In the first period, 1640–1690, the Cree lived in the eastern woodlands of northern Ontario and Quebec, where they experienced their first contact with European fur traders. In the second phase, 1690–1774, the Cree became dependent on European goods after the English established trading posts in Cree territory along the shore of Hudson's Bay. Due to a depletion of natural resources, the Cree took on a middleman role in the fur trade, and, armed with guns, began to move west. During the third period, 1740–1820, many Cree bands moved onto the prairies, but did not completely sever their ties to the woodlands and their middleman role in the beaver fur trade. In the last period, 1820–1880, the Cree adopted new cultural forms and established themselves as "a true Plains tribe," engaging in continuous plains-style warfare.[5] According to Mandelbaum, then, Cree dependency on the fur trade motivated their westward expansion, and access to guns facilitated their acquisition of new lands in southern Saskatchewan and central Alberta, as they forced the Blackfoot and Gros Ventre west and south, respectively.

The 1970s ushered in a new era of fur trade history, as historians began to examine the central role that First Nations people had played in the trade.[6] Historians still maintained, however, that the Cree migrated west due to the impact of the fur trade. For example, Bishop stated that "the expansion of the French traders north and west of Lake Superior during the eighteenth century marked the beginning of major population shifts westward, involving the Cree, Ojibwa and other Algonquians."[7] In addition, like earlier historians, these scholars recognized the close relations of the Cree and Assiniboine, but nevertheless insisted on portraying these two groups as distinctly bound tribal entities, even though some acknowledged the existence, role, and importance of intermarriage.

Simultaneously, some scholars began to challenge the migration theory. According to Gillespie, Smith, and Russell, the "root" of the Cree migration theory is a misinterpretation of Mackenzie's journal by other fur traders/explorers, and, later, by scholars.[8] Gillespie noted that Mackenzie's statements about the Cree migration were vague, containing inaccurate and ambiguous information, which therefore "demand[s] cautious evaluation."[9] Although historical evidence shows that the Swampy Cree moved westward due to the fur trade, James E. G. Smith argued that "they cannot alone be responsible for the population of all western regions within such a remarkably brief period."[10] Russell provided the first major critique of Mandelbaum's—and therefore Mackenzie's—historical account of the Plains Cree. According to Russell, the notion that the Cree migrated west after European contact, as Mandelbaum suggests, "is plausible and attractive; [Mandelbaum] is able both to describe and explains the movement of the Cree ... [however] he omits, passes over, or misinterprets the evidence."[11] Russell contends that the "underlying problem with Mandelbaum's history of the Cree and their neighbours is not the insufficient information but that he interpreted the material within a body of preconceptions."[12] These preconceptions were in part derived from a reading of Sir Alexander Mackenzie.

The point to be taken is that the western limits of the Cree at contact cannot be ascertained from the historical records. Granted, Russell and Smith did not argue that there was no movement. Smith, for example, maintained that the Swampy Cree migrated west after European contact. However, he asserted that other Cree groups "had been long present in the west: it is merely the name Cree that was at this time extended westward to apply to these divisions, previously known by such generic terms such as Southern or Upland Indians."[13] The implication is that the Cree did not move west due to the emergence of the fur trade. Smith's contention, as will be discussed later, has been supported by archaeological research.

Origins of the Assiniboine

The ethnographic literature concerning the Assiniboine has been relatively sparse in comparison to that dealing with the Cree and other northern plains groups.[14] To date, no one has completed a thorough examination of the Assiniboine ethnohistory. However, a number of scholars have included the Assiniboine as a part of their larger individual studies: Arthur Ray's 1998 fur trade study provided probably the most extensive summary of early Assiniboine history; David Miller's 1987 dissertation included a significant literature review of the Assiniboine; Russell had an important chapter in his 1991 book dealing with criticism of early Assiniboine history; and DeMallie and Miller included a short discussion of the pre- and early historic periods in the 2001 *Handbook of Indians of North America*.[15] Most scholars who have studied the peoples of the northern plains have included Assiniboine history in their works.[16] As Russell stated on the lack of ethnohistorical research on the Assiniboine, it "is puzzling that the Assiniboine, despite being the most numerous group on the northeastern plains and parklands in the eighteenth century, have been so greatly ignored."[17]

Scholars have generally agreed that the Assiniboine were originally a part of the Yanktonai Sioux, but broke away at some point and later established close relations with the Cree. There is much speculation about when exactly the Assiniboine separated from the Yanktonai, with estimates ranging from prior to 1640 to as late as the 1750s.[18] Nevertheless, there has been agreement that after the Assiniboine separated from the Yanktonai, they were closely associated with the Cree.[19] The reason given for this association is the assaults that the Assiniboine suffered after the Cree obtained arms from the British through the Hudson's Bay Company. The Cree intensified their attacks on the Sioux, including the Assiniboine groups. The Assiniboine, who were located between the main Sioux group and the Cree, were exposed to a higher level of attacks. The theory is that the Assiniboine population was much smaller than the Cree, and therefore made peace with the Cree through intermarriage, though few have dealt with the social and cultural impact of these intermarriages. The contention that the Assiniboine were a smaller group contradicts Russell's claim that they were the most numerous group in the region. Nonetheless, the Assiniboine/Cree alliance is believed to have occurred between 1670 and 1690 as a result of the fur trade. The consequences of this alliance for the Assiniboine were that it provided access to British goods and obliged them to join the Cree in attacks against the Sioux.[20]

The historical interpretation indicates that the Assiniboine in the mid-seventeenth century occupied the Lake of the Woods area, known as the "Boundary Waters," and eastward to Lake Nipigon, north of present-day

Thunder Bay, Ontario.[21] They then moved northwest toward the Lake Winnipeg region in Manitoba and, by the 1800s, their territory had stretched from Lake Athabasca in the north to northern Montana in the south.[22] The assumption by all these scholars has been that the Cree led the Assiniboine west, although, as Russell (1991) stated, "the question of primacy is often vaguely treated or ignored."[23]

Some scholars have taken exception to the notion that the Assiniboine territory included the Boundary Waters area.[24] Russell noted that, "since it was always realized, even in the 1600s, that the Assiniboine had split off recently from the Sioux, it was generally considered that the Assiniboine were located in northwestern Ontario and adjacent northern United States."[25] These scholars argued that the Assiniboine territory was in the Lake Winnipeg region and west into the Touchwood Hills region of southern Saskatchewan. That Kelsey clearly showed the Assiniboine to have been living in this region was, to Wheeler, clear evidence of the Assiniboine territory. He argued that "the Parkland ecozone from Lake Winnipeg to the Touchwood Hills in Saskatchewan is the more probable territory referred to in these [early] references. A Parkland-Plains seasonal cycle for the Assiniboine is consistent with the bulk of the historical information for this group."[26]

There is no consensus as to when the Assiniboine separated from the Sioux. Nonetheless, it is widely accepted that the Cree and Assiniboine were closely allied for many years; yet most scholars have not focused on the nature of that relationship, preferring to portray them as two distinct groups.

Origins of the Saulteaux

The third group whose heritage is claimed by the Cowessess First Nation band membership is the Saulteaux. This section demonstrates that, as with the treatment of Cree and Assiniboine, scholarship to date has treated the Saulteaux as a distinct cultural group on the northern plains, and has not focused on intercultural relationships with their social and political organization. The predominant historical view of the Saulteaux has been that they migrated from the east after the introduction of the fur trade. According to Bishop, in the 1650s and 1660s the Ojibwe migrated from the Sault Ste. Marie region along the southern and northern shores of Lake Superior toward eastern Minnesota in the south and the Lake of the Woods region in the north. Historians have deduced that this migration was motivated by a desire either to escape the expansionist Iroquois or to search for Cree and Assiniboine middlemen.[27] Due to ongoing hostilities with the Sioux, the southern Ojibwe were prevented from going directly west into central Minnesota. The westernmost point of the eastern woodlands is approximately fifty miles east of the Red River in the north, thereby making the Red River Valley the boundary of the northeastern prairies, with the Ojibwe east of the Red River and the Sioux to the west. This region became a "no man's land" known as the "War Road," with neither Ojibwe nor Sioux entering it for fear of attack. As a result, many southern Ojibwe moved north to the forks of the Assiniboine and Red rivers (present-day Winnipeg; see Map 1) and established semi-permanent hunting territories. From there, they migrated periodically back to the Minnesota woodlands to avoid being attacked by the Sioux.

Hickerson viewed the conflict between the Ojibwe and the Dakota in functionalist terms, whereby the conflict served to regulate the deer population for each group.[28] Peace between the two groups resulted in over-hunting and depletion of the deer population, leading Hickerson to state, "success in war must have also meant starvation."[29] Scott Hamilton and Bruce Cox questioned Hickerson's functionalist claim about Ojibwe/Dakota warfare. Hamilton judged Hickerson's explanation to be oversimplified: "This functionalist interpretation creates a serious theoretical problem as it implies an explanation of the 'origin' of the phenomenon divorced of its historical and social context and centering upon environmental context."[30] Both Hamilton and Cox pointed out that there was a "long tradition of warfare" between the two groups that was not only tied to access to resources, but was also seen as "a vehicle to prestige and wealth, and ... social and economic" success.[31]

The Ojibwe were, and still are, divided into patrilineal clans. Clans were evident on Cowessess in the early 1900s. Scholars have debated whether clans within Ojibwe society were a pre- or post-contact phenomenon. Fred Eggan believed that when the Ojibwe began to migrate, they "maintained their kinship system and cross-cousin marriage, with its intense local integration but either added or borrowed a patrilineal clan system."[32] Hickerson asserted that the introduction of the fur trade prompted the Ojibwe to take part in large-scale trading, which subsequently changed their social structure, as small Ojibwe villages were transformed within one generation from unilineal descent groups to large, bilateral villages.[33] Smith, however, argued that there is no evidence to support Hickerson's claims of the changing Ojibwe social structure in the seventeenth century. He asserted that nowhere in the historical literature of the sixteenth century is there any description of clans among the Ojibwe. Bands are not described as totemic until the eighteenth and nineteenth centuries, but even these groups did not perform the usual functions of clans.[34]

Other scholars have argued that the Ojibwe had clans prior to European contact.[35] According to Bishop, there is little evidence to support either position. His interpretation of the historical documents, based on his "understanding of the vectors of change," led him to believe that the Ojibwe had clans in the pre-contact period. "To assume that the Ojibwa borrowed the clan-totem system seems unlikely, given the devastating effects of the fur trade, intertribal rivalry, and resource deprivations during the postcontact period."[36] Furthermore, he questions what, if Ojibwe clans were a post-contact phenomenon, might explain the absence of clans among the Cree, "since many Cree experience historical and ecological influences similar to the Ojibwa."[37]

There has also been some debate on the extent of the Ojibwe westward migration. Complicating matters are the numerous terms used by earlier observers for various First Nations groups. As Bishop and Smith noted, it is difficult to tie early historic names to contemporary groups due to "the major population shifts precipitated by the Iroquois wars and the fur trade which led to movements and mixing of groups so that by the middle of the eighteenth century, many original tribal and group designations were lost. Therefore, various Algonquian groups in northern Ontario today must be understood as blends and amalgamations of earlier distinct people."[38] Many scholars agree, for example, that *Kilistinon* (variously spelled), as used by Europeans in the early historic period, refers to the Cree.[39] Likewise, there has been considerable debate and speculation about prior terms used for the Ojibwe.

Adolph Greenberg and James Morrison refuted the idea of the Ojibwe post-contact migration to the Boundary Waters area. They, along with Schenck, argued that that the Ojibwe had occupied land west of Lake Superior from contact at least, and that a westward movement of people did not occur.[40] They argued that the term Ojibwa, not the people, moved west with Europeans, who applied it to several different groups. Furthermore, they stated that the use of the terms Cree and Ojibwa "has created a false impression of cultural homogeneity or discreteness, disguising local ecological and social variability in ethnic categories," with the term Cree applied to a wide variety of people, including Ojibwe groups, while Ojibwa was applied more narrowly.[41]

In 2002, Bishop wrote a lengthy article in response to Greenberg and Morrison, in which he carefully re-articulated his Ojibwe migration argument. He asserted that the evidence employed by Greenberg and Morrison contradicted their own argument. Bishop stated that, "to make their case for ethnic continuity, they present a barrage of examples, some often very useful ones, but completely disconnected from the cultural-historical contexts that would give the examples meaning."[42] By doing so, Bishop contended that it allowed them to arrange the evidence to support their claims. He pointed out that many ethnologists, like Skinner, Speck, and Hallowell, had conducted extensive fieldwork in the early twentieth century in which Ojibwe informants had confirmed the Ojibwe migration:

> For some, statements made in the early 20th century may not be convincing proof of an Ojibwa migration. Were the Indian informants themselves confused about their past, or did the anthropologists simply get it wrong, perhaps they misunderstood what they had heard or thought they had heard. Because oral testimony sometimes distorts, conflates and exaggerates, it could be argued that it is simply unreliable and therefore should be dismissed. This view, however, would not be accepted by most ethnohistorians. Thus, unless one wishes to reject Ojibwa attestation given to scholars such as Skinner, Speck and Hallowell at a time when there was no politico-legal agenda involved, one is forced to conclude that Ojibwa oral history should at least be compared with the historical accounts.[43]

For Bishop, based on the available archival evidence, the Ojibwe migrated into the Lake of the Woods region after contact. When they moved there, they absorbed the remnant members of the larger Cree population, who themselves had moved west in response to the fur trade. Before turning to a discussion of scholarship on the Métis, it is worthwhile to acknowledge the archeological contributions to understanding the origins of the Cree, Assiniboine, and Saulteaux.

Archaeology and the Emergence of Plains First Nations People

Like historians and anthropologists, archaeologists have not reached a consensus to explain the emergence of Cree, Assiniboine, and Saulteaux as plains peoples. Archaeologists have identified numerous prehistoric cultural complexes in various eras, but linking those complexes to historic groups has proven controversial.

Archaeologists and linguists have hypothesized that the proto-Algonquian culture had its origins in the Columbia Plateau region. Approximately 3,800 years ago, perhaps due to attacks by Sahaptin speakers, whose descendants became the Nez Perce, the Algonquian began to migrate eastward. Peter J. Denny described this migration as having commenced from where "the Snake River plains ends at the Divide.... I think the migrants turned south and then east along the upper Missouri River, proceeded south to about the James River (in South Dakota), and then went east into the hilly country which gives rise to various southeastwards tributaries of the Mississippi."[44] From here, the group split into two, with one group settling just south of Lake Michigan and the other proceeding south to the Wabash Valley. Two thousand years ago, an Algonquian branch migrated in a northwest direction toward southern Manitoba. Roughly 2,300 years ago, two distinct languages, Blackfoot and Cree, emerged from the proto-Algonquian language. As Blackfoot and Cree languages are so distinct from one another—many originally believed that Blackfoot was not an Algonquian language—it is generally accepted that the Blackfoot ancestors were the first to migrate back westward. Scholars generally agree that the archaeological cultural complex known as "Old Wives" was the antecedent to the Blackfoot.[45]

The cultural complexes that have incurred much debate as to their affiliations are the Selkirk and Blackduck complexes. Many archaeologists have regarded Selkirk as being associated with the Cree,[46] and their range as far-reaching. According to Wright, from as early as 810 AD, their territory extended north to South Indian Lake in northern Manitoba, west to Lac Île-à-la-Crosse in Saskatchewan, south to the Saskatchewan River, and east to the northwestern portion of Ontario.[47] Wright continued: "Archaeological evidence strongly suggests that the Cree had a long period of cultural development in the region under consideration and that they are not easterners who pushed west and northwest in response to the fur trade."[48] Binnema has added that, although the archaeological evidence is clear about the pre-contact migration of the Cree, this does not rule out subsequent post-contact migrations.[49]

Early archaeologists, such as Lloyd Wilford and Richard MacNeish, have argued that the Blackduck complex, situated in the Boundary Waters region, was associated with the Assiniboine.[50] James V. Wright and K. A. C.

Dawson both dismissed the Assiniboine connection. Wright pointed out that the prehistoric and early historic Sioux possessed a Mississippian culture. Yet, pictographs associated with Algonquian culture can be found in the Boundary Waters region. Wright reasoned that if "Blackduck is Siouian then the Assiniboine must have shared in a basic art style related to common cosmological views with their Cree and Algonquian neighbors."[51] Dawson concluded, in response to Bishop and Ray's assertion that the Assiniboine were located in the Boundary Waters region and that the Ojibwe moved into that region in the post-contact period, that the "unbroken archaeological record does not support the view of a recent intrusion of an alien peoples, nor does a review of the historical record which clearly places the Assiniboine around Lake Winnipeg with only transitory appearances in Ontario in the context of intercourse for the purpose of trade."[52] Though some scholars, such as Evans, Pettipas, and Denny, have contended that Blackduck is associated with the Cree,[53] what is clear is that a majority of archaeologists associate Blackduck with Algonquian peoples, not Siouian, as had previously been thought.

Though early archaeologists associated the Assiniboine with the Blackduck complex, many now believe that they are associated with the Mortlatch tradition. The Hidatsa and Mandan have been marginally linked to the Mortlatch complex, and the evidence, according to Binnema, shows that the Assiniboine are even more closely related to it. The linkage of the Assiniboine to the Mortlatch tradition means that they, much like the Cree and Ojibwe, had been present on the northern plains much longer than previously thought. Their presence on the plains is significant, as Binnema has stated, "for this suggests that the ancestors of the Assiniboines participated in extensive trade with both the Cree and the Hidatsa communities for several centuries before Euroamericans arrived."[54]

Some ethnohistorians have rejected the arguments of archaeologists regarding the prehistoric location of the Cree, Assiniboine, and Saulteaux.[55] Bishop, the most vocal in his opposition to the new archaeological perspectives, contended that at the time of contact the Ojibwe were located no farther west than Michipicoten Bay on the northeastern shore of Lake Superior:[56] "There is no evidence to support the view that the different Ojibwa groups extended beyond the Michipicoten Bay region prior to the Iroquios wars of the mid-seventeenth century."[57] Furthermore, Bishop and Smith speculated that Assiniboine and Cree cultural contact, not Ojibwe and Cree, in the

Boundary Waters regions accounts for the presence of mixed Blackduck and Selkirk sites.[58] According to Bishop (1982), this new archaeological perspective has "underestimated the impact of European colonialism, especially the fur trade, on native people."[59] Bishop attributed the discrepancy between the ethnohistorical and archaeological views to archaeology's "continued heavy reliance upon field-obtained data, gathered not just decades but centuries after the first European influence were felt, to interpret prehistoric Indian life."[60] Bishop called for archaeologists to employ an interdisciplinary approach, "thereby allowing archaeologists to avoid employing models which apply to the post-contact period, as much as they may appear to be aboriginal on the surface."[61]

Origins of the Métis

Like the Plains Cree, Saulteaux, and Assiniboine, the Métis have been the subject of significant discussion surrounding when, where, and how they emerged as a distinct people. A review of the literature shows that the predominant themes include a varying mixture of race and cultural factors to explain their emergence. The constant in this discussion is that Métis emergence occurred when they were no longer identified as being First Nations, as there is a tendency to highlight the racial and cultural differences between them.

For the early chroniclers of the Métis, such as G.F.G. Stanley, Arthur S. Morton, Marcel Giraud, Harold Innis, W.L. Morton, and Joseph Howard, race was of primary importance.[62] Their writings were couched in notions of social evolution, which regarded Europeans as intellectually and morally superior to Indians. These scholars viewed mixed ancestry people in a slightly better light than Indians, but nonetheless still considered them to be inferior to Europeans. Also, it is implied that First Nations people were never of mixed European and First Nations ancestry. The contact between the Métis and Europeans was seen as a symbol of "a clash between primitive and civilized peoples."[63] For Stanley, the racial inferiority of Indian and Métis peoples was accepted as fact. For example, he stated, "by character and upbringing the half-breed, no less than the Indians, were unfitted to compete with the whites in competitive individualism of white civilization, or to share with them the duties or responsibilities of citizenship."[64] Thus, even in a mixed race population, scholars continued to carve sharp lines of distinction based on racialized notions.

The 1816 Battle of Seven Oaks has often been heralded as the birth of the Métis as a "New Nation."[65] For the most part, though, these writers viewed the French Métis and English Halfbreeds as being separate from each other. For example, Frits Pannekoek rejected Irene Spry's argument that the two mixed-blood groups in the Red River Settlement had a close relationship.[66] Scholars also assessed the relationship between Métis and First Nations groups to be rooted more in their biological linkage rather than in any meaningful social or cultural bonds. Finally, though, treatment of the pre-Red River Métis was cursory; their emergence has been seen by historians as a strictly western Canadian plains phenomenon.

Beginning in the 1970s, researchers began to probe further into Métis history. Scholars such as Jennifer Brown, Olive Dickason, John Foster, Harriet Gorham, Jacqueline Peterson, and Sylvia Van Kirk examined the issue of Métis ethnogenesis.[67] These studies increased our understanding of the fur trade and Aboriginal people as first articulated by Ray.[68] These authors depart from the economic historical approach of previous historians, and look instead at the impact of social relations between Aboriginal people and European fur traders. As a result, gender was seen as playing a more prominent role in these studies. Race and culture were still used as markers for group differentiation, but usually within a class context.

Reinforcing Van Kirk's work, Brown challenged researchers to examine the roles that First Nations women played in Métis identity formation.[69] She utilized the concept of "matriorganization," first articulated by Charles A. Bishop and Shepard Krech III, to acknowledge that European fur trader husbands had lived, even briefly, with their Indian wives. Brown also noted that more mixed-blood boys than girls were pulled out of their home environments and provided with a European education. The implication was the development of "semi-autonomous female headed famil[ies]," which Brown urged researchers to examine more fully to gain a deeper appreciation of Métis ethnogenesis.

John Foster identified the processes that allowed mixed-ancestry people to move from "proto-metis" into "full-blown Metis" identities.[70] He asserted that the relationships between European fur traders and First Nations men played a crucial role in this process. Foster established a two-stage process in developing a Métis identity involving the independent traders, usually of French origin and known as Freemen—or, as Foster labeled them, the outsider adult males. The first stage saw the outsider adult male marry into an

Indian band and develop a close relationship with the adult male members of the band and with other outsider adult males. This led the Freemen to establish their own bands with their country wives and families after having become assimilated enough in the band's social and political culture.

Foster attributed the ethos of the adult French Canadian males as the motivating factor for leaving their wives' bands and establishing their own. This ethos among French men "emphasized the necessity of being a man of consequence in one's own eyes and in the eyes of one's fellows [referring to other adult French Canadian males]."[71] In this milieu, the outsider adult males were characterized as having a large degree of assertiveness, apparently in contrast to First Nations men.

By 1988, there was a call for researchers to move away from the "Red River myopia" that had focused on the activities of Louis Riel and the Red River Métis to the exclusion of other Métis groups.[72] In the 1990s, Métis history began to expand beyond Red River, with a number of studies examining the American Métis experience.[73] Since 2000, a number of studies using genealogies have focused on Métis ethnogenesis.[74] The construction of genealogies provides researchers with "a framework for detailed study of families, such as the Desjarlais, and enabled me to identify kin groupings, to postulate sociopolitical alliances, to track the migration of Métis individuals and extended families into different regions, to examine the socioeconomic status of these families over time, and to trace the process of acculturation as they responded to changing socioeconomic circumstances and adopted Indian, Métis, or Euro-Canadian modes of behaviour to survive."[75]

In her book, Devine, like Foster, applied the concept of "Proto-Metis," to every French man who "had established himself, his country wife, and his metis children in a group apart from the aboriginal parent band, they continued to cultivate aboriginal values, attitudes, and modes of behaviour."[76] In other words, they were not quite Métis because they still lived the lifestyle of First Nations people. For Devine, the emergence of a Plains Métis identity in Red River occurred after 1818, with the arrival of Christian missions that served to unify the Métis in permanent settlements. In the Athabasca region, a separate Woodlands Métis identity emerged in the 1870s with the signing of Indian treaties that separated Indian and Métis people.[77]

Swan provided another road to the Red River Plains Métis—other than the Great Lakes, as discussed by Peterson. Swan delineated the Jerome family genealogy, which showed that they had moved from north-central

Alberta to Pembina, North Dakota, south of the Red River settlement. Swan claimed that the Métis demonstrated identifiable cultural traits in southern Saskatchewan by the 1790s, thirty years before the Catholic mission was established in Red River. For Swan, the existence of Métis culture on the prairies demonstrated that "the ethnic markers of a mixed culture evident in the Great Lakes [were] also happening in the North West."[78] She agreed with Devine and Foster regarding the existence of the Proto-Métis, though she used the term "Indianized Frenchmen" to describe the fathers of the mixed-blood children who became the Métis within two or three generations.

Macdougall examined how the Métis in northern Saskatchewan utilized the Cree concept of *wahkootowin* to create their own distinct identity.[79] According to Macdougall, *wahkootowin* means "relationship" or "relative" in Cree. However, she used the term as a theoretical construct to explain internal community behaviour that was expressed inter-generationally and through both the extended family and the two dominant institutions in northwestern Saskatchewan, the fur trade companies and the Roman Catholic Church.

Unlike Devine, Macdougall argued that, "Metis people were not united by external forces like the fur trade, the Church or nineteenth century national-istic movements but rather by the relationships created and nurtured through wahkootowin. Metis wahkootowin created and shaped identity, community, which in turn, forged their place within the fur trade and the Church."[80]

Macdougall expanded on Brown's idea of the importance of Métis women to the development of the Métis, and introduced a different per-spective of Métis ethnogenesis. Macdougall saw Métis women in northern Saskatchewan as being "the centrifugal force that incorporated successive waves of outsider males who carried with them the surnames that came to mark the northwestern Saskatchewan communities and identified the fami-lies locally and patronymically."[81] In this respect, Macdougall diverged from Foster, Devine, and Swan. For her, instead of Proto-Métis, the French men and Indian women who married and had children were a "proto-generation," while their children were the first generation of Métis. That first generation was born in the late 1700s, with the second born by the 1820s.[82]

In the last twenty years, the discussion of Métis ethnogenesis has devel-oped a sophistication that provides a more complex view of Métis history. The simplistic and racist images of Métis people promoted by earlier scholars have been brushed aside and replaced with one of Métis people exercising agency in light of economic, political, and social challenges. Recent studies have attempted to move toward describing the process of Métis ethnogenesis as a cultural development, yet most largely continue to describe this process within a racialized context. The Métis are portrayed as being neither white nor Indian, but a new race, although most scholars currently use the term "nation" instead of race. Scholars have implicitly operationalized the clear distinction made between the Métis and various First Nations groups, despite the close social ties. In addition, scholars have appeared to view Métis cultural expression as a monolith, precluding the possibility of a diverse range of Métis culture.

A review of the literature dealing with the emergence of Cree, Assiniboine, Saulteaux, and Métis peoples reveals assumptions, established patterns of interpretation, and competing explanations that serve the scholars' purpose, but do not accurately represent the lived experience of the people being examined. Specifically, the view of these groups as being distinctly bounded may facilitate the mapping of territories and movements, but it oversimplifies the interethnic relationships and essentializes the cultural groups. The pattern of interpretation of dominance, dependency, and westward migration limits the historic view to a mere four centuries. The competing explanations, however, demonstrate that there is room for new interpretations. Very few, with some more recent exceptions, attempt to provide an Aboriginal cultural perspective or understanding of the events.

Aboriginal People of the Saskatchewan Plains, 1800–1870

Regardless of when the Cree, Assiniboine, Saulteaux, and Métis arrived on the prairies, by the early 1800s bands from each of these groups were making their presence felt on the northern Plains. Scholars have discussed in some detail that political, military, and economic alliances among bands from these four groups gave them an advantage in asserting their interests in a highly competitive region. Scholars have acknowledged that alliances based on kinship were facilitated by similar social organizations that allowed for incorporation of individuals from other ethnic/cultural groups. Seldom has the multicultural makeup of the band been explained; instead, the tribal perspective has been privileged.

Scholars have noted that all four groups operated as sets of linked bands, which were politically autonomous units lacking tribal-level political organization.[83] A band's membership was highly fluid, relatively small in size and highly mobile, usually dispersing and gathering with the seasons. Leadership for each group was based on the influence of a respected male. As Katherine Pettipas stated of the Saulteaux, "the system of ranked leadership was not formalized to the point of precluding an individual's rise in the power structure, and the fact that some enjoyed more privileges associated with their status than others was at least tacitly acknowledged."[84] Band size was influenced by the leadership qualities of a chief, but was also related to kinship ties. Individuals could freely move between bands. Chiefs did not possess coercive power, but instead relied on their skills to arrive at consensus. Generosity was highly valued, and as a result chiefs had to accumulate wealth, then give it away. A person who demonstrated skills as a good hunter and/or warrior was usually able to accumulate wealth, and could count on support from his relatives as his core members; as his reputation and effectiveness as a chief grew, so, too, did band size increase.[85] New members without kinship ties married into the band and ensured their status with other members. The result was that, as Mandelbaum stated about the Plains Cree, "numbers of each band were constantly augmented by recruits from other bands of Plains Cree, or often other tribes."[86] Interestingly, Mandelbaum, like most scholars, recognized that the bands were culturally mixed, but nevertheless he continued to speak of them as distinct tribal units.

The simultaneous occupation of territory by the four groups is described in the historical literature. By the beginning of the 1800s, Plains Cree bands were located in four clusters in present-day Manitoba and Saskatchewan. On the eastern edge, along the Assiniboine River and just east of Brandon House, there were some forty lodges. Just west of this location, at the forks of the Assiniboine and Qu'Appelle rivers, were another twenty-five lodges. Seventy-five lodges were located in the Touchwood Hills region. Finally, one hundred lodges were located between the south and north branches of Saskatchewan near the confluence of the Battle River.[87]

Ray explains that the Assiniboine bands, comprised of over five hundred lodges, were spread out from the Souris River in North Dakota in the south, the Assiniboine River in the Brandon House area to the east, along the Qu'Appelle River up through the Touchwood Hills, past the South and North Saskatchewan Rivers, and along the Battle River.[88] By the 1820s, there were also some thirty-four lodges of Assiniboine, Cree, and Métis residing north of these groups in the Edmonton House district.[89]

According to Peers, by this time the Saulteaux had established themselves in southern Manitoba after many years of "commuting" back and forth from the Red Lake, Leech Lake, and Rainy Rivers regions.[90] They were living in territory that included the southeastern shore of Lake Winnipeg, south along the Red River to Pembina, west to Turtle Mountain, and north into the Interlake region.[91] Also, according to Peers, they were reported as being farther west along the Qu'Appelle River, and up the North Saskatchewan River as far as Edmonton House and Lac La Biche.

By the beginning of the 1800s, there was a sizeable Métis population in the same region as the other three groups, either working for the fur trading companies or living in bands and operating as independent traders.[92]

What becomes apparent, scholars have shown, is that these groups occupied overlapping territories. One region, however, may have had a larger population of one group than another. For example, Ray stated that nearly two-thirds of the Assiniboine were located between the Souris and Qu'Appelle valleys.[93] The Saulteaux, meanwhile, were heavily concentrated in the Red River region, yet they had a presence in the Turtle Mountain area just east of the Souris River Valley. In this period, Cree and Assiniboine switched from being trappers and traders to being suppliers of food provisions for the Hudson's Bay Company.[94]

By the early 1800s, Plains Cree and Assiniboine bands, augmented by a few Saulteaux and Métis bands, had formed a formidable military alliance. Stonechild, McLeod, and Nestor have called this the Iron Alliance.[95] Their main enemies, according to Milloy, were the Gros Ventre, Blackfoot, Sioux, and Mandan/Hidasta. Their hostilities with the Sioux traced back many decades. At the beginning of this period, John McDonnell, a fur trader with Northwest Company, recorded a battle in the late 1790s on the southern shore of Lake Winnipeg, where the Sioux are said to have massacred a large camp of Cree, Assiniboine, and Saulteaux. In 1804 and 1805, the Cree, Saulteaux, and Assiniboine formed war parties of up to three hundred warriors against the Sioux.[96]

The close relations among the groups were highlighted by their military exploits. The Cree/Assiniboine bands and the Gros Ventre underwent considerable change between the 1770s and 1780s. In the early 1770s, the two groups were on amicable terms, with the Cree acting as middlemen for the Gros Ventre in the fur trade.[97] The Gros Ventre lands, located in south-central Saskatchewan, were known for an abundance of furs. By the end of the 1770s, according to Fowler, the Cree/Assiniboine began to usurp Gros Ventre lands. Although the Gros Ventre scored many victories, overall they suffered devastating losses at the hands of the Cree/Assiniboine. As a result, the "Gros Ventre responded to their predicament by boldly setting off for new territories," settling along the upper Missouri, east to Yellowstone River,[98] while the Cree/Assiniboine seized their southern Saskatchewan homelands.

The origin of the Cree and Blackfoot tension is somewhat unclear. According to Milloy, the root of their conflict had to do with the nature of Cree/Assiniboine relations with the Gros Ventre. As the Cree and Assiniboine moved into central Saskatchewan, they initiated intense fighting with the Gros Ventre. Though the Blackfoot were Gros Ventre allies, they did not come to their aid for fear of being cut off from the European goods that the Cree/Assiniboine middlemen had to offer. By the 1790s, however, the European fur traders were able to bypass the Cree/Assiniboine middlemen and trade directly with the Blackfoot. As a result, the Blackfoot severed their trade alliance with the Cree/Assiniboine and were now free to protect their weaker allies, the Gros Ventre, thereby maintaining access to Gros Ventre horses.[99] David Smyth took exception to Milloy's work, especially the claim of a Blackfoot and Cree/Assiniboine alliance. As Smyth pointed out, there is no evidence in the historical record to support a claim of a Blackfoot and Cree/Assiniboine military alliance: "The texture of Blackfoot-Cree relations in these two decades is indistinguishable from that of almost any period in the first three-quarters of the nineteenth century."[100]

Between 1810 and 1870, hostilities between the Cree/Assiniboine/ Saulteaux/Métis and the Blackfoot confederacy increased until the defeat of the Iron Alliance in 1870. The Iron Alliance and the Blackfoot Confederacy had entered a somewhat tentative peace between 1820 and 1825, marked by only periodic outbreaks of violence. By 1825, however, the peace was severed completely after the Blackfoot defeated a group of Beaver Hills Cree near present-day Edmonton. Beginning in the 1850s, the buffalo herds began to slip out of southern Manitoba and Saskatchewan, reaching only into southern Alberta and northern Montana, and giving rise to more inter-tribal warfare. During the 1840s and early 1850s, the Sioux became a potent force, having been at war with the Red River Métis, but suffering a significant defeat in 1851 at the Battle of Grand Coteau.[101] By the late 1850s, the Sioux began to move westward into the Missouri/Yellowstone river area, attacking the Assiniboine.

In the 1850s and early 1860s, a number of peace agreements were attempted. The Cree leader, Maskepetoon, arranged one such peace with the

Blackfoot, which was subsequently breached in 1858 and then shattered in 1860.[102] Nevertheless, Maskepetoon continued to work for peace. By the late 1860s, the Iron Alliance had moved into the Cypress Hills in southwest Saskatchewan and southeast Alberta, so as to be closer to the buffalo that had all but disappeared from other parts of Saskatchewan. In the 1870s, buffalo were still to be found in abundant numbers in the Cypress Hills, according to Norbert Welsh, an English Halfbreed buffalo hunter who said he had hunted them there.[103] There were still plenty of buffalo in southern Alberta, in the heart of Blackfoot country, into the late 1870s. Issac Cowie, a Hudson's Bay Company fur trader, noted that one Iron Alliance contingent included "Crees and Saulteaux, the semi-Stoney and Cree 'Young Dogs' of Qu'Appelle and Touchwood Hills a few English and French Metis ... also some Assiniboines from Wood Mountain and a few from the North Saskatchewan ... containing a mixed population of probably two thousand five hundred or three thousand people of whom about five hundred were men and lads capable of waging war."[104]

Their movement, so close to Blackfoot territory, did not sit well with the Blackfoot, who launched several successful attacks. In April 1869, Maskepetoon again attempted to reach a peace. However, the Blackfoot killed him and everyone in his party, including two of his sons and a grandson.[105] The next year, some eight hundred Cree, Saulteaux, Assiniboine, and Métis warriors led by Big Bear, Piapot, Little Poplar, and Little Pine set out on a major offensive against the Blackfoot. The Iron Alliance thought that the Blackfoot had been ravaged by disease and would not be able to withstand such a large force. Unfortunately (from the Alliance's perspective), this was not the case, as they proceeded into a trap. Alliance losses are estimated to have been between two and three hundred, while the Blackfoot may have lost some forty lives.[106] In the spring of 1871, the Iron Alliance sent tobacco to the Blackfoot to arrange a peace, which was agreed upon by the fall of that year.[107] The peace was cemented following the protocols of smoking the pipe, gift exchanges, and adoptions. As Milloy concluded, "except for occasional incidents of horse stealing, this agreement remained unbroken."[108]

Saskatchewan's Aboriginal People up to 1885

An understanding of the nature of northern plains peoples' intercultural relationship is augmented by a description of the reasons that the Iron Alliance entered into treaty negotiations, of the actual negotiations, and of Aboriginal/

Canadian relations after negotiations were concluded. In particular, the Iron Alliance was a willing and informed party to the treaty negotiations, and the negotiations fell within a First Nations treaty-making framework. This framework called for both parties to enter a reciprocal relationship with assumed responsibilities based on kinship roles. A review of how the relations between First Nations and the Canadian government played out provides insights into how, from a First Nations perspective, kinship works and how it was to guide interaction.

Just as they had concluded their peace with the Blackfoot, the Iron Alliance had to contend with a new threat to their political, economic, and social interests. By the 1860s, Canada looked to the West as a means of emulating the tremendous development that was occurring in the United States.[109] In 1869, Canada purchased the Hudson's Bay Company's (HBC) rights to Rupert's Land, which included much of western Canada, and precipitated events leading to the creation of the province of Manitoba under the guidance of Métis leader Louis Riel. By 1873, the Canadian government had signed Treaties One, Two, and Three with the Ojibwe of northwestern Ontario and southern Manitoba. The purchase of Rupert's Land by Canada, the creation of the province of Manitoba, and the signing of Treaties One, Two, and Three all impacted the interaction between the Canadian government and Saskatchewan's Aboriginal people.

The Cree, Assiniboine, Saulteaux, and Métis of Saskatchewan were well aware of the treaty negotiations taking place in Ontario and Manitoba, even though they themselves were not a part of those talks. As the Ojibwe had done, the Iron Alliance also desired to enter into a relationship with the Canadian government through treaties. There were several specific reasons for this. First, they were aware of the implications of Canadian expansion and settlement, as they had witnessed the devastating effects of American settlement on Native Americans.[110] Second, the First Nations leaders wanted to diffuse the dangers of the whiskey trade, which had intensified after the killing of at least twenty Assiniboine, including the mutilation of Chief Little Soldier in the Cypress Hills (known as the Cypress Hills Massacre) by American whiskey traders.[111] Third, Saskatchewan's Aboriginal people needed to recover from the deleterious impact of their prolonged warfare (especially with the Blackfoot), an outbreak of smallpox in 1870, and a serious decline in the buffalo herds of the northern prairies.[112] Finally, by entering into a treaty relationship, the Iron Alliance hoped to have their Aboriginal rights acknowledged and protected.[113]

Writers have demonstrated that the First Nations leaders were well aware of what was at stake, and entered into negotiations, hoping to extract the best possible deal for their people.[114] As they entered into negotiations with the Crown, the Iron Alliance operated within the framework of their cultural protocol of dealing with an outside group. An important component of this protocol was that, before an agreement could take place, outsiders were expected to accept a kinship role and assume the responsibility of reciprocity that came with that role. The treaty, then, represents, in part, the creation of a relationship between First Nations and Canada based on socially constructed roles and responsibilities grounded in First Nations' kinship practices. It was also clear, however, that the Canadian government failed to understand the significance of entering into such a relationship from a First Nations perspective.[115]

That the Cree and Saulteaux chiefs who negotiated Treaty 4 were operating from their cultural understanding of reciprocity and kinship is demonstrated by the use of the pipe in the negotiations. The written account of the negotiations shows that Alexander Morris, lieutenant governor of the Northwest Territories and chief treaty negotiator for the Crown, did not completely understand the meanings and significance of First Nations treaty making. For example, in the Treaty 4 negotiations, unlike the Treaty 3 talks, the pipe was not offered to Morris. He told the Gambler, one of the Saulteaux spokesmen, that the Ojibwe of the Treaty 3 "gave me the pipe of peace and paid me every honor. Why? Because I was the servant of the Queen."[116] This was a misunderstanding regarding the significance of the pipe. The presence of the pipe had less to do with Morris's status as the Queen's representative than with sanctifying the reciprocal relationship being negotiated and based on the promises made.[117] Even though Morris had claimed that the pipe was not used in the Treaty 4 negotiations, Ray, Miller, and Tough noted that caution "is required on this point; documentary record of Treaty 4 negotiations has no evidence of ritual or ceremony, but ... that record is not necessarily complete."[118]

Reciprocity was a crucial component of First Nations treaty-making. By offering food and gifts prior to treaty negotiations, Morris adhered to the protocol of reciprocity established in the fur trade ceremonies that preceded the actual trading of furs.[119] But Morris did not understand that gift-giving was a key gesture that signaled entry into a formal relationship. As Friesen stated, "[t]o the commissioner as to most Canadians then and now, the treaties were considered a 'once and for all' way of clearing the land of the legal obligations of Indian title." For the chiefs, on the other hand, the treaties "represented the beginning of a continuing relation of mutual obligation."[120]

The treaty negotiations lasted from 8 to 15 September 1874. At the signing, the chiefs were satisfied with the terms of the treaty, even though they did not obtain all that they had requested, such as including the Métis in the treaty. For example, The Gambler said to Morris, "Now when you have come here, you see sitting out there a mixture of Half-breeds, Crees, Saulteaux, and Stonies [Assiniboine], *all are one*, and you were slow in taking the hand of the Half-breed."[121] This request was not for the inclusion of distant relatives, but for close relations: brothers, sisters, cousins, fathers, mothers, aunts, and uncles. Morris, however, told the gathering that the Métis would be dealt with separately.

Nevertheless, the negotiations fell within First Nations' treaty-making framework based on reciprocity and kinship. When the chiefs said that they were taking the mother's hand, referring to Queen Victoria, they were allowing Canada to enter into their kinship circle. By accepting the chiefs' hands, the Canadian government agreed to the role and responsibilities that kinship entailed. The chiefs may have believed that they had reached a meeting of the minds with the Canadian government based on mutual obligation and reciprocity when they signed the treaties, but they "would realize that the government was operating outside [their] treaty making framework a few years later when the Canadian government failed to fulfill their commitments of the treaties."[122]

By the late 1870s, many chiefs became dissatisfied with either the lack of treaty implementation or the terms of Treaties 4 and 6 (the former was signed in 1876 and covered the North Saskatchewan River region in central Saskatchewan and Alberta). Few chiefs had selected a reserve, but instead gravitated toward the Cypress Hills in search of the last buffalo herds. The chiefs most outspoken against the treaties were Big Bear, Little Pine, and Piapot. Piapot, leader of the Cree-Assiniboine Young Dogs, signed an adhesion to Treaty 4 in 1875 only after he had been assured that the treaty would include provisions for farm instructors, tools and equipment, and medical assistance. Big Bear and Little Pine were influential chiefs from the Treaty 6 region. Neither chief signed Treaty 6, however, because of concerns over the loss of autonomy that the treaty implied. As complaints about the lack of treaty implementation increased, the standing of these chiefs also increased among as many as half of the Saskatchewan bands.[123]

The large concentration of bands in the Cypress Hills greatly concerned government officials, a concern intensified by development of hostilities in the United States. On 25 June 1876, a combined Lakota and Cheyenne force defeated Lieutenant Colonel George Custer at Little Bighorn. After the conflict, the Lakota and Cheyenne split up in smaller groups and headed in different directions. Chief Sitting Bull went north toward the Cypress Hills and Canada. In November, Sitting Bull's people, numbering close to two thousand, arrived in the Wood Mountain area, thirty miles east of the Cypress Hills.[124] A year later, in June 1877, the U.S. government attacked Chief Joseph's Nez Perce people to force them to relocate from their Idaho reservation. The Nez Perce fought and eluded U.S. troops for several months, but finally surrendered at Bear's Paw Mountain, some fifty miles south of the Cypress Hills. Though a majority of Nez Perce were forcibly removed from the area, some one hundred, under the leadership of Chief White Bird, managed to cross the Canadian border and reach the Cypress Hills.[125]

By 1877, a large concentration of Aboriginal people was located in close vicinity of the Cypress Hills. Sitting Bull's Lakota band and a Dakota band that had arrived in Canada in 1863 were living just east of the Cypress Hills. Meanwhile, the Nez Perce, Plains Cree, Assiniboine, Saulteaux, and Métis bands were living in the Cypress Hills, and the Blackfoot, Bloods, Peigan, and Sarcee of the Blackfoot Confederacy occupied areas just west of the region. Hugh Dempsey has estimated that at this time there were more than five thousand First Nations people in the Cypress Hills.[126] Edgar Dewdney, the commissioner of Indian Affairs for the Northwest Territory, estimated that in 1880 some seven to eight thousand Canadian First Nations people were in the Milk River region of Montana.[127] The presence of all these people concerned Canadian officials for two reasons. First, they feared the creation of an inter-tribal confederacy, and, second, they feared that Louis Riel, now an American citizen living in Montana just south of Cypress Hills, would recruit disaffected Indians. Though councils with the Blackfoot, Cree, and Sioux were held, no confederacy materialized.[128]

In 1880, a number of chiefs, including Piapot, Lucky Man, and Cowessess, as well as some Assiniboine chiefs, requested that their reserves be located in the Cypress Hills.[129] This decision, no doubt, might have been influenced by the new Indian Commissioner Dewdney's announcements of new policies regarding Indian Affairs in the northwest. When Dewdney was first appointed Indian commissioner, he told the chiefs that he would distribute rations to them because there was a lack of game in the region.[130] For First Nations, this followed the kinship obligation that the Crown had agreed to assume when it signed treaty. However, Dewdney later implemented policies designed to assert control over those chiefs who were agitating for revisions of the treaties. He announced that rations would not be provided to those First Nations individuals who had not accepted treaty and that the government would recognize any adult male as chief who was able to garner a following of one hundred people.[131] The policy had the desired effect, as a number of new bands were created. Some individuals who had belonged to bands such as Big Bear's and had favoured revisions to the treaties decided to accept Dewdney's offer. Others who had not signed treaties, notably Big Bear and other chiefs, such as Little Pine, who had accepted treaty but wanted them revised, refused to accept Dewdney's proposal.[132] Dewdney also stated that bands whose chiefs had selected reserves would not receive their annuities until they returned to those reserves. By the end of the summer of 1880, however, only the Assiniboine reserve had been surveyed, while a majority of the Plains Cree band traveled to Montana to hunt buffalo.[133]

In the summer of 1881, due to pressures faced in the U.S., many Indians returned to the Cypress Hills and were informed of Dewdney's new policies. Near riots ensued as starving First Nations demanded that rations be distributed.[134] Additionally, Canadian Assiniboine chiefs who had taken treaty refused to accept their annuity payments until those from northern reserves received annuities. Chiefs Lucky Man and Little Pine also requested that Thomas Wadsworth, the Inspector of Indian Agencies, "pay every native in the country."[135] Interestingly, the chiefs, as they had done in the treaty negotiations, also made an appeal for their Métis relatives to be allowed to enter the treaties, suggesting the closeness between these groups.[136]

These tensions convinced Dewdney that the government could not afford to allow a large concentration of people in the region. Dewdney therefore decided to close the agency farms, relocate farm instructors, and not survey the Cypress Hills reserves that had been promised to various bands.[137] Even more significantly, Dewdney decided to close Fort Walsh, which had acted as the distribution centre for rations. In effect, this implemented a policy of starvation aimed at subjugating the chiefs.[138] Dewdney did, however, allow annuity payments at Fort Walsh in November 1882. Nevertheless, the Indian agent in charge of dispensing the payments, Allan McDonald, who would later become the Indian agent for Crooked Lake, to which Cowessess band belonged, "expressed his desire to 'punish' the Indians, and he gave them barely enough rations to survive."[139]

Dewdney's starvation policy had a devastating effect on the First Nations population. Chief Big Bear, the last chief to sign treaty, had been forced to move his band to the Battleford region to establish his reserve. His band's twenty-one day journey was arduous, as a majority of the 550 people had to walk. Big Bear's granddaughter described the journey: "The trek to our former home was a hard one to live through because of the lack of food and the scarcity of game. We traveled forever northwards and ran into severe storm. Deaths were numerous. We stopped only briefly to bury our dead; amongst the victims were my mother and sister."[140] The number of people who died as a result of Dewdney's starvation policy has never been officially tallied or recognized by the Canadian government. Nevertheless, in his report to the Department of Indian Affairs, Dewdney was pleased with the result that his starvation policy had had:

> I look upon the removal of some 3,000 Indians from Cypress Hills and scattering them through the country as a solution of one of our main difficulties, as it was found impossible at times to have such control as was desirable over such a large number of worthless and lazy Indians, the concourse of malcontents and reckless Indians from all the bands in the Territories. Indians already on their reserves will now be more settled, as no place of rendezvous will be found where food can be had without a return of work being exacted, a fact which tended materially to create much discontent among those who were willing to remain on their reserves, as well as to increase the laborious duty of our agents.[141]

Chapter 7 will deal with how Dewdney's starvation policy impacted Cowessess band at the time it was implemented and during the Treaty Land Entitlement negotiations in the 1990s.

The relocations did not end the efforts of the chiefs to agitate for revisions to the treaties, but they were severely undermined by the events of 1885. While the chiefs were attempting to renegotiate their treaties, the Métis of the south branch of the Saskatchewan River in Batoche (located fifty miles north of Saskatoon) were attempting to have their land claims recognized under the leadership of Riel. The Canadian government sent troops to "put down the rebellion," and on 15 May defeated the Métis general/war chief Gabriel Dumont at the Battle of Batoche, ending Métis hopes for the acknowledgement of their Aboriginal rights.

The aftermath of 1885 was devastating to Aboriginal people in Saskatchewan. Métis leaders were imprisoned, and Riel, a U.S. citizen, was tried, convicted, and hanged for treason. Though there were First Nations involved in the fighting alongside the Métis, most chiefs did not participate or condone violence as a means of settling their grievances. Nonetheless, the Canadian government used the threat of violence to assert total control over First Nations. First Nations leaders like Big Bear and Poundmaker were sentenced to prison. Seven First Nations men were hanged for murders that took place in incidents outside the actual rebellion but which were nonetheless associated with it by most Canadians at the time. The Canadian government used these events to justify amendments to the *Indian Act* that sought to repress Indian cultural and political activities. The architect of these repressive policies was Edgar Dewdney.

• • •

Scholars have for the most part failed to convey the complexities of Aboriginal societies in southern Saskatchewan. This point will be clearly shown in the following chapter. This is not to say that the ways in which scholars have generally discussed Aboriginal people have no value. However, Aboriginal people as tribal entities with distinct cultural boundaries have created problems for the identification of contemporary people—for both insiders and outsiders.

3

Multicultural Bands on the Northern Plains and the Notion of "Tribal" Histories

The experiences of Cowessess First Nation members do not reflect scholars' interpretations of Saskatchewan's Aboriginal people. As has been shown, scholars have emphasized "tribal" histories that highlight intertribal contact and relations, but nonetheless maintain distinct tribal boundaries. This tribal history approach masks the importance of kinship in band formation and maintenance. This approach is useful for understanding general historical trends of specific cultural and linguistic groups, and provides the context for multicultural bands and mixed-ethnic groups. However, it does not quite acknowledge that most Aboriginal groups in the northern plains of Saskatchewan were multicultural in composition. Why were they multicultural, and why have scholars failed to convey this multiculturalism? Aboriginal groups were multicultural because their customary laws allowed them the flexibility to include other people into their groups. The customary kinship practices of Cowessess people and other groups were spelled out in the stories of Elder Brother. However, many scholars have not recognized or understood, or have simply ignored the Law of the People. Without this fundamental understanding of Aboriginal culture, many scholars have had to resort to extrapolating relations at the band level to relations at the tribal level, thereby distorting our view of Aboriginal societies.

A few authors, such as Susan Sharrock and Patricia Albers, have examined multicultural groups, but not to a degree that helps explain the multicultural nature of the Cowessess band.[1] Sharrock discussed the ethnogenesis of the Cree/Assiniboine, and Albers outlined the merger and alliance of the Cree,

Saulteaux, and Assiniboine. However, there is no evidence that the Cowessess band developed a singular distinctive culture. Sharrock's and Albers' conclusions also fail to explain how the Métis, a group supposedly culturally and racially distinct from First Nations, became incorporated into bands.

The tribal history approach ignores the importance that kinship played in band formation and maintenance. In contrast to the fluidity of bands, according to Sharrock, "the membership or composition of each tribe or aggregation of bands has been equated with the members of an ethnic unit, with the speakers of an interintelligible language, with territorial co-residents, and with a society comprising the carriers or practitioners of a particular culture."[2] Tribes were culturally and politically bounded entities.

Extrapolating band-level relations from those at the tribal level has presented a confounded view of Aboriginal societies. As a doctoral student, Neal McLeod, a member of the James Smith First Nation, located just south of Prince Albert, Saskatchewan, wanted to write a history of the Plains Cree. He soon realized, however, that his project would not be as straightforward as he first thought:

> I had always assumed that my Reserve, James Smith, was a part of the "Plains Cree nation" because that is how my family identi-fied.... However, as I began to talk to various old people from my Reserve, I became very aware of the contingency of the label "Plains Cree" had for my band. I became aware of the ambiguous genealogies that permeated my own family tree, as well as the nar-rative ironies that emerged when one tried to create a "national" discourse. In addition to the discovery of my own family tree, I became increasingly aware that the situation of James Smith was widespread, and the assertion of a pure, essentialized "Cree" identity (or even a Plains Cree identity) was extremely misleading and limiting.[3]

McLeod came to realize that the people on his reserve, like many in Saskatchewan, were of mixed ancestry. He found that the "reserve system solidified, localized and indeed simplified the linguistic diversity [and there-fore the cultural diversity] which once existed in Western Canada."[4] McLeod discovered that members of James Smith were descendents of Plains Cree, Saulteaux, Métis, and Dene people. The tribal-specific approach fails to ex-plain the existence of multicultural bands such as Cowessess and James Smith in the pre-treaty period. Contrary to the tribal view, most Aboriginal bands in the northern plains of Saskatchewan were kin-based and multicultural. Plains Cree, Saulteaux, Assiniboine, and Métis individuals shared similar cultural kinship practices that allowed them to integrate others into their bands.

To be clear, multicultural bands like Cowessess did not develop a singular hybridized culture such as those described by Sharrock and Albers, but rather were able to maintain multiple cultures. This is not to suggest that cultural sharing did not occur, but because there were significant numbers from various cultures within the bands, these individuals were not forced to acculturate to another group. A few examples from Cowessess provide insight into its multicultural nature. In 1914, anthropologist Alanson Skinner published an article that described clan systems among the Saulteaux of Manitoba and Saskatchewan. During his visit to Cowessess, a band member informed Skinner that the Saulteaux members of the reserve belonged to one of two clans, the Blue Jay and the Eagle.[5] Thirty years after settling on the reserve, then, the Saulteaux members of Cowessess band were still known to belong to clans. The Plains Cree members of the band, however, did not belong to these clans, which were something foreign to their society. Skinner also collected a series of Plains Cree Elder Brother stories.[6] He published these stories as being Plains Cree in origin, but noted that some were collected from Saulteaux members and were about the Saulteaux cultural hero, Nanabush. Finally, there is anecdotal evidence to suggest that some cultural sharing occurred between Plains Cree and Saulteaux band members. One band elder once told me that many of the old people, such as my grandfather, spoke a "half-breed Cree" language. This language was not, as I had assumed, a mixture of Cree and English or Cree and French, but rather a mixture of Cree and Saulteaux. Although this elder could understand the language, she did not consider it her language, for she was Assiniboine. That individual band members spoke, or at least understood, more than one language—a number of band members also spoke Michif, the Métis language—and Plains Cree and Saulteaux members maintained their own trickster/transformer stories is illustrative of the band's multiculturalism.

Individuals from various cultures were able to coexist in the same band because they shared fairly similar cultural attributes. A central cultural trait was the way in which kinship was practised. The argument presented in this chapter, then, is that the scholarly focus on tribal affiliation ignores the importance of kinship ties as the central unifying factor for Aboriginal groups on the northern plains. Group formation, I contend, was played out at a band level, not a tribal level.

This chapter is divided into three sections. The first critiques the use of the term "tribe" as put forth by scholars since the 1960s. This is followed by an application of the critique to the standard histories of northern plains people. These tribal histories continue to overshadow the role of bands as the primary political and social units in which northern plains people organized themselves; and, thus, continue to influence how contemporary Aboriginal groups are viewed. The third section explores the ways in which scholars have discussed Métis distinctiveness in comparison with First Nations groups and argues that these discussions have obscured the close relations between Métis and Plains Cree, Assiniboine, and Saulteaux. Scholars and politicians have created and perpetuated a racialized view of the Métis that ignores their kinship links and cultural similarities with First Nations people. J.R. Miller has challenged researchers to think beyond the artificial differences between the two groups: "Investigators of both Indian and Métis history topics really must ask themselves how much longer they are willing to allow obsolete statutory distinctions that were developed in Ottawa in pursuit of bureaucratic convenience and economy to shape their research strategies."[7]

That the term "tribe" is problematic is not a new notion; Morton Fried was the first to point out certain flaws with it. As summarized by Sharrock, Fried identified two important shortcomings of the term: "1) the validity of tribe as a general stage or level of sociopolitical integration is questionable; and 2) tribe, by non-specific definitions, cannot be correlated completely with any extant or historically well documented, bounded sociocultural unit."[8] For Sharrock, the non-specific definitions of tribe are problematic because of "the confounded idea that a tribe is at one and the same time, an ethnic unit, a linguistic unit, a territorial co-residence unit, a cultural unit and societal unit…. Seldom are these units discretely bounded and correlative in membership composition."[9] Patricia Albers also questions the use of the term tribe and highlights the importance of kinship:

> The historical situation of the Plains Cree, Assiniboine and the Ojibwa did not conform to typical tribal models where territories were divided, claimed and defended by discrete ethnic groups, nor did it fit descriptions in which political allegiances were defined primarily in exclusive ethnic terms. Ethnicity in the generic and

highly abstract sense of a "tribal" name did not always function as marker of geopolitical boundaries. Given a pluralistic pattern of land use and alliance making, most of their ethnic categories did not have a high level of salience or any a priori power to organize and distribute people across geographic space. What appears to have been more important in defining the geopolitics of access to land, labor and resources were social ties based on ties of kinship and sodality in their varied metaphoric extensions and expressions.[10]

However, as mentioned above, Albers does not give serious consideration to how Métis fit within this group dynamic. For Ray Fogelson, tribe is an inaccurate reflection of Aboriginal societies, and so he prefers the term "community."[11] The "idea of communities," he writes, "is preferable to the idea of tribes, since tribes are politico-legal entities rather than direct face-to-face interactive social groups. Furthermore, in aboriginal and neo-aboriginal times, there were very few true tribes, in the sense of institutions with clear lines of political authority, chiefs, councils, and strict membership criteria.... Tribes were not primordial polities but institutions created to facilitate interactions with states."[12]

Regna Darnell further asserts "that 'tribe' is a highly suspect and thoroughly ethnocentric category, particularly when applied to nomadic hunter-gatherer traditions."[13] Theodore Binnema identifies a particular problem with employing the notion of tribe when studying group relations: "By focusing on a single group such as Crees, the Kutenais, or the Crow, we risk overlooking the important network of relationships that existed between ethnic groups."[14] For most Aboriginal people in general, and for Plains Cree, Assiniboine, Saulteaux, and Métis specifically, the network of kinship relations was more important than ethnicity for group identity formation.

In her study of Northern Cheyenne relations with the United States government, Christina Berndt argues that one of the results of the use of the term "tribe" is that it becomes easier to diminish the political integrity of Aboriginal people:

> Viewing Native nations as tribes has provided both scholars and government officials with a set of categories that facilitate their efforts to contain, define, and control Native people. Yet, Americans' perceptions of the American Indian tribes reflect a

certain ambiguity about acknowledging the sovereignty status of Native nations.… Representing Indian peoples as tribal nations provides an ambiguity that allows both scholars and officials to construct them either as bounded entities with a uniform membership, culture, and territory or as chaotic, boundless, irrational entities lacking national formation depending on the agenda of the moment.[15]

Berndt asks how Aboriginal nationhood as a sovereign category might be conceptualized "without relying on nation-state assumption."[16] Relying on scholars such as Tom Holm, Dianne Pearson, Ben Chavis, Vine Deloria Jr., Clifford Lytle, David Wilkins, Tsianina Lowmawiama, and John Carlos Rowe, Berndt articulates a sovereign Native nationhood model with kinship as its foundation to explain the political and social organization of the Northern Cheyenne.[17] In a fashion similar to the Iron Alliance, Berndt shows that the Cheyenne used kinship to enhance political, military, economic, and social ties, enabling them to migrate from the eastern woodlands onto the plains: "They were also able to create multiple alliances with outsiders—sometimes even with enemies. They were able to intermarry outsiders and adopt enemies and remain a people. The flexibility of kinship organization allowed them to spread across vast geographic distances and incorporate a wide range of outsiders into their families and yet always remain unified."[18] Therefore, the term tribe does accurately describe the Northern Cheyenne social and political organization.

Though Berndt's application of kinship is very useful to guide an examination of contemporary Cowessess kinship, there are some slight differences between the two studies. The fact that she is examining kinship as a critical ingredient to understanding the Cheyenne from a sovereign nationhood model leads her to describing the Northern Cheyenne as a complex, multilingual, multicultural nation. In some ways, this is similar to the Cowessess situation. In the early and pre-reserve period, Cowessess was also multilingual and multicultural. Cowessess, however, was not a nation, though it may fit within Berndt's conception of nationhood. However, it was one band out of many in the Iron Alliance in southern Saskatchewan that were comprised of a similar social and political organization.

Very much like the Northern Cheyenne, the formation of the Iron Alliance was based on kinship facilitated by similar social organizations, which allowed for the incorporation of individuals from other cultural groups and thereby challenged the notion of concretely bounded tribal units. Unlike the Northern Cheyenne, however, the groups within the Iron Alliance operated as sets of linked bands—politically autonomous units lacking tribal-level political organization.[19] In 1937, for example, anthropologist David Rodnick described historic Assiniboine social and political structures, highlighting the role that kinship played in group formation and maintenance:

> The band was the political unit in Assiniboine life. It was autonomous in nature and completely sovereign. Individual affiliation within the band was loose, since it was relatively simple to form new bands, or for an individual to leave one and join another. An individual called himself a member of the band in which his parents had lived at the time of his birth. Upon marriage he could either elect to remain in his own or else join the band of his wife's people. Due to the fact that such affiliation was not too infrequently changed, the members of a band were normally related to one another.[20]

Describing Plains Cree, Assiniboine, and Saulteaux of the Iron Alliance as tribes or nations does not quite fit, as it was with the bands that social and political power rested. The way in which kinship operated in these bands allowed the flexibility needed to survive and thrive on the northern plains.

The Plains Cree, Assiniboine, and Saulteaux bands all followed the Dakota-type kinship system, in which a person's kinship role determined their responsibility to others.[21] A dominant part in this structure was the provision for marriages. The cross/parallel and arranged systems formed the basis of marriages for many Aboriginal groups. Peers and Brown describe the cross/parallel system thus: "Parallel cousins are the children of one's father's brother or mother's sister (i.e. of same-sex siblings); cross cousins are the children of one's father's sister and mother's brother (i.e. of siblings of different sex). Concomitantly, all relatives of one's own generation were grouped either as siblings/parallel cousins (for whom the term was the same); or else they were cross cousins, and potential sweethearts and mates."[22] Opposite-sex cross-cousins were eligible, but not exclusive, marriage partners. While people were not confined to marrying their cross-cousins, they were freed from the taboos and responsibilities imposed on opposite-sex siblings. By contrast, parallel cousins treated each other as siblings, and were therefore compelled to follow social taboos that strictly forbade marriage. Parallel cousins were also obliged to fulfill supportive roles for each other, roles that were not the primary responsibility of cross-cousins.[23] Anthropologists, however, have not commented on how cross/parallel cousin regulations applied (if at all) to second cousins.

Arranged marriages were an important component of the Dakota-type kinship system. These marriages occurred either through mutual agreement between parents or by purchase, whereby the groom's family bestowed large amounts of gifts on the prospective bride's family.[24] Arranged marriages allowed bands to create political, economic, and social alliances with other cultural groups, including Europeans.[25] Multicultural, kinship-based bands were part of a strategy to ensure survival. Albers states, "Widening the range of contacts and resources to which local groups had access was a sensible strategy for accommodating the rapid political, economic and demographic changes taking place in their midst."[26] Kinship alliances between Aboriginal groups accomplished the same objective as it did in the fur trade. Van Kirk describes the function of kinship in the fur trade: "From the Aboriginal point of view, cross-cultural unions were a way of integrating the Euro-Canadian stranger into Native kinship networks and enmeshing him in the reciprocal responsibilities that this entailed."[27]

The notion that tribal boundaries were concrete has been facilitated by the way scholars have described kinship patterns.[28] These writers acknowledge that traditional kinship made an individual's acceptance as a new band member a relatively easy process. For example, Mandelbaum states that for Plains Cree bands, "any person who lived in the encampment for some time and who traveled with the group soon came to be known as one of its members."[29] Most new members could trace a kinship link to someone in the band, but this was not always the case. In situations where there were no kinship ties, "marriage into the band usually furnished an immigrant with the social alliances necessary for adjustment to the course of communal life. Thus the numbers of each band were constantly augmented by recruits from other bands of Plains Cree, or from other tribes."[30] Mandelbaum recognizes that members of other "tribes" were incorporated into Plains Cree bands, but the implication of this was that these outside tribal members became acculturated to the Plains Cree culture, which ensured that the latter's cultural boundaries were maintained. The result of these scholars' treatment of Saskatchewan's Aboriginal peoples has been to essentialize their identities and blur their multicultural composition.

Even while some scholars have challenged the notion of the term tribe, others have continued to describe inter-group relations at a tribal level. An example of this approach has been used to describe relations between the Saulteaux and Assiniboine. According to Laura Peers and Harold Hickerson, the Saulteaux were on good terms with the Cree, but their relations with the Assiniboine were somewhat more tenuous.[31] They suggest that the cause of the less favourable relations between the Saulteaux and the Assiniboine was competition for depleted resources in the region. Peers supports her position by quoting from the autobiography of John Tanner, an American who had been kidnapped by the Shawnee from his Ohio home as an adolescent in 1792, and who was later adopted into an Odawa family. Tanner wrote that the Saulteaux saw the Assiniboine as filthy and brutal, and that "something of our dislike may perhaps be attributed to the habitually unfriendly feeling [that] exists among the Ojibbeways" toward the Assiniboine.[32] Peers also cited the explorers Lewis and Clark, who stated in 1804 that there was a partial state of war existing between the Saulteaux and Assiniboine.[33] Yet, Peers fails to note that by the turn of the century Tanner and his family were living with Cree and Assiniboine in the Pembina Mountain region. Interestingly, Hickerson states that the Cree were not happy with the Saulteaux's westward expansion, an aspect of their relations that Peers ignores, perhaps better to highlight the closeness of the two groups. Even though the Cree were not happy with the Saulteaux presence, Hickerson nevertheless notes that the three groups set out together to fight the Sioux.[34] That scholars have often used inter-band relations as examples of inter-tribal relations perhaps helps to explain this seemingly contradictory evidence.

Evidence of warfare of any kind between the Saulteaux and the Assiniboine is rather sketchy. For example, the Lewis and Clark reference to a partial war that Peers uses is vague. Lewis and Clark provided lists of characteristics of various First Nations groups of the northern plains, and stated that the Red Lake, Pembina, and Portage la Prairie Saulteaux warred with the "Sioux (or Darcotas) (*and partially with the Assiniboine*)."[35] They referred twice in the same manner to conflicts between the Saulteaux and Sioux, but, despite providing detailed descriptions of battles between other groups in their journal, made no references to any actual conflicts between the Saulteaux and Assiniboine.[36] That the Saulteaux and Assiniboine continued joint economic, military, and social activities at a time when they were supposed to be near to war suggests that their relations were more peaceful than usually described. This is not to suggest that there were no tensions, but rather that any tensions probably occurred at a band level and were not strong enough to result in violence at a tribal level.

There is much more evidence to indicate that the Saulteaux and Assiniboine had a very close relationship. For example, in the late 1790s, Tanner and his family arrived in Red River from Michilimackinac, and later met with many Cree and Assiniboine: "We were at length joined by four lodges of Crees. These people are the relations of the Ojibbeways and Ottawwaws, but their language is somewhat different so as not to be readily understood. Their country borders upon that of the Assiniboins, or Stone Roasters; and though they are not relations, nor natural allies, they are sometimes at peace, and are more or less intermixed with each other."[37]

In 1804, some three hundred Saulteaux and Assiniboine warriors left Red River for Pembina in search of Sioux.[38] The following year, the Saulteaux traveled with the Assiniboine and Cree to Mandan villages to trade for horses. The Saulteaux also acquired horses from the Assiniboine by trading their medicine. Of the Assiniboine, Tanner wrote that so "many Ojibbways and Crees now live among them that they are most commonly able to understand something of the Ojibbway language."[39] That the nature of the inter-group relations was a band consideration, not a tribal one, is highlighted by Tanner's description of one Cree band's threat of violence against his family "on the account of some old quarrel [that they had] with a band of Ojibbways."[40] This threat of violence by one Cree band against a Saulteaux band highlights the political autonomy of the bands. As Hickerson and Peers outline, the Cree and the Saulteaux had a long-lasting relationship, but this does not mean that periodic conflicts between individual bands did not occur. David Rodnick points out that occasional conflicts occurred even between similar cultural groups. He explains that among the Assiniboine, "Inter-band feuds of momentary duration took place occasionally. These, however, were conflicts between two large families, rather than actual band affairs."[41] Tanner's experience with that particular Cree band is a clear indication that tensions occurred between bands, but this did not equate to tribal conflict, a notion that scholars have ignored.

The history of Aboriginal people of southern Saskatchewan during the 1870s and 1880s is commonly portrayed as the history of the Plains Cree.[42] Although the Saulteaux, Assiniboine, and Métis are present in these and other histories, scholars have usually placed them in the background, subordinate to roles played by Plains Cree. For example, Sarah Carter emphasizes the Plains Cree in her study: "Plains Cree bands in the district covered by Treaty 4, concluded in 1874, are the focus of this study. They lived west of the Saulteaux of the parkland and included Saulteaux, Assiniboine, and mixed-bloods among their number."[43] While Carter acknowledges bands comprised of members from other cultural groups, they are nevertheless portrayed as essentially Plains Cree.

The picture painted by historians is somewhat misleading, because the designation Plains Cree often masks a reality of multiculturalism among the bands, especially given that many of the prominent chiefs of this period were of mixed ancestry. For example, Little Pine's mother was Blackfoot and his father was Plains Cree.[44] According to Hugh Dempsey, Poundmaker was the son of an Assiniboine man and a Métis woman who had been adopted by Blackfoot Chief Crowfoot.[45] Chief Big Bear's father is considered to have been a renowned Ojibwe medicine man named Black Powder, who was originally from Ontario and the chief of a mixed Cree and Saulteaux band. The exact ethnicity of Big Bear's mother is not known.[46] Piapot, leader of the Young Dogs, was Cree-Assiniboine.[47] According to Doug Cuthand, Chief Sweet Grass, one of the leading spokesmen in the Treaty 6 negotiations, was Gros Ventre, and his mother, according to Allan Turner, was a Crow woman.[48] Pasqua was Plains Cree, but he was also chief of a predominantly Saulteaux band.[49] Although most scholars have been aware of the mixed ancestry of these chiefs and their bands, they have usually presented most of them as essentially Plains Cree, ignoring both their multicultural backgrounds and those of the bands they led.

Scholars have also gone to great lengths to emphasize the differences and tensions between Métis and First Nations. John Milloy, for example, points to Plains Cree frustrations with Métis buffalo hunting practices. He cites fur trader John McLean, who noted that the Plains Cree responded to incursions into their hunting territory by attacking small groups of Métis and lighting massive prairie fires to dissuade them from utilizing their hunting territory.[50] Peers contends that the "Métis hunts continued to deplete the dwindling bison herds, and, under such conditions, decades-old resentment against them escalated into real hostility."[51] She also states that the Saulteaux presence in large, mixed encampments was not resented in the same way as the presence of the Métis because the Saulteaux "used and indeed emphasized their kinship with the plains [sic] Cree to gain access to the bison."[52] According to

Greg Camp, the European cultural influence of the Métis caused friction between them and the Saulteaux in the Turtle Mountain region.[53] Although the Turtle Mountain Chippewa had complained to fur traders and American officials about Métis hunting practices, they had become economically and socially intertwined with the Métis. Nonetheless, Camp states that "the mixed-blood presence south of the [American] border was no less a threat to the food supply of the full-bloods."[54]

Describing relations between the Assiniboine, Plains Cree, Saulteaux, and Métis in the Cypress Hills, Sharrock cites fur trader Isaac Cowie, who mentioned a combined encampment of these groups, where the "Indians kept the Métis under constant surveillance, besides subjecting them to many other 'annoyances.'"[55] This action was apparently due to a level of distrust that the other groups had for Métis hunting practices. In describing the relations between these groups, Sharrock states, "based on a documentable degree of interrelatedness, the Assiniboine were most closely interrelated with the Cree-Assiniboine [a new, distinct ethnic group that emerged from the inter-action of the Cree and Assiniboine], and the Cree with the Saulteaux. The united Assiniboine and Cree-Assiniboine acted as a unit in opposition to the Cree and Saulteaux forces, and the entire northeastern plains grouping acted in opposition to the half-blood Métis."[56] Sharrock's assessment appears to have been influenced by Cowie's own negative view of the Cree-Assiniboine, known as the Young Dogs. Cowie had had some unpleasant interactions with some Cree-Assiniboine and placed them in contrast to other groups. He wrote, "The Young-Dogs might be most fittingly expressed by calling them the sons of the female canine."[57] In discussing the factors that led to the creation of a distinct Cree-Assiniboine culture, Sharrock outlines the problems with tribal categories, but by privileging Cowie's views in describing the interactions between the Cree-Assiniboine band and other bands, she reifies the very tribal boundaries that she seeks to challenge. Her descriptions disregard the fact that most of the other bands at Cypress Hills were cultur-ally mixed groups, even though they may not have developed a hybridized culture like the Young Dogs. The problem, it appears, is that, for Sharrock, bands were monocultural, not multicultural. This misconception led her to discuss the differences among First Nations groups and between Métis and First Nations groups.

The emphasis on tension between Métis and First Nations groups belies the fact that these groups were closely related, and is underscored by the actual level of conflict that existed in comparison to other Aboriginal groups. That the Plains Cree, Assiniboine, and Saulteaux fought many battles against other First Nations is well documented. Although there may be references to conflict between the Plains Cree, Assiniboine, and Saulteaux and the Métis, there are no actual accounts of any battles. This suggests that the Plains Cree, Assiniboine, and Saulteaux treated the Métis differently than, say, how they treated the Blackfoot, where stolen horses could spark a violent response. The Plains Cree, Assiniboine, and Saulteaux were concerned about Métis buffalo hunting practices, but they attempted to settle the situation by expressing their concerns to fur traders, keeping the Métis under surveillance and subjecting them to "annoyances," or lighting prairie fires. Considering the central importance of the buffalo to their own economic, social, and spiritual well-being, it is surprising that there are no accounts of the Plains Cree, Assiniboine, and Saulteaux waging war on the Métis. At most, there were only small attacks.

The close relations between First Nations and Métis people meant that Plains Cree, Assiniboine, and Saulteaux bands were unwilling to wage war against the Métis, even though the latter were infringing on an important social and economic resource. These ties help to explain why there were Métis who fought alongside their First Nations relatives in battles against other First Nations groups. The level of tension and the different treatment, vis-à-vis other Aboriginal groups, between Plains Cree, Assiniboine, Saulteaux, and Métis has been glossed over by scholars whose work has unjustifiably emphasized differences between First Nations and Métis. Any tension that occurred between Métis bands and the Cree, Assiniboine, and Saulteaux bands does not appear to have been any more significant than tensions that occurred between the bands of these First Nations.

The reason for the lack of warfare is likely to have been due to kinship ties between the groups. The close relation between First Nations and Métis is highlighted by the degree of intermarriage. As noted earlier, Chief Poundmaker's mother is reputed to have been Métis. This was not a lone example. Chief Little Bone, or Michel Cardinal, was of Saulteaux/Métis ancestry, and had many wives who were either Saulteaux or Métis, or both.[58] Chief Gabriel Cote, or the Pigeon, was the son of a Saulteaux mother and a Métis man.[59] Heather Devine suggests that Chief Cowessess may have been Marcel Desjarlais, who was of Saulteaux and Métis ancestry.[60] The father of another Cowesses chief, Louis O'Soup, was named Michel Cardinal.[61]

Although the Métis had developed a separate culture, it contained enough common points that they were able to marry into these bands without any significant disruptions to either group.

The close relations and similar cultural features between the Métis and the Plains Cree, Assiniboine, and Saulteaux is also illustrated by the fact that many bands contained Métis members and by the chiefs' desire to have Métis included in the treaties. During the Treaty 4 negotiations in 1874, for example, Chief Kamooses (also spelled Kanooses) requested that the Métis be included in the treaty.[62] Two years later, at the Treaty 6 negotiations, Chief Mistawasis also requested that his Métis relatives be included in the treaty.[63] In 1881, in the Cypress Hills, Chiefs Lucky Man and Little Pine made similar requests.[64] Also in 1881, the governor-general, the Marquis of Lorne, visited the Northwest Territories and met with First Nations leaders at Fort Qu'Appelle. The spokesperson for the assembled chiefs was Louis O'Soup. Among the list of grievances O'Soup presented to Lorne was a request that the Métis be included in the treaties.[65] O'Soup, who had been a headman and later chief of Cowessess, will be discussed in more detail in the next chapter. Even after the government refused to enter into treaty negotiations with the Métis, many simply joined their relatives in bands that had been recognized as Indian. This would not have been possible were they not closely linked by kinship and culture.

There can be little doubt that the presence of the Métis has added a certain complexity to intra-Aboriginal relations. This complexity has been due in no small part to outsiders' attempts to understand the impact of the racial make-up of the Métis. Since the 1970s, as noted in the previous chapter, scholars have purported to understand the Métis by concentrating on their cultural rather than racial attributes, the practice of earlier scholars.[66] Nonetheless, the notion of race is still embedded in discussions about Métis people. That is to say, scholars have implicitly categorized Métis as a racial category distinct from First Nations people. For example, Métis are frequently described as cultural brokers, cultural mediators, or bicultural because of their ability to straddle First Nation and European cultures. However, First Nations were also cultural brokers, cultural mediators, and were bicultural or even multi-cultural. There were many First Nations people and groups who, to varying degrees, acculturated themselves to various European practices and values. These individuals or communities, however, have not usually been viewed as cultural mediators in the same way as have the Métis. The difference is that historical and contemporary outsiders have viewed the Métis and First Nations through racialized lenses.

Although recent scholars of Métis history are beginning to look "beyond Red River" and provide new views of Métis history, many tend to have simply replaced Red River Métis with Plains Métis as representing the prototypical Métis.[67] As Brenda Macdougall states in her study of the Île-à-la-Crosse Métis in northern Saskatchewan, "It would seem that Red River myopia has given way to a Plains—whether Canadian or American—myopia that still constrains our ability to recognize the diversity of the Metis experience in Canada. It is an unwillingness to acknowledge that the ethnogenesis of a new people was dynamic, occurring in different regions at different times as the fur trade expanded and contracted."[68] As a result, the undertaking of massive buffalo hunts, the acceptance of Roman Catholicism, French language usage, the wearing of a combination of European and First Nations clothing, and other markers are viewed as cultural standards for all Métis. The presence of such a dominant expression of Métis culture has made it difficult to acknowledge the possibility that a diverse range of Métis cultural forms exists.

The scholarly discussion of the existence of proto-Métis bands also heightens the racial and cultural differences between Métis and First Nations groups. The flaw in this thinking, however, is that when First Nations groups adopted and adapted European culture, they were not considered anything less than First Nations. And, indeed, First Nations' cultures have changed. The difference, however, is that there is an implicit racial component when discussing the Métis that is absent when discussing First Nations' cultural change. The concept of proto-Métis is predicated on the interpretation that there have always been significant differences between Métis and First Nations cultures. It is built on the assumption that the Red River Métis culture is the only Métis culture and those Métis groups who exhibited a higher level of First Nations cultural characteristics than European must therefore not be Métis. This denies not only the diversity of cultural expressions, but any possibility that Métis culture has the ability to change in response to temporal and spatial factors in the same way as First Nations' groups. Depending on the location and period, various Métis groups responded differently to external factors, which means that more than one kind of Métis culture must have emerged.

One challenge to the race-based theories of ethnogenesis is to view the freemen not as "Indianized Frenchmen," as Ruth Swan states, but as actual Métis.[69] Historians do not considered the freemen to be Aboriginal because they were Europeans. However, upon marrying into First Nations bands, the freemen became sufficiently culturally competent to gain the confidence of their male in-laws. If they were unable to demonstrate an ability to secure the physical and cultural survival of their wives and children, it is unlikely that the freemen's new relatives would have allowed them to form their own bands. The freemen would have been immersed in First Nations culture, but they would not have expunged their French cultural heritage; they would have become bicultural. They would have passed to their children aspects of their French culture, but they also would have transmitted the cultural norms of their First Nations in-laws to ensure that their children could operate successfully within this social and cultural environment.

While the French freemen brought both their French culture and acquired First Nations cultural knowledge into their marriages, First Nations women continued to pass on their own cultural knowledge to their children. Macdougall describes the role that women played in the development of Métis culture: "As Aboriginal women married outsider adult male fur traders, they brought to their marriages attitudes and beliefs—indeed, a worldview—about family and social life that influenced the creation of a Metis socio-cultural identity. Furthermore, that these families lived in the lands of their maternal relatives and, as was the case of the Île-à-la-Crosse Metis and spoke the languages of those maternal cultures certainly shaped their worldview."[70] Macdougall further states, "Far removed from emerging centres of Red River and non-Native settlement, in regions such as northwestern Saskatchewan the reality was that family life, and in particular these female-centred family networks" were central to the advent of Métis culture.[71] It was the women's kinship links that enabled new bands to be established, and it was the maintenance of these links that allowed the bands to survive. By highlighting the role of Aboriginal women, Macdougall not only challenges the emphasis placed on the French freemen, but also sheds light onto the importance that First Nations cultural practices had in Métis cultural development. The weight given to Métis Europeanness has unfairly overshadowed First Nations culture in the emerging Métis culture. I suggest that this overshadowing is due to the scholarly tendency to view Aboriginal people at a tribal level, not a band level, and to view the Métis in racial terms instead of cultural terms.

By viewing these new Métis groups from a band level instead of a tribal level, it becomes apparent that they were culturally different from their parent band because of the bicultural nature of the freemen and, to a lesser extent, their First Nations wives. This cultural difference between the new Métis and First Nations bands may not have been as great as it would be in later years, when some Métis groups underwent significant cultural change. Certainly, this does not mean that all freemen would have been Métis. However, acknowledging the "Métisness" of the freemen eliminates the issue of race when discussing Métis culture, and allows for change, adaptation, and a range of Métis cultural expression. Viewing Métis from a band perspective also challenges the notion that Métis cultural expressions differed greatly from those of First Nations. Realizing this, perhaps, helps to explain continued political, military, economic, and social alliances between these groups.

Nicole St-Onge has suggested that scholars have overlooked Métis/Saulteaux relations during the mid-nineteenth century in St. Paul des Saulteaux, located on the western edge of the Red River colony.[72] St-Onge states that scholars since the early 1980s have accepted the notion that the Métis "had endogamous tendencies by the early and mid nineteenth century with men occasionally bringing native-Indian wives into the community and Métis women also occasionally incorporating Euro-Canadians, white merchants and voyageurs in the fold."[73] However, her examination of church and census records shows that, in contrast to previous research, there was actually a high rate of intermarriage between the two groups. The prominence of a notion of Métis endogamy emphasizes the cultural differences between the Métis and Saulteaux and other First Nations groups. This difference is epitomized by the (mis)characterization of buffalo hunting as belonging to the Métis and fishing, trapping, tapping for syrup, and salt-making to the Saulteaux. However, as St-Onge points out, Métis women who married Saulteaux men became involved in Saulteaux economic activities. The intermixing of these two groups "indicates that, prior to 1870, ethnic identities were fluid, relational and situational."[74] The Métis and Saulteaux shared sufficient cultural kinship practices to allow for the incorporation of new members: "Given the practices of incorporation and inclusiveness of both the Métis and Saulteaux, there was no reason or necessity in the course of their lives for residents of the Northwest to limit themselves to one identity. If mechanisms existed in both Métis and Saulteaux communities to incorporate European outsiders into extensive family networks, it was all the easier for people already closely allied to merge with either or both communities as circumstances dictated."[75] St-Onge reminds us that First Nations and Métis groups had the social mechanisms to integrate Europeans into their groups, yet the idea that First Nations and Métis could join each other's group has not been considered. Scholars simply have not recognized that the two groups shared similar cultural kinship understandings. However, as St-Onge states, an "initial conclusion advanced here is that converging histories, economic pursuits and kinship ties were blurring the ethnic distinction between the Métis and their close allies, the Ojibwa-Saulteaux, and perhaps others, as the nineteenth century progressed."[76] Scholars' inability to see the cultural similarities is due to a tendency to highlight the cultural differences between First Nations people and Métis people. That tendency itself has been fueled by an implicitly racial view of these groups. St-Onge's findings, then, are significant because they help to explain how Métis individuals could be incorporated into bands, and even become leaders.

The legal status of Métis, as Miller has noted, has guided the scholarly agenda and popular conceptions of the Métis. The Métis as a group did not sign treaties with the Canadian government nor are they considered Indian under the *Indian Act*. As a result, the Métis fall under a different legal classification than First Nations. Unlike First Nations, the Métis are the responsibility of provincial governments. In recent years, there have been legal arguments put forth that the Métis should be considered Indians under Section 91(24) of the Canadian Constitution.[77] However, this argument is greatly undermined because, for over two centuries, outsiders have viewed the Métis as "not Indian," regardless of close relations or cultural similarities. Some First Nations people also continue to hold the view that Métis are "not Indian." From this perspective, it follows that Indians are more culturally Aboriginal than Métis, and therefore have a stronger claim to Aboriginal rights, thus raising the issue of cultural authenticity. For some First Nations leaders and First Nations people of Métis ancestry, then, acknowledging the close relationship with the Métis or Métis ancestry could be viewed as detrimental in terms of rights and entitlements. These contemporary tensions are similar to the historic tensions, for access to resources is the central issue.

This is not to suggest that no First Nations leaders have acknowledged their ties to the Métis. In September 2007, for example, comments by Richard John, the former chief of One Arrow First Nation, illustrate that the close ties between First Nations and Métis have not been forgotten by some contemporary First Nations. According Blair Stonechild and Bill Waiser, the Métis forced Chief One Arrow and other First Nations to participate in armed conflict against the Canadian government at Batoche during the 1885 Resistance.[78] According to John's family history, however, Chief One Arrow willingly joined the conflict. John notes, "There are friendships [between residents of One Arrow and the neighbouring Métis at Batoche] right through to this day. We help each other and it has been that way from prior to 1885."[79]

What is the implication of viewing Aboriginal groups from a band perspective rather than a tribal perspective? Should scholars discard tribal terms completely? There is agreement among some ethnohistorians that tribal designations are a European construction and were applied to Aboriginal groups somewhat haphazardly.[80] However, abandoning tribal categories would not only be difficult, it may not even be desirable. Plains Cree, Saulteaux, Assiniboine, and Métis cultural groups did and continue to exist. While they shared many similarities, there were undeniable cultural traits that differentiated them. It was these cultural differences that made the bands and the individuals in the bands multicultural. Even individuals who were not of mixed ancestry were multicultural. It will not be an easy task to ascertain how many bands were multicultural, or, if they were, to what degree they were multicultural. In addition, given the colonial imposition of the outsider's definition, many contemporary Aboriginal people have, as McLeod notes, "essentialized" their cultural identities. For many Aboriginal people, specific cultural affiliation is vital to their identities.

However, contemporary kinship patterns, at least among Cowessess people and probably for other First Nations as well, ensure that band members' collective identity survives. Cowessess people's attitudes are shaped within the context of family/kinship connections, not by externally defined tribal or cultural affiliations. A person's family name places that person within the familial reserve context. This is not to claim that cultural affiliation is totally ignored, but that it is not the primary identifier that connects people, certainly not in the way that family/kinship does. For Cowessess people, family/kinship ties are of greater importance to identity than place of residence, gender, cultural affiliation, or notions of race. Members may say to outsiders that they are Plains Cree or Saulteaux, but what is really important is to which families they are related. This kinship pattern is historically based and it is what most historians have not fully articulated.

The concept of tribe, with its well-defined cultural boundaries, and the notion of Métis as a culturally and racially distinct group from First Nations does not explain the multicultural composition of many Saskatchewan First

Nations. The role and function of kinship practices corresponds to the values embedded in the Law of the People, provides a greater understanding of Saskatchewan First Nations, and helps to explain the motivation of historic intra-Aboriginal relations in the northern plains.

4

The Multicultural Composition of Cowessess First Nation

That scholars have misinterpreted the cultural identities of Saskatchewan's Aboriginal people is demonstrated by the experiences of members of Cowessess First Nation from the early reserve period to more recent times. When Cowessess First Nation members first settled on their reserve, the band was comprised of Plains Cree, Assiniboine, Saulteaux, English Halfbreeds, and Métis, based on the Law of the People. In the early reserve period, members of Cowessess First Nation, as with all First Nations, faced tremendous pressures to alter their political, social, and economic culture to reflect Euro-Canadian cultural ideals. In many ways, Cowessess members adapted relatively smoothly to the changes, replacing aspects of their traditional cultural ways with Canadian cultural practices. For example, they had developed a fledgling but sound agricultural economy and were the first First Nation in Saskatchewan to adopt a democratically elected band government. However, after 1885, the federal government used the *Indian Act* and Indian Affairs to implement increasingly repressive policies intended to intensify pressure on First Nations to assimilate. Cowessess members resisted by both ignoring these demands and organizing politically to protest against them in ways that demonstrated determination to protect the authority of their band government. Even with the pressure to change, there were aspects of their pre-reserve culture that Cowessess members did not change. The band persisted in practising their customary form of inclusionary kinship as set out in the stories of Elder Brother, through marriage and adoption, thereby remaining a mixed-ancestry band into the twentieth century. This chapter, then, illustrates that the cultural boundaries drawn between Aboriginal groups is a fiction that has served the purposes of scholars and government officials, but has had no relevance to the actual lives of the people examined.

Adaptation and resistance in the face of the Canadian government's colonial efforts are central themes in Cowessess in the early to mid-reserve period, from the 1880s to 1945. Even in the midst of these turbulent times, traditional kinship practices, which the Elder Brothers stories emblemized, persisted. This chapter is divided into two sections. Both discuss the challenges the band faced due to government regulations, and to a lesser extent, the racism of everyday Canadians. The first section outlines the early reserve period, focusing primarily but not exclusively on the experiences of Louis O'Soup, a Cowessess political figure whose influence was felt throughout southern Saskatchewan. O'Soup is important, not only because of his leadership, but also, for our purposes here, because of the compelling evidence of the prominence kinship played in guiding his actions. The second section looks at conditions on the reserve from the 1920s to just after World War II. In this period, the prosperity Cowessess had enjoyed in earlier years declined and assimilation through the residential schools intensified. However, the band continued to resist government intervention into their lives. In addition, kinship practices are still exercised in accordance with the Law of the People—in particular with regard to Cowessess relations with the Métis living just off the reserve and with eastern European immigrants. Off-reserve migration of some members began after the war, with some losing touch with the home community.

The Cowessess Band and Louis O'Soup, 1870–1913

From the brief biographical information available about the early life of Chief Cowessess, it is known that he was chief of a mixed band of Cree, Saulteaux, Assiniboine, Métis, and Halfbreeds who hunted and trapped in the region between southwest Manitoba and the Cypress Hills. He is considered to have been of Saulteaux descent, and his band, identified as belonging to the Calling River People, was centred in the Qu'Appelle Valley.[1] He was a signatory to Treaty 4—his name is spelled "Ka-Wezauce" on the treaty document—but did not take part in the public negotiations.[2] He was said to have been very old, probably in his eighties, when he died in 1886. According to Harold Lerat, a Cowessess elder who published a band history in 2005, Chief Cowessess never accepted Christianity, nor was he given a Christian name.[3] Heather Devine, in tracing the Desjarlais family, noted that one of the sons of Joseph Desjarlais was Marcel Desjarlais (b. 1803), also referred to as "Gwiwisens." She stated, "During my research, I noted that Marcel 'Gwiwisens' Desjarlais bears a name identical to that of a Saulteaux-Cree Chief named Cowessess. ... Because direct references to Marcel Desjarlais disappear from the records after 1847, the possibility that Marcel Desjarlais might, in fact, be Cowessess is compelling."[4] In the 1830s, the Desjarlais band migrated from the Athabasca region to the region bounded by the Swan River in the north, Turtle Mountain in the south, the Qu'Appelle Lakes in the west, and Lake Winnipeg in the east, and were closely associated with another Métis band led by Michel Cardinal, also known as Okanase (Little Bone).[5] This is the same region in which the Cowessess band was based prior to taking treaty in 1874. Cowessess and his band were also among those who moved to the Cypress Hills in 1876.

More is known about Louis O'Soup, a Cowessess headman. He was an important First Nations political figure for nearly forty years, notable for lobbying for treaty rights and economic and social improvement for First Nations people. O'Soup was well regarded as an orator, and the esteem in which he was held is probably reflected in his name, O'Soup, which means "black fat" in Saulteaux, referring to the choice meat of an animal that was reserved for men of prestige. O'Soup, as Sarah Carter stated, "was of Metis and Assiniboine ancestry, yet he identified himself, and was regarded as ... Saulteaux."[6] O'Soup was born in the late 1830s in the Swan River region, and was the eldest son of Michel Cardinal and his Assiniboine wife. He married a Nez Perce woman named Omasinakikewiskwew. His wife was perhaps one of the Nez Perce who sought refuge in the Cypress Hills after they fled Bear Paws Mountains in 1877. Peter Neufeld noted that "at least five of Chief Okanase's [Michel Cardinal's] sons played significant roles as chiefs on the prairies, and the dynasty of leaders has continued to the present."[7] Two of O'Soup's brothers were Chief Mekis, who signed Treaty 2, and Chief Keeseekoowenin, who signed an adhesion to Treaty 4 in 1875 and established a reserve in southwestern Manitoba. Furthermore, according to Carter, O'Soup and Cowessess were full brothers. Their thirty-year difference in age makes this assertion unlikely but not impossible, especially if they were half-brothers. Lerat, however, suggested that Cowessess and Cardinal (Okanase) might have been half-brothers, which would have made Cowessess the uncle of O'Soup.[8] Though it is uncertain whether Cowessess was Marcel Desjarlais or a blood relative of O'Soup, what does become clear is that the two men lived in the same region and had close contact with each other.

While at Cypress Hills, O'Soup was chosen to be spokesman for the First Nations in their efforts to lobby the government for assistance in farming and helping offset starvation. He requested that the Cypress Hills First Nations be provided with a blacksmith for each band, assistance to break the land once Indians had settled on a reserve, free movement between the U.S. and Canada, and that chiefs and headmen receive a log house, horse, and buggy.[9]

At Cypress Hills, Chief Cowessess requested that a certain area be surveyed for his reserve. He had been persuaded to select another parcel of land, as Dewdney and John Setter, the newly appointed farm instructor, deemed his first choice unsuitable. He finally agreed on land next to Chief Piapot. His band was given two axes, four hoes, a spade, eight bushels of potatoes, and began to farm while waiting for the land to be surveyed. Although the government's Indian reserve surveyor, Allen Patrick, was commissioned to survey Cowessess' reserve at Cypress Hills, this was not done because the government began to have second thoughts about the concentrated number of Indians in the region. The Cowessess band's initial experience with farming was considered promising, which was fortunate because the buffalo herds had all but disappeared from the region.[10]

However, the Cowessess' band faced internal troubles, as O'Soup was attempting to replace Cowessess as chief.[11] In 1877, O'Soup led 106 members to Fort Qu'Appelle, where they accepted their annuities, while Cowessess remained at the Cypress Hills.[12] In 1880, after he had split from the Cowessess band for over three years, O'Soup had a reserve surveyed for his band at Crooked Lake in the Qu'Appelle Valley in southeastern Saskatchewan. The reserve was surveyed for a population much larger than was required for the size of his band, and it is speculated that O'Soup had hoped that more people would join him from Cowessess' people, who were still in the Cypress Hills.[13]

In 1881, the governor general, the Marquis of Lorne, visited the Northwest Territories, meeting with First Nations leaders in Fort Qu'Appelle. O'Soup was one of those leaders. Carter noted that, "O'Soup wore a magnificent outfit, now housed in the Museum of Mankind in London, which featured a beaded bull's eye chest-rosette characteristic of Plains Saulteaux ceremonial dress."[14] After Lorne presented O'Soup with a watch, O'Soup gave the governor general his shirt. Lorne later sold the shirt to the British Museum, where it now resides. During his talk with Lorne, O'Soup outlined many grievances that the chiefs had with the treaties, including their claim that during the treaty negotiations the Indians were promised relief from starvation and compensation from lands stolen, neither of which had happened. O'Soup further stated that, with the disappearance of the buffalo, the five-dollar annuity was insufficient to sustain them; the Indians needed more help to be successful in farming. Importantly, O'Soup advocated, as other chiefs had, that their Métis relatives be included in the treaties. Because of these and other complaints, O'Soup told the governor general that many chiefs wanted to break the treaties. The governor general's response was to assure the chiefs that the government would take these complaints seriously, urging them to follow the advice of their Indian agents, to trust that Dewdney would look after their welfare, and cease any talk about breaking the treaties.[15]

Meanwhile, back at the Cypress Hills, Cowessess and the other chiefs were facing pressure to leave the region. By 1881, Cowessess' band was farming relatively successfully, but still had not had their reserve surveyed. At one point, Cowessess, angry over the issue, resigned as chief, but later changed his mind. At the same time, he was attempting to both gain more band members and persuade current members not to join O'Soup at Crooked Lake. Another band, led by Zach Lerat (pronounced le-*rah*), known as the "Chief of the Half-Breeds," arrived from Turtle Mountain, seeking to unite with another band in the Cypress Hills. Harold Lerat stated that a French-Canadian missionary gave his great-grandfather Pitawewekijik the name Lerat in reference to his ability to swim as well as a muskrat.[16] Cowessess allowed Zach Lerat (perhaps Pitawewekijik's son) to join his band, assuring him that there were more members in his band than in O'Soup's. Another reason, besides political gain, why Lerat joined Cowessess' band may have been due to kinship ties. Pitawewekijik's second wife was Emilie Siinpiins Desjarlais;[17] if Cowessess was Marcel Desjarlais, they may have shared some kinship connection. Regardless, Cowessess' move to recruit members indicates that perhaps he was contemplating a move to Crooked Lake in response to a lack of rations available at Cypress Hills, and to a desire of some band members to reunite with O'Soup's members.

While Cowessess was recruiting band members, Indian Agent Allan McDonald tried to convince O'Soup to resign as chief and let Cowessess and his followers join him at Crooked Lake.[18] According to Lerat, McDonald told "O'Soup that Little Child [Cowessess] would not live forever, so he should let Little Child bring the band back together and step down so that the old man could be chief at Crooked Lake."[19] O'Soup agreed to step down and receive Cowessess in friendship. In May 1883, after traveling by train and horse and wagon, Cowessess arrived at Crooked Lake with eighty-six band members, while another 182 members remained at the Cypress Hills with Headman Okaness (who eventually took a reserve in the Touchwood Hills; he is not to be confused with Michel Cardinal, also known as Okanase). Tyler notes that it is difficult to say for sure what happened to the band members who stayed with Okaness, suggesting that some had joined other bands.[20] Cowessess band members have told me, however, that many died from starvation at Cypress Hills, and others died attempting to walk to Crooked Lake. This will be discussed further in Chapter 6.

By 1883, most First Nations people were settled on reserves, yet starvation continued to be a severe problem. At the end of November 1884, the Department of Indian Affairs compounded the situation by cutting back on rations to reserves. On the Crooked Lake reserves, which include Sakimay, Ochapowace, Kahkewistehaw, and Little Bone, Indian Agent McDonald claimed that the people were not suffering from starvation, stating in his 1883 annual report that, "Little Child went to his reserve with the intention of remaining permanently this spring and the short time he has been at work shows that he intends sticking with it, and he has already shown a good example to Indians who have lately gone on the reserves."[21] In addition, the annual report for that year noted that Cowessess' band had sold four hundred bushels of potatoes at a dollar per bushel, which suggests, as McDonald claimed, that starvation was not occurring on the Crooked Lake reserves. However, Tyler and Andrews each noted that the Hudson's Bay Company trader at Crooked Lake claimed that there was no game in the area,[22] and that, in Tyler's words, "the rations issued were so skimpy that many children, at least, had actually died of starvation, and that he [the HBC trader] had been forced to give away food from his store from time to time to see many of the families through the winter."[23] During the winter of 1884, furthermore, a surveyor reported starvation on the Kahkewistehaw reserve, which neighbours the Cowessess reserve. Nevertheless, McDonald announced further cutbacks to the rations supplied to the Indians.[24]

Clearly, contrary to McDonald's assertions, there was a lack of food on reserves, which caused much stress—stress which in 1884 led to a well known "incident" on neighbouring Sakimay First Nation, in which O'Soup's leadership skills were called upon to assist. The starvation at Sakimay led to a food storage house being seized by a number of men led by Yellow Calf. Lerat found an interesting account of the incident by Kanaswaywetung (Old Man Two Voice) in the Oblate archives, probably recorded in the 1930s:

> So they got together and planned a raid and went up to the agency and asked again. They now threatened to help themselves to the ration house and when Mr. Keep [sic] refused, one man whose name was Chackekqwaquian picked up an axe and called the other Indians. He broke the ration door and Mr. Keep who tried to stop him, grabbed him, but he wasn't strong enough as he was thrown down and choked while the other Indians ran in, took out flour, bacon, tea, etc. and whatever they saw, they filled up their bob sleighs and drove away shouting and yelling.[25]

Keith, who was the farm instructor, sent for the police despite O'Soup's requests to the contrary. Three men—Alex Gaddie, a Cowessess band member, Cowessess' son (whose name is unknown), and O'Soup—acted as mediators between the police and Yellow Calf, a Sakimay band member and the spokesman for the group. Chief Cowessess, who by this time was very old and nearly blind, did not attend, but according to Northwest Mounted Police Inspector Deane, Cowessess "expressed regret at the late occurrences—said that the young men would dance instead of working, and that punishment would serve them right."[26] A two-hour meeting was held, with Gaddie acting as interpreter. Gaddie, an English Halfbreed, was probably the son or grandson of Magnus Birston, an HBC employee from the Orkney Islands. Birston had a son, William Birston, who was known simply as Gaddie and whom Cowie described as "a great, big, genial fellow, who could turn his tongue and his hand to anything."[27] The meeting ended with the police requesting that the leaders of the group be surrendered to them.

The next day, another detachment of police arrived at Sakimay with Indian Agent McDonald and went to the house where the young men waited. Police superintendent William Herchmer "gave orders for the police to fall in and draw their pistols. Immediately, the Indians responded by training all of their rifles on the police." Disgusted with this action, McDonald left. Herchmer began to move towards the house when the door flew open and a young man pointed a double-barreled shotgun at his head. No one moved for several moments until Herchmer "decided that talking might be more profitable than force, after all."[28]

Later that night, another meeting was held with Hayter Reed, assistant Indian commissioner. The meeting was long, with little progress made. O'Soup then stood up and gave a powerful speech, stating that the Indians "justified their actions on the grounds that because they were starving and their request for rations had been refused, they had no choice but to help themselves to the stores."[29] O'Soup added that one of the men had reasoned that, "if he were allowed to starve—he would die—and if [he] were doomed to die he might as well die one way as another."[30] According to Gaddie, it was the best speech he had ever heard.[31]

The result was that the three men were charged and tried for the offense, but all were given suspended sentences. The government was also more liberal with rations afterward.[32] Charges against Yellow Calf were dropped, because Hayter Reed believed that he "had acted in the interests of humanity, from the first to the last."[33] Yellow Calf's niece, Hilda, who married Alec Pelletier, a Cowessess band member, said of her uncle, "Our father *Osowopeeshkez* was a smart man. There have not been many Indian leaders like him."[34] The incident on the Sakimay Reserve focused media attention on the starvation of Indian people, but nonetheless, as Andrews concluded, "in its aftermath there was no revision of over-all Indian Policy."[35] As for O'Soup, his reputation as an orator was enhanced, as Hayter Reed wrote that he "was an able orator and shrewd councilor [and] is the man to whom the Indians look for guidance."[36]

In 1885, Riel and the Métis tried to recruit as many First Nations and Métis people as they could to join their cause. There is evidence to suggest that O'Soup was interested in assisting Riel. For instance, in the fall of 1884 O'Soup responded to a request for a meeting with Riel: "Dear Friend: I have heard that he wishes to see me, Louis Riel, and also who is making the meeting with Metis and Indians. If I have to do anything tell me at once. If he has need of me, Louis Riel, send me one as soon as possible."[37] The letter was originally written in French and signed by O'Soup, suggesting that he, or someone close to him, was literate in French. According to Indian Agent McDonald, were it not for Gaddie, Nepapheness, and other Cowessess band members, O'Soup would have led a party from Crooked Lake to join Riel.[38] There were war dances held on the four Crooked Lake reserves, which resulted in the Indian agent providing more rations to placate them. According to Hayter Reed, except for one or two men who fought in the rebellion, the Cowessess band was considered loyal to the government.[39] These two men are not named, but they could be the two with the last name Trottier who fought at Batoche. Trottier is a family name found on Cowessess, but contemporary band members traced the Trottiers who fought at Batoche to the Métis community of Val Marie, located in southwestern Saskatchewan. However, a Bill Trottier, whose father was killed at Batoche by the Canadian forces, was left orphaned and was placed in the care of the priest at Fort Qu'Appelle, where he trained as a shoemaker and later married into Cowessess.

The connection based on familial ties between Cowessess band and Turtle Mountain led to O'Soup receiving an invitation to meet with Saulteaux and Métis people at Turtle Mountain in North Dakota in the fall of 1885. He approached Indian Agent McDonald for permission to attend this meeting, but was refused. Undeterred, O'Soup left the reserve on the pretense of going deer hunting in the Moose Mountain area. Instead, he went to Broadview, the closest town, and caught a train to Oak Lake, where someone met and took him to Turtle Mountain. The Turtle Mountain people sought his oratory skills in their attempts to gain federal recognition by the American government. He agreed to go to Washington, D.C. as part of their delegation after one of their leaders, Joseph Rolette, agreed to be his interpreter on a planned trip to Ottawa to lay out his grievances with the Canadian government. O'Soup returned to Cowessess and waited for word of the delegation's departure. Unfortunately, McDonald intercepted the letter from Rolette and did not pass it along, and thus prevented O'Soup from going to Ottawa. One outcome of the Turtle Mountain peoples' request for assistance was that a number of Canadian First Nations people moved to Turtle Mountain, including sixty-eight Cowessess band members.[40] One of the Cowessess band members who moved was Chicon Pelletier (my maternal great-great-grandfather's brother), who was perhaps one of the progenitors of the Turtle Mountain Chippewa Peltiers. That the persistent kinship ties made it possible for people to move back and forth is illustrated by the example of Pitawewekijik, also known as Pierre Lerat, who went to Turtle Mountain in the late 1880s and returned to Cowessess in 1901 when he was about eighty years old.[41]

In 1886, O'Soup was chosen as one of four chiefs—along with Ahtakakoop, Kahkewistehaw, and Mistawasis—to visit Ottawa to witness the unveiling of a monument to Joseph Brant.[42] The three older chiefs, all treaty signatories, chose O'Soup as their spokesman to speak to reporters, allowing him the platform to put forth their grievances to the Canadian public. He appealed to Canadians' sense of sympathy for the less fortunate in an interview that appeared in the *Montreal Gazette*:

Now if you saw the state of those poor Indians out there you would feel something in your heart to have pity on the poor. And again there is another thing. We have to live on reserves with people we don't understand. I don't see why they cannot find agents and instructors who live in the country. The reason I mention this is that it was one cause of the big trouble last year [probably a reference to the Yellow Calf incident, and also to the Riel rebellion]. Some men don't care of the poor Indian. They push him out of the door or give him a blow. They know we don't know anything and they don't take notice of us. We are not like dogs; we are human beings.[43]

The trip fulfilled O'Soup's long-held desire to go to Ottawa. McDonald had written in 1881, "[W]hat is to be done about O'Soup? I never meet with him without him bringing up the subject of his visit to Ottawa."[44] Although he and the other chiefs were able to visit Parliament and see the wonders of a modern Canadian city, there is little evidence that their grievances received any response.

From 1885 to 1907, Cowessess reserve faced assaults upon their economic, political, social, and cultural structures. Immediately after the Battle of Batoche in 1885, Hayter Reed, the assistant Indian commissioner, instituted many restrictive policies, including the pass system. He also sought to undermine the tribal system through the allotment of reserves.[45] Chief O'Soup was of two minds about allotment, and as a result, by 1890 Cowessess was allotted.[46] In 1889, Hayter Reed implemented a new farming policy that reduced the area under cultivation to one acre and prohibited the use of labour-saving machinery.[47] The rationale for this policy, in place until 1897, when Reed was dismissed as deputy superintendent of Indian Affairs, stems in part from Reed's notions of social evolution. Reed believed that, for their own good, First Nations people should not skip a stage in their development from savagery to barbarism to civilization. Reed stated in 1889, "The fact is often overlooked, that these Indians who, a few years ago, were roaming savages, have been suddenly brought into contact with a civilization which has been the growth of centuries. An ambition has thus been created to emulate in a day what white men have become fitted for through the slow progress of generations."[48] His reasoning was that, because First Nations people were not at the same stage of social evolution as white people, they were not equipped to compete with white people. Carter stated that Reed believed First Nations farmers "should not be equipped with the machinery that would allow them to compete."[49] Reed expected First Nations farmers to produce crops to fulfill their subsistence, not commercial, needs, and that they therefore required only one acre of land.

In addition, the *Indian Act* included the permit system, which required First Nations to first gain permission from an Indian agent before leaving the reserves to "sell, slaughter or barter."[50] Further, an 1895 amendment to the *Indian Act* banned many aspects of the sun dance.[51] By the late 1800s, the government established and funded on-reserve residential schools operated by various religious denominations.[52] Cowessess' residential school opened in 1898.[53] Indian Affairs also increasingly used its power under the *Indian Act* to disallow particular chiefs and councilors. Starting in 1900, non-Natives increased calls for opening reserve lands to settlement. In many cases, Cowessess band members were able to resist these challenges, such as when O'Soup left the reserve to go to Turtle Mountain without permission, but in other cases their attempts to maintain control of their reserve were severely undermined.

Although Carter argued that Reed's peasant farming policy, not First Nations people's aversion to farming, led to the destruction of reserve agriculture after 1897, there is evidence that First Nations farming in Saskatchewan generally, and on Cowessess specifically, actually continued to prosper into the twentieth century. A study published in 1999, for example, showed that the number of acres under cultivation and the bushels of crops produced in the Treaty 4 region of Saskatchewan increased dramatically between 1897 and 1915. The number of livestock owned by these reserves also showed a slight increase in this period.[54] As early as 1882, Cowessess band members demonstrated a strong inclination for farming. Men such as Aisacan, Ambrose Delorme, Francis Delorme, Equequanape, Baptiste Henry, Alex Gaddie, Nepapheness, Louis O'Soup, Pierriche Pelletier (my maternal great-great-grandfather), Joseph Sparvier, and Zac Lerat were noted as being successful farmers,[55] while Joe Lerat, Ed and Augustin Pelletier Wahpekaneraup, and Wapamouse (my maternal great-great-grandfather) were described as having significant numbers of livestock.[56] Their success in farming enabled band members to purchase farm equipment without funds from Indian Affairs. Even after Reed implemented his farming policy, Cowessess farmers continued to purchase their own machinery, as well as build their own grist mill in 1891, in clear violation of Reed's policies.[57] The band did not feel the impact of Reed's policy because Indian Agent McDonald refused to enforce it. Despite tremendous pressure from Reed, McDonald believed that the peasant-farming policy was counterproductive to the assimilation objectives of Indian Affairs. The quality of Cowessess livestock was recognized, for example, when in 1888 O'Soup took three first-prize awards at the Broadview Fair for his milk cow, three-year-old steers, and fattest steer.[58] The success of Cowessess' farmers should not be understood to mean that they enjoyed the same economic prosperity as non-Native farmers, for they did not, as they still faced many bureaucratic and economic obstacles. However, farming was an effective means of meeting their economic needs. As Tyler pointed out, by 1897, the last year that Reed's policy was in place, nearly all the families on Cowessess depended on farming to survive.[59] In spite of government policies, Cowessess' people and other First Nations communities continued to increase their agricultural output until the dustbowls of the Depression (which one researcher suggested had more to do with the collapse of Indian agriculture than Reed's repressive policies).[60]

In 1887, the political structure on Cowessess changed, as a parliamentary Order-in-Council approved a request from Cowessess to switch from a traditional leadership model to an elected chief and council. Cowessess was apparently the first band in the northwest to adopt an elected council, and in the fall of 1887, O'Soup, who had succeeded Cowessess as chief when he passed away in 1886, was unanimously elected chief for a three-year term.[61] Though Cowessess had accepted the new government structure, the Indian Affairs office still held considerable influence, maintaining the power to approve all elections. In 1894, Reed, who wanted to do away with the position of chief so that First Nations people would not have leaders to stand up to the Indian Agents, offered Cowessess a wagon in exchange for abandoning those positions.[62] O'Soup was in favour of eliminating the positions of chief and council, and using the saved money for the benefit of the whole band.[63] However, a majority of band members were opposed to this idea and rejected Reed's offer.[64] After the refusal of the department's offer, McDonald informed the band that, under the *Indian Act*, the band was entitled to elect a chief but no headmen, even though they had previously been electing four headmen. Joseph Lerat responded to McDonald, saying that by accepting democratically elected chiefs Cowessess had in effect lost the right to have four headmen, as had been recognized by treaty. McDonald replied that, "as a special act of generosity the government would allow the band to elect two headmen, but that Department reserved the right to annul this privilege at any time."[65]

Meanwhile, as early as the 1880s, residents in the neighbouring towns of Whitewood and Broadview had petitioned to open reserve land to white settlement. While McDonald was the Indian agent, he advocated on behalf of the Indians, mainly because he was committed to First Nations assimilation. For him, reserve land was a means to train First Nations in agriculture and thereby accelerate their assimilation. However, by the early 1900s, with new department personnel in place, the possibility of land surrenders moved closer to reality. In 1906, another petition was put forward, asking that the southern portion of the Cowessess reserve closest to the white towns be opened for settlement. At this time, the Cowessess reserve contained 49,920 acres of land. In 1907, William Graham, the Indian commissioner, handled all the negotiations and was able to obtain land surrenders from Pasquah, Muscowpetung, and Kahkewistahaw First Nations.[66]

The evidence shows that there were some inconsistencies in the negotiations for the Cowessess land surrender. According to Tyler, land surrenders could only occur with the consent of fifty percent plus one of all adult male band members. Lerat outlined the discrepancies of the surrender.[67] First, only twenty-nine of the eligible thirty-eight or thirty-nine actually voted. Alex Tanner's sons told Lerat that their father did not go to the meeting because he was against the surrender. Another person who had been recorded as having voted yes to the surrender did not exist. Furthermore, two men, Francis and Norbert Delorme, were recorded as receiving their sixty-six dollar share of the sale, but were not recorded as having voted. The vote was 15–14 in favour of the surrender, with Alex Gaddie, who acted as interpreter, casting the deciding vote. Gaddie's farm was a part of the surrendered land and he expected to be compensated for the improvements he had made. He was eventually awarded thirty-three dollars as compensation. Finally, on the land surrender document, where it was originally written, "That he is a Chief of the said band of Indians," the word "Chief" was crossed out and replaced, handwritten, with "Indian." Consequently, it was Gaddie's mark, not Chief Joe Lerat's, on the document. As Lerat stated, "They decided that Gaddie could sign the surrender, instead of the chief, and then the numbers just don't add up." The total land surrendered was 20,704 acres (see Map 2). Though there was clear wrongdoing by the government, Lerat placed a share of the blame for the illegal surrender on Gaddie.[68]

Unlike the economic adaptations that were readily made, the social adaptations in the kinship patterns ordering community relations were not abandoned or replaced by Canadian social values and patterns. Cowessess band continued the pre-reserve practice of accepting new members into the band well into the 1900s. Sometime during the 1890s, for example, two men, Wapamouse (also spelled Wapahmoose) and Patrick Redwood, transferred into the band. Wapamouse was the son of Chief Wahpemoosetoosis (White Calf), who had signed Treaty 4. When Wahpemoosetoosis left Cypress Hills, he moved to the reserve led by his son, Chief Star Blanket.[69] Redwood was a carpenter who married a Cowessess woman. There were also a number of white children who were adopted by Cowessess families. O'Soup, who suffered the loss of three daughters from, perhaps, starvation during the winter of 1881, adopted a boy of Irish descent. The boy's parents had apparently deserted him and he was left with the priest at the Qu'Appelle Industrial School, where the adoption was arranged.[70] According to Janice Acoose, O'Soup adopted her paternal grandmother, Madeline, also of Irish descent.[71] Madeline later married the famous Saulteaux long-distance runner Paul Acoose from the neighbouring Sakimay First Nation.[72] According to band elders, a number of Cowessess families traveled to Winnipeg around 1905 and adopted up to seven white children, including Mariah Lerat, Harold Lerat's mother. Lerat confirmed that Gus Pelletier and Annie Two Voice adopted his mother, but he believed, contrary to his sisters, that she came from Qu'Appelle, not Winnipeg.[73] However, the people whom I interviewed did not know the identities of the other children, and a few people mentioned that only Mariah was adopted from Winnipeg. One respondent was positive that Mariah was a teenager when she was adopted, implying, therefore, that she was not culturally an Indian. The other interviewees, however, said that she was, in fact, still a baby when she was adopted.

The band also accepted individuals who had either elected to enfranchise, or who had transferred to other bands but later decided to re-apply to be treaty Indians and band members. For example, Harold Lerat's grandfather's brother, Pierre Lerat, who had married a Métis woman named Cecile Desjarlais, enfranchised and was given $160 in Métis scrip. He later requested to be a treaty Indian and was allowed back, but with his annuity payments withheld until the scrip money was paid back.[74] Many Métis and Halfbreeds who had married Cowessess members applied to be let into treaty: "Even though there were bureaucrats that did not agree with allowing half-breeds into treaty, the deal ended up that if the half-breeds came back into treaty, their annual treaty money for all members of the family would be held back until the amount paid to them in scrip was recovered."[75]

In the late 1890s, O'Soup transferred to the Pine Creek Indian reserve near Lake Winnipegosis and lived with Chief Gambler's band.[76] O'Soup had a longstanding friendship with the Gambler, dating back to at least 1874, when both men were headmen. In 1907, he applied to be allowed back to Cowessess. A vote was held in which his application was defeated 17–8. Another vote was passed unanimously in favour of not allowing any more transfers into the band. However, when O'Soup again applied to go back to the reserve the next year, only one person out of twenty-nine voted against his return.[77] Although there was some animosity against allowing new members into the band, the band nevertheless continued the cultural practice of inclusion from pre-reserve times. As Lerat stated, the inclusive attitude of most band members "just shows how welcomed children were on the reserve, whether they were Indian, Metis or white, it didn't matter."[78]

By the end of the first decade of the twentieth century, Cowessess First Nation had made significant strides in agriculture and education. This does not mean, however, that band members were satisfied with government policies. As Delia Opekokew stated, "While the history of the Cowessess Band reveals that its people made sincere attempts to co-operate with government officials, there was also a tradition of reasoned protest against those government policies which the members of the band considered to be contrary to their interests."[79] In 1910, Cowessess band members began to organize meetings with other Treaty 4 reserves to discuss the government's failure to fulfill the treaty obligations. One of the chiefs' complaints was that the residential school system was not meeting expectations for their children's education. As Chief Joe Lerat stated at a meeting held on Cowessess reserve, there was "too much work for children and not enough book learning."[80] In 1911, a delegation of nine First Nations leaders from Saskatchewan and Manitoba went to Ottawa to meet with the minister of the interior responsible for Indian Affairs and the deputy superintendent of Indian Affairs to discuss their criticism of the government. O'Soup, who, according to Carter, "had been clearly instrumental in organizing this delegation over several years," was again the spokesman, with Gaddie acting as interpreter. He presented to the minister letters from Piapot, Gordon, Leech Lake, Valley River, White Bear, Ochapowace, and Muscowpetung reserves.[81] He then told the minister that,

> I was very young when the Treaty was made, but I was in with the
> crowd that he [Alexander Morris] made the bargain with. When
> I heard what was said I thought to myself 'Oh, we will make a
> living by the promises that are made to us…. For many years we
> have put our children to school and there is not one yet that has
> enough education to make a living. [The only way to make a living
> was to farm, for which they had to] go to their parents for a start
> and their parents have nothing to give them, and the young men
> is [sic] reported as lazy. But he has nothing to scratch the ground
> with, and cannot farm.[82]

One of the specific issues that O'Soup raised with the government included
the loss of Indian status for women who married non-Indians, which had
happened to his daughter. He also argued that the land where Treaty 4 was
signed, known as Qu'Appelle Flats, was First Nations land. In fact, in the
1990s, that parcel of land was given reserve status for use by all Treaty 4 bands.
Celebrations are held there each year during the week of 8 to 15 September
to commemorate the signing of Treaty 4. According to Carter, he was not
happy with the fact that a customs official seized some of his ponies, because
he could not afford to pay the duties. "You take our little ponies from us," he
said, "although we gave you the country and you are making money on the
country we gave you and we have not money to pay for the ponies."[83] The
Indian delegates also raised concerns about the government undermining
Indian control of their own lands and the outlawing of traditional Indian
ceremonials.[84]

Indian Affairs officials attempted to downplay the significance of this visit
by labeling the leaders and O'Soup as "misguided malcontents."[85] They ac-
cused O'Soup of making "mischief among the Indians and [creating] discord
between them and those working with them for the Department."[86] However,
the legacy of this trip was that their articulation of their treaty rights became
the foundation upon which the twentieth century treaty rights movements
was built. Opekokew stated that the visit "was one of the most important
organized protest movements by the Indians of Saskatchewan since 1885. It
was entirely an Indian movement which demanded changes in the manner
in which government officials administered Indian people. As such, it was
the forerunner of more permanent Indian organizations, which had as their
goal the preservation of Indian rights, and the betterment of the conditions

under which Indians lived."[87] Government Indian policies did not change as a result of this visit, though O'Soup's request for a wooden leg was granted (he had lost his leg a few years earlier in a train accident). The stage, however, was set for other, later Saskatchewan First Nations' organizations, such as the Allied Bands, the Protective Association for the Indians and their Treaties, the League of Western Indians, the Association of Saskatchewan Indians, the Union of Saskatchewan Indians, and the Federation of Saskatchewan Indian Nations, all of which emerged between the 1920s and 1960s. These organizations assumed the roles and responsibilities laid down in 1911, namely to continue to lobby for the fulfillment and recognition of treaty and Aboriginal rights.

Sometime between 26 February and 9 July 1913, O'Soup passed away on the Cowessess reserve. In many ways, O'Soup embodied the complexity of the Cowessess band. Cowessess was originally a mixed Plains Cree, Assiniboine, Saulteaux, and Métis band. O'Soup's mother was Assiniboine, his wife was Nez Perce, he had strong ties with the Turtle Mountain Métis, and he was able to speak several languages, including French. Being multicultural, he could operate within many cultural contexts. Interestingly, he either could not speak English, or did not speak it well, but still functioned quite easily within an Anglo-Canadian setting. The identity ascribed to him by both his European contemporaries and current scholars, however, was Saulteaux.

The multiculturalism of the historic Cowessess band is reflected in contemporary band members' self-identification. As one interview participant pointed out, "I say we're a mixed band, but we're also [pausing to think] we're mixed." This respondent compared Cowessess band members' ethnicities with other First Nations groups: "There is Cree, Métis, Saulteaux, it doesn't make any difference to me. It's like different tribes belonging to one band opposed to the Blackfoot and the Bloods, they are all Bloods." These band members also reflected the majority of responses:

> Well, if somebody asks me, you know, they say, "Where are you from?" And I go, "I'm from Cowessess." And they go, "Oh." And what, they don't say, "Nationality," they say, "What tribe?" And I say, "Well, I'm Cree and Saulteaux," 'cause my mom's Saulteaux and my dad is Cree.

> Half and half, not half and half, but it's mixed. It's the Cree and the Saulteaux, because my *kohkum* used to speak both languages,

okay. My *kohkum* married onto Cowessess in the early twenties, I think—1920s, she married onto there.

We're a Saulteaux reserve, you know. There's a high percentage of mixed blood and I don't know myself the history of the reserve as much as I should. I know that there's a strong influence from the fur trading days. Looking at the North West Company, which was a French-based trading company, and the Hudson's Bay Company, a Scottish-based company, my ancestry ... at some point there was an insertion of Scottish blood along the way.

Though many people referred to a Métis and Halfbreed presence on the reserve, few, such as the third interviewee quoted above, acknowledged that they themselves were descended from Métis or Halfbreeds. Few identified themselves as Assiniboine, though many mentioned that they had uncles, aunts, or parents who were Assiniboine. What is demonstrated, nevertheless, is the multiculturalism of the Cowessess band. From O'Soup's narrative, the understanding emerges that for Cowessess people in the pre- and early reserve period, the greatest importance in social organization and inclusion was not so much what ethnic group one belonged to, but rather the kinship relations that tied people together. Even for contemporary band members, as will become evident later, kinship continues to be an important identifier.

Cowessess Band in the Twentieth Century

During the period from just prior to the First World War to the beginning of the Second World War, the government intensified enforcement and administration of Indian policies, which compounded the economic, cultural, and social stress felt by Cowessess band members. Yet, the social and kinship connections of Cowessess people remained relatively strong

In the 1920s, the number of students attending Cowessess' residential school increased from sixty to seventy. This increase in student population did not, however, increase the quality of education. Many students' days were divided into a half day of labour for the school, doing farm work, cleaning, sewing, or cooking, and a half day of instruction in the classroom. One Cowessess elder, who attended the residential school in the early 1940s, outlined his school schedule: "I remember getting up at 5:00 in the morning to milk cows and we had to be back at 6:00 am for breakfast and then go back to work. That would go for one week, and then the next week we went to three hours of classes. I know [learned] a little bit. I could read. My spelling was my downfall." His father became frustrated with the lack of education that his son was receiving and decided to pull him from school: "My dad said, "You are not going to school no more. You will learn more here." I said, sure, I'll agree with that. So the priest came up and said, "You better go back to school. Fine if you don't go back, then you will go to jail." My dad said, "I don't care." The next day, he came back with the Indian agent. Because I was sixteen, I was able to stay home. For next year I farmed with my dad [and he] taught how to hunt and trap." The poor education that the students received fell far short of First Nations leaders' vision of education that would prepare their children to make a living. Indeed, in the late 1920s and early 1930s, the Allied Bands advocated higher educational standards and maintenance of First Nations culture within reserve schools.[88]

High rates of runaways and the existence of gangs at the Cowessess residential school reflected the harsh treatment that students suffered at the hands of the priests and nuns. Lerat remembered how the older boys dealt with the treatment they received: "I was cheeky enough to know that I didn't want to be in school. I wanted to go out in the barns, even on Saturday, but Earnest [Lerat's cousin] said no, I could not go out there because the bigger boys always had a gang fight in the pump house while the farm instructor was away. There were two gangs."[89] These experiences are reminiscent of those described by Basil Johnston concerning his time at a Spanish residential school in Ontario,[90] and by students of a Chilocco Indian Boarding School in Oklahoma,[91] which suggest just how common and widespread such experiences were among Aboriginal children at this time.

The residential schools were designed to eradicate First Nations cultures, and for many who attended them, the cultural impact was immense. Though many First Nations practices remained intact, many others were at least partially diminished. Another Cowessess member who attended the Cowessess residential school described his notion of kinship:

> Through boarding school we never learned [about family]. Family was already separated, the girls on one side, the boys on one side. We couldn't speak our language. So having that separation and being in boarding school, there were a lot of our cultural teachings that were taken away, so we were brainwashed with their knowledge and lifestyle. That took away a lot of our given right

to know about our own relatives and family about the way things should be. But as I grow older, I start to understand this and now today when elders speak about all my relations, I understand that now. It's not just one, it's not just my immediate family, it's not my cousin, it's everybody. We are all one. I understand that now.

As will be examined more fully later in the book, the residential school experience has had a direct, negative impact on kinship relations.

In the 1930s, First Nations language use began to decline among young people, due mainly to assimilative efforts by the priest and nuns at the school. As mentioned earlier, the late elder Adele Asaican stated that a majority of Cowessess people spoke what she called a "half-breed Cree." For her, this meant a blended language of Cree and Saulteaux. This blended language might, perhaps, explain the very existence of the name "Cowessess," a fusing of the Saulteaux word for little child—"kawazauce"—with its Cree equivalent, "awasis." At any rate, after three decades of residential school experience, parents and family members were not inclined to encourage their children to speak their historic language, for fear of mistreatment. Harold Lerat (2005) first attended residential school in 1937, and explained how he lost his language:

> When my dad went to school he was not allowed to speak Saulteaux or Cree. The kids would get beaten if they did, so when his older kids went to school, Dad said not to speak Cree or you will get beat up. The older ones all spoke the Indian languages at home, but because Elsie and I were in school after our parents died, we lost our language. I learned a few words when relatives came to visit, but back then kids had to be quiet when you had company so I would go out of the room, and because I stayed away, I didn't learn.[92]

As a result of these kinds of experiences, a majority of Cowessess elders who attended school from the 1930s onward do not speak their parents' language.

At the same time, agriculture on Cowessess declined as the Depression turned farm fields into dust bowls. Though a few band members were able to continue to farm, most Cowessess people had to find alternative sources of income. Many were able to work on government-sponsored work relief programs, which involved building roads, digging ditches, and cleaning up garbage. Others were able to eke out a living by cutting and selling firewood to the nearby white towns. Women and children made money by picking berries and seneca root, or by killing gophers for white farmers and ranchers. Many men worked for those white farmers who were still able to produce crops. The men would travel illegally to various farms by boarding freight trains, risking trespassing fines if caught by railway officials. Hunting and trapping was still used to supplement income.

By the 1930s, band members, who had been lauded for the great strides they had made in the 1880s and 1890s, had become mired in poverty and despair, which government officials attributed to the supposed racial characteristics of Aboriginal people. At this time, the priest at Cowessess lobbied for more financial support, stating that, "The Indians are generally poor; the half-breeds living around them are still poorer, so our chances of collecting money among them are small indeed."[93] In 1941, the superintendent of Indian Affairs, M. Christianson, noted the decline of Cowessess' fortunes: "Cowessess Reserve is really desperate.... It is deplorable to think the Cowessess Reserve were at one time fairly prosperous Indians. They had quite a few more cattle; they did considerable more farming and are fairly intelligent Indians, more on the half-breed type.... Cowessess, as I have said before, is a real worry as the Indians are not only very hard up but also disgruntled."[94]

Christianson did not link government policies to the reserve's socio-economic situation. Instead, he implied that Cowessess people possessed some sort of character flaw that prevented them from achieving better success: "[W]e had a greater production farm on this reserve, consisting of 3,000 acres. This land was turned over to the Indians and then went back to weeds, as well as several hundred acres the Indians farmed themselves."[95] His linking of Cowessess peoples' intelligence to biology, rather than to their own determination, was common among government bureaucrats. The "biological" make-up of Cowessess, of course, had not changed to any great degree from the 1890s. They had not suddenly become biologically "more Indian." Interestingly, during this same period, provincial government reports and newspaper editorials routinely described those living in Métis communities as lazy, shiftless, and unintelligent.[96]

Relations between those living on the reserve and those living in the Métis community of Marieval continued to be strong well into the post-war years. One elder who was interviewed said that some of her relatives married men from the "Métis side": "My aunts married Métis people. We used to go visit them. My mother and them were close. ... You see, the Métis lived over here on the other side of the [Qu'Appelle] River." One Second World War veteran, who grew up in Marieval, adjacent to the reserve across the Qu'Appelle River, described their relations with Cowessess people during the 1930s as being very close. People from Marieval, he said, would go to the reserve to play baseball, attend church, and participate in community dances.[97] The persistence of intermarriage between these communities facilitated their close relations. In fact, this particular veteran had married a Cowessess woman, and his mother, too, was from Cowessess.

The presence of the Roman Catholic Church on Cowessess also contributed to the close relations, as many people from both sides of the river were Catholic and faithfully attended mass and other church functions. The church also acted as a unifying factor with the non-Aboriginal population, as French-Canadian and Polish newcomers also attended the reserve church. A possible explanation for the parishioners' multiethnic nature was the existence of the Ku Klux Klan, which flourished in 1920s Saskatchewan, and which targeted French-Canadian and eastern European immigrants because they did not speak English and were Catholic.[98] The multiethnic parish, however, was disturbed by the racist attitudes of these white people—even though the Klan considered them to be non-white. In 1921, a petition was submitted to the priests to create a separate parish for the Indians and Métis parishioners due to the racist attitudes of some French Canadians.[99] This did not occur, and in 1934 the priests indicated that five Polish, seven French, thirty-four Métis, and one 107 Indian families attended the church on Cowessess.[100] One Cowessess member mentioned that many French Canadian, German, and Métis are buried in the Cowessess graveyard.

The Second World War marked a dramatic time for Cowessess people and Aboriginal people in general. Aboriginal people enlisted in the Canadian military in large numbers. According to Indian Affairs, there were 3,090 status Indians who had enlisted in the Canadian military during the Second World War.[101] However, these numbers are somewhat suspect, as some Indian agents were more diligent than others in maintaining the integrity of their records.[102] According to a local history, fifty men from Cowessess enlisted.[103] Some of these, however, could have been from Marieval. Reasons for enlisting ranged from patriotism and the lure of earning a regular income to a sense of excitement and wanting to be with friends and relatives who enlisted.[104]

Returning home after the war, the Indian veterans found that little had changed on the reserve. Indian Affairs still controlled every aspect of reserve life. In the immediate post-war period, employment opportunities were the same temporary, labour-intensive jobs that had been available prior to the war. One band member stated that he and his family moved to Montana because they had been starved off the reserve, a reference to the tight control that Indian Agent Kerley still had over reserve residents: "Well, there was no jobs to speak of. But I was fortunate enough to be able to work with my uncle who was digging wells. So it was in February 1955 that we dug our last well and we had no more wells to dig. No employment of any type. There was no such thing as welfare in them days. So I got to say that we were starved off the reserve and we were starved right out of Canada. That's when we went to the States."[105] Another band member, however, characterized this description of the state of the reserve as an exaggeration, stating that there were plenty of work opportunities.

Nevertheless, by the end of the 1940s and beginning of the 1950s, many band members had begun to leave the reserve. One elder mentioned that he was fifteen in 1947 when he left the residential school to work on his father's farm. He explained how working for his father led him to leave the reserve: "But the way it was back in them days, it was hard to sell anything. You had to get a permit to sell anything. I had a bin full of wheat and I couldn't sell it, and I had cattle of my own that I raised and everything and I couldn't even sell them because you always had to have a permit. This was when I decided I would leave everything to my dad and join the army, but then I ended up working instead in Regina for ten years before moving to British Columbia." Some women left because they were forced to—women who married non-status Indians still had to leave the reserve according the *Indian Act*—while many others left in search of jobs. When returning veteran Samson Pelletier pressed Indian Agent Kerley for change, he was told to leave the reserve (though one band member believes that Kerley paid Pelletier to leave). The late Edwin Pelletier left because his neighbour continually allowed his animals to eat Pelletier's crops. He went to Regina, where he stayed for many years before returning to the reserve in the 1970s and becoming a highly respected band councilor and elder. Another elder who also farmed on the reserve said that he left in the early 1950s. He said that after the war they were "still using horses, then the tractor came along. Then there was not enough land for the three of us. So I left." For the next twenty years, this elder lived and worked on a farm owned by a non-Native man. Many band members moved to Regina, others to regions within the province, or to other provinces, and even the United States in search of gainful employment.

In spite of the strain of a multitude of outside forces, many retained their connections to the reserve by visiting regularly, but those who moved farther away simply lost touch with the reserve. Yet, even many of those who were unable to return to the reserve nevertheless kept their Cowessess connection alive with their families through stories of their life on the reserve. Many elders interviewed on the reserve had left at some point in their lives but decided later that they preferred to come home. One elder had been away for nearly forty years before he decided to return:

> What really started me thinking about coming home was when I had a dream of my grandmother. She spoke Cree with a little French in it in my dream. I was talking to her and she told me that my home was over there [Cowessess] and I really started thinking that maybe I should go back home.
>
> I liked it [moving back to Cowessess] because that was home. I didn't like the city. I was glad to get that house on the reserve. I felt good. I felt at home. I fulfilled what my grandmother told me.

As Harold Lerat stated, "No matter where the Cowessess people go or what they do, the thing that holds us all together is our past. Little Child's legacy is here on this land, in our hearts and our memory."[106]

5

Cowessess Band Members and the Importance of Family Ties

The previous chapters of this book have examined how scholarly and legal descriptions of Aboriginal people have contributed to a perception that distinct and impenetrable boundaries exist between Saskatchewan Aboriginal peoples. The history of Cowessess shows the mixed ancestry of its members, highlighting the artificiality of these imposed boundaries. This chapter explores the ways in which contemporary Cowessess band members have, to varying degrees, maintained the customary kinship practices the Elder Brother stories embody. The customary kinship practices of Cowessess people have been altered; it is difficult to ascertain just how well contemporary Cowessess people actually know the Elder Brother stories. Nonetheless, based on interviews and participant observation, this chapter will show that even though members may not know the Law of the People, the concepts embedded in it persist. The Law of the People therefore still guides kinship practices, social interactions, and community and individual identity for many Cowessess First Nation members.

The first set of interviews for this research occurred with a focus group of seven elders living on the reserve. I began by giving them informed consent forms to complete while I explained the purpose of the research and the interview process. I also explained my personal background and connections to Cowessess. After these preliminaries, I was set to interview the six elders present (one was absent, at this point). After double-checking, I found that the tape recorder was not working. With the elders' permission, I instead made handwritten notes during the interview. I asked the first question: "What does the term 'kinship' mean to you?" At that point, the final elder came in and sat beside me, so I repeated the question. The newcomer promptly responded that kinship "doesn't mean nothing" to him. This was followed by an uncomfortable silence—uncomfortable for me, at least. I was not sure if he was speaking on behalf of the others, and whether all my questions were going to be answered in this brusque manner. I began to say something when this same elder said, "Wait a second here. Who are you anyway? Where're you from?"

This research was not so much about my identity—though there can be no denying that that was a part of it—but, more importantly, who we are as Cowessess people. I told him who I was, which led to a long discussion among the elders about my grandfather and grandmother (that is, his first wife), and how people in the room were related to them or knew about them. The rest of the interview went smoothly, with the elders contributing a great deal to the various topics I raised.

The elders' discussion of my grandparents illustrates how, for many Cowessess members, particular notions of the traditional kinship system have persisted. Through government policies and legislation and church-run residential schools, First Nations people from the late nineteenth century and well into the twentieth century were under tremendous pressure to abandon their traditional culture and assimilate to the values of the dominant Euro-Canadian society. The assimilation policies, however, never quite achieved Duncan Campbell Scott's stated goal of absorbing Indians into the Canadian body politic. Traditional cultural practices, such as languages, ceremonies, and kinship patterns, were greatly affected but never totally eradicated.

The interviews and informal discussions raised a number of themes and serve as a means by which to organize the following chapter. First, band members discussed the social and economic motivations for leaving the reserve. Specifically, people mentioned the existence of social dysfunction, the lack of on-reserve economic opportunities, and comparisons between urban and reserve living as reasons for leaving the reserve. The next theme that arose was the negative impact that assimilation policies, abetted by the residential school system and the *Indian Act*, as well as the realities of contemporary life, have had on marriage practices and language maintenance, and how they have contributed to changes in traditional kinship roles and responsibilities of family members. Even faced with these pressures, however, Cowessess people have maintained many aspects of their kinship roles and responsibilities. Cowessess people put their belief in the importance of family into practice in varied ways. Central practices that act to maintain family connections as identified by Cowessess people include the ways in which family responsibilities are carried out; the roles of elders as agents of socialization; the important link between past, present, and future, which are sustained through family and community gatherings; the way some members define family in ways that challenge imposed legal or racial classification of Indians; and strategies adopted by members living in the urban context, such as living in close physical proximity to family members. What becomes evident for Cowessess people is that, even though kinship patterns have changed due to outside forces and contemporary realities, aspects of the traditional roles and responsibilities based on family ties have persisted.

Impact of Dysfunction and the Reserve Economy on Kinship Practices

Kinship practices on Cowessess First Nation have undergone tremendous change since the pre-reserve and early reserve eras. A major catalyst for these changes was the residential school. Several generations of Cowessess people attended the residential school, where students were separated from their families and endured harsh treatment and forced assimilation. One long-term effect of these experiences has been social dysfunction, which has challenged the viability of traditional kinship practices.

In the interviews I conducted with Cowessess members, the residential school experience and alcoholism were seen as having a negative impact on kinship relations. For example, one urban member directly linked residential schools and alcoholism on kinship relations. She stated that, "there have been alcoholism, residential schools that have had a really big impact on our ability to bond. ... My father was a heavy drinker and he had two brothers who drank for a while, and quit. ... Then there was the impact of residential school on some of them being taken away to residential schools. ... So it's very difficult to say how things would have been if we weren't so harshly impacted by those two factors." This professional, urban woman explained to me that the level of dysfunction she witnessed on the reserve impacted both her and her family:

> There's so many dysfunctional people living on the reserve that [family] responsibility can become very negative, because people turn on each other and that's where all the backbiting and every-thing comes from. I think that it's a two-way thing, 'cause on the

reserve, you live there for a while, and if anything is going to make you leave it's going to be the negativity that you encounter.... And it's just so much dysfunctional behaviours because of alcoholism and this residential school stuff, and it's just poverty and living in poverty and the cycle of poverty. It's just very difficult for any of the values of kinship and responsibility and community to shine through.

One middle-aged woman, who has lived both on- and off-reserve, and who currently resides in an urban area, explained the impact of the trauma faced by her family:

> It's difficult [maintaining family connections], because we were brought up to think that way. But because I think [of the difficulties], it had a lot to do with trying to protect just your immediate family. I know myself, as a mother, I don't have much to do with one of my brothers because he's a bad alcoholic. And he's got three sons, so as much as I love my nephews and I love those boys and they love me, I don't see them as much ... because I try to keep my children away from what's happening there. As much as you love them, you can't rescue them. You're there to support them, but you cannot live their lives and make the choices for the parents. And so I see, as a parent now today, I understand much more clearly why my family may have been more isolated from some of my other, uh, cousins, my first cousins, than I would otherwise have been.

For this woman, the dysfunction that existed on the reserve was the reason she left the reserve and did not plan to move back: "Like, for myself, I would never move back to the reserve, you know. My husband is white and, like, we met here in Regina—but not because of that [that she wouldn't move back]. When I left the reserve, I had too many bad memories, and I said I would never, ever move back, no matter what. Not even for a million bucks. I would never move back to the reserve, 'cause it's just too many bad memories down there for me."

Interestingly, it was the female urban members who mentioned the issue of dysfunction. None of the male urban members, nor any reserve members, discussed social dysfunction. This may be indicative of the urban women's reserve experience, as they all stated that the level of dysfunction was a direct reason for them either leaving or not returning to the reserve. This woman, however, mentioned that part of the reason why her uncle and aunt had left the reserve in the 1950s had to do with the dysfunction evident there: "Well, my first cousins, I can remember their mom and dad—who's my aunt and uncle—they took them off the reserve when they were young and they moved to the States. But at that time, well, I think the reason why they did it is because of all the alcohol [abuse on the reserve]." Even though some reserve members did not mention this issue in the interview, there were nevertheless indications that social dysfunction was a community concern. During different gatherings, alcohol and drug abuse and family violence arose as topics of discussion. However, the level of social dysfunction on the reserve was not the only reason given by those interviewed about why people left.

For many, a lack of employment opportunities on the reserve was, and still is, a major reason for moving to an urban area. One man, whose parents left the reserve in the 1950s, echoed many urban members' feelings about the lack of economic prospects on Cowessess: "The economy on the reserve has never been good. Jobs have been very far and few between. And, you know, around the surrounding communities, around the reserves, there are often very, I guess, large gaps between the two cultures, the two peoples—the white peoples, the Indian people of the reserves. You often cannot find work even in an adjacent small town because there is—I hate to call it bigotry and racism—but I think it's still probably alive and well." For this interviewee, economic and social factors pushed people away from the reserve. Not only were there insufficient employment opportunities on the reserve, the possibility of obtaining employment in the local towns was also dishearteningly bleak due to the racist attitudes of some townspeople. Overall, the lack of employment and educational opportunities and the existence of social dysfunction were significant reasons for members to leave the reserve.

Change and Continuity of Kinship Patterns

Assimilation pressures altered Cowessess members' attitudes toward some kinship practices, leading to changes in, or even elimination of, certain practices. Anecdotal evidence suggests that certain traditional marriage practices, such as cross-cousin and arranged marriages, continued to occur on Cowessess until the 1950s.[1] My grandfather, Samson Pelletier, for example, married his second cousin, Elizabeth Pelletier. Samson's mother, Rosin

Pelletier, was a cousin of Paul Pelletier, the father of Elizabeth. Paul Pelletier and Rosin Pelletier's fathers were brothers, which made Paul and Rosin parallel cousins, and therefore ineligible as marriage partners under the traditional kinship system. Samson and Elizabeth, however, were cross-cousins in the second generation. In a conversation with another band member, it was stated that there were second cousins in his father's family who had married. As alluded to in Chapter 3, anthropologists have not dealt with second cousins in their discussions about cross-cousin marriages. Accordingly, whether or not second cousins fell within the cross-cousin marriage criteria is uncertain. Nevertheless, cross-cousin marriages occurred on Cowessess up to the 1950s.

Arranged marriages were not common on Cowessess after 1900, but they did take place well into the mid-twentieth century. One band member recalled two arranged marriages. These marriages shared two important features. In both cases, the women came from other reserves and were considerably younger than their husbands. In the first example, the woman married an older man even though she did not love him. Once her children were old enough, she left her husband and settled with another Cowessess man whom she did love. In the second case, a father disapproved of the woman that his son had planned to marry. The father then arranged for his twenty-eight-year-old son to marry a girl thirteen years his junior from a neighbouring reserve. They were married in the mid-1950s, had a number of children together, and remained married until the husband's passing in the late 1960s. There have apparently been no arranged marriages on Cowessess since this last marriage. Interestingly, the ethnic or tribal groups of the marriage partners was not of great concern; rather, importance was placed, as it was in earlier periods, on the fact that the women came from another band.

Attitudes toward marrying close relations have changed considerably since the 1950s. In an editorial that appeared in the *Saskatoon Star-Phoenix,* Doug Cuthand explained the attitude toward marriage held by most contemporary Saskatchewan First Nations people: "Reserves are composed of groups of families who gathered under the leadership of their chief more than a century ago. So, in order to avoid the shallow end of the gene pool, marriage to close relatives is taboo and our elders counsel young people to seek partners from other communities."[2] Many Cowessess members interviewed, whether they lived on- or off-reserve, explicitly addressed intermarriage when asked about the roles and responsibilities of relatives. One reserve resident, a middle-aged man, noted that, "My family always stresses our roles and responsibilities that we will not date one another or whatever. That we are family and that shouldn't happen. We are very strong in that belief that we don't intermarry with one another because of our family tree and how far it extends back." Another reserve resident, a woman in her sixties, stated, "Relatives, aunts, and uncles, first cousins, second cousins, third cousins can't be messing around like in relationships or anything. We tried to keep track of that." A man in his thirties, who lives on the reserves, stated, "I wound up with a cousin myself, but that's because our parents didn't tell us who our people were." This statement points to the fact that sexual relations with cousins is not tolerated, but that for some families, it has become difficult to keep track of all their relatives. An elder who lives on reserve added that marrying cousins was not allowed because "years ago they were strict" about who married each other. Although this elder did not say who "they" were, it seems likely that he was referring to church officials.

This change in attitude toward marriage could be related to a number of factors, the first being the internalization of the notion that intermarriage is morally wrong or biologically detrimental. The Catholic Church, which enforced Christian rules of marriage and introduced new marriage taboos between biologically related individuals, denounced traditional kinship patterns. Many Cowessess people mentioned, for example, that they had been told by the priest that common-law marriage partners would not be allowed to be buried on the reserve cemetery. The ardent belief expressed by Cowessess members about marrying close relatives may also be related to a negative non-Native stereotype of First Nations people, namely that First Nations people intermarried at a high rate. This stereotype suggest spiritual, physical, and mental shortcomings among First Nations people, no doubt making them sensitive to being labeled in such a manner.

Another factor that may have contributed to the change in attitude toward intermarriage is related to the historical treatment and contemporary realities of First Nations people. Whereas parallel cousins were traditionally not considered eligible marriage partners, they were a crucial source of support because they filled the same roles as siblings.[3] Clearly, today cross-cousins are not seen as suitable marriage partners, but they do appear to fill the same supportive roles as traditional parallel cousins. Historical trauma has impacted how families interact with each other. Many of those interviewed mention that all cousins are treated the same, as though they are siblings. Traditionally, parallel cousins, as Brown and Peers note, "played several supportive roles. They called each other's children by the same term that they used for their own children and acted as siblings when dealing with each other's parents."[4] Parallel cousins then fulfilled the same roles as siblings. Today, however, while cross-cousins are no longer marriageable, they do fulfill the financial, emotional, or other kinds of supportive roles that, historically, parallel cousins would have filled exclusively. For example, one young urban member outlined her understanding of family responsibilities: "I think with First Nations people, when someone can't take care of them [their children], then the grandparents or the aunts have to help bring them up." Interestingly, she made no distinction between the aunts being her parents' siblings or her parents' cousins. That cross-cousins can fill the historic parallel-cousin role is important because, if they were unable to do so, there would be considerably fewer available support systems in place, since too many people, dealing with the fallout of colonization, are unable to carry out their historic obligations. Nonetheless, many Cowessess members have maintained the roles and functions of parallel cousins.

The membership criteria of the *Indian Act* have also altered some band members' views of who is considered a relative. Traditionally, the goal was to incorporate as many people as possible into one's kinship relations, a goal that served as a survival strategy. In times of stress, such as a lack of resources or a military threat, people could call on kin from their band or other bands for assistance.[5] Although the incorporation of people into kin networks is still evident, for some there are limitations as to who can be viewed as a relative. One reserve resident mentioned that his sister had married a "non-status Indian" man, and, even though the husband is non-status, he is considered a brother-in-law and an uncle to his wives' relatives. When asked if the husband's siblings are considered relatives, however, the response was, "With him, that is where the line ends. His children are a part of the family tree, but his brothers and sisters, they are not our relatives, just him." When asked if his brother-in-law were a status Indian, would his siblings be considered relatives, the response was, "Yes, to an extent."

For some Cowessess people, the Aboriginal language shifts and traditional language loss experienced by Cowessess people may have also caused a change in kinship relations. Language shift occurs when a generation of children in a family or community learns, as its first language, something other than its ancestral tongue.[6] The cultural concepts are not translated verbatim, and especially in Cree/Saulteaux/Assiniboine languages the kinship terms do not correspond to those expressed by English kinship terms. For example, Mandelbaum noted that the Cree term *ntosim* refers to both son and sister's daughter's husband.[7] An individual's responsibilities corresponded to his or her kinship role. In traditional kinship practices, a person who filled the sister's daughter's husband role was considered a son; he would have had greater responsibilities to his wife's parents *and* her uncles and aunts than a person in the same role in a contemporary Western kinship context. It follows that the loss of language negatively impacts traditional kinship roles and responsibilities. Some research participants, like this one, noted the loss of language on Cowessess and its impact on conveying traditional values: "We have no language. If we have no understanding of what it means to be, to have that close connection to our community and that understanding of where we fit, then, really, we're no different [than people in mainstream society]." Another participant linked the effect of residential schools to the loss of language: "I think that it [the experience with residential schools] really hit us hard. Very few of us [Cowessess members] speak any [First Nations] language and yet my father spoke four [First Nations] languages and my mother spoke three [First Nations] languages plus the Métis, you know, the Métis dialect. So, they never thought of it important enough to teach us any of it except for the odd words you picked up when you hear the elders talk. I can pick up some of what they're saying." She further described the impact that not learning the language had had upon the communication of ideas between her and her father, an impact she believes has led to cultural loss:

> My dad used to say that we would probably lose a lot from the language, because he used to tell us "Uh, just, I can't explain it to you. I wish you understood" when I was growing up. He'd say, "I wish you understand it in Cree. I can explain it better." So I'm sure, we were losing a lot of our culture, and a lot of the elders that I know keep telling me we have to learn the language, like Saulteaux or Cree: "Learn one of them, 'cause you don't understand things, I can't tell you things that I would be able to tell you." So, as far as kinship, I don't know. I think kinship is very much alive and well. I think it's just covered up a lot by a lot of other issues, but I think with the kinship and part of being Indian, there's no doubt in my mind that the two are very closely related. That's what makes us different.

This urban woman also made the connection between language loss and culture loss:

> I do feel like I've missed something, because … when I go back, I see relatives, or when I go visit my grandma, they'll be talking in Cree or in a language foreign to me. And I won't be able to participate, and that's what I feel like I lost. When I was a child and I used to listen to [the language]. I used to understand bits and pieces. I used to never be able to talk it, but I used to understand the words and what I was told to do: you know, go clean this and you go and do this, and I'd do it. But I mean, I can't speak it. I think that's what I miss—and our ways. I have to be directed, because I don't know specifically what I'm supposed to be doing, and that's what I feel like I'm missing is that language, the culture, and our traditions.

Such views support the popular notion that the loss of language necessarily equates to the loss of culture.

However, the research data counters the conclusion of a cause-and-effect relationship between loss of Aboriginal language and loss of traditional kinship roles. In fact, there were indications in the interviews that the loss of language has not altered kinship roles and responsibilities. In the above quote, while the participant links the loss of culture with the loss of language, she acknowledges that kinship is still important to Cowessess people. In answering what the terms "kinship," "kin," and "family" meant to her, this woman responded in a way that sheds some light on how Cowessess people conceptualize kinship roles and responsibilities:

> Now you're using them all in the same context, so what I'm going to say is that, to me, the terms "kinship" or "kin" or "relative" all represent family. How do I define family? To me, I define my close immediate family as being my father's children and my father's siblings' children. But I don't get to see them very often, but when we're all together we all treat each other very much like family. I'm called *kohkom* [grandmother] by my first cousin's grandchildren. I'm their *kohkom*, as well. So it's, it's close. We consider each other very close in that term, I guess, that is how I would define it. …
> So, I think kinship may be defined a little bit differently than

the mainstream, but that's just the way that we were brought up. Blood and family connections were important.

This respondent's notion of immediate family closely corresponds to what Peers and Brown call "immediate extended family" in their description of traditional Ojibwe kinship patterns.[8] For the respondent, her immediate family extended beyond her nuclear family to include her cousin's grandchild, and spanned four generations. Her notion of kinship suggests that there might be an overemphasis on the link between the loss of language and the loss of a distinct Aboriginal identity and culture. There is no doubt that there are certain ideas contained within Aboriginal languages that cannot easily be translated into English, and so language loss necessarily does contribute to a certain level of culture loss. At the same time, there are many concepts, such as kinship roles and responsibilities, that exist in the realm of action, not only in name. People belonging together in a kinship group share an understanding of relatedness, and the English translation, though not explicitly complete, carries an implied meaning that is understood within the community.

For those members who had left the reserve to live in the city of Regina, they mentioned that a disconnection exists between them and the reserve. It is believed that this disjunction is caused by the lack of support that the band provides its urban members. Indian Affairs policies prohibit bands from using band funds to benefit urban members except to support post-secondary study. Some, like this participant, face the dilemma of remaining on the reserve and having access to band funding but few employment opportunities, or leaving the reserve to work and being cut off from band financial support:

> I know a lot of urban Indians that feel disconnected [from the reserve]. They [the band/Indian Affairs] don't provide anything for the urban Indians. It's [support] always for the Indians on the reserve. But us living off the reserve, we're still band members. So, I think that they should still have benefits and provide for the urban Indians, because a lot of the Indians are leaving the reserve to get work because there's nothing on the reserve. There is no economic development and they can't provide enough jobs for all the Cowessess members, so that's why they have to leave. But I think they should still provide and keep them informed on what's happening on the reserve.

Others mentioned that living in the city has led to a disconnection between them and their families on the reserve. As one interviewee noted, "I guess it would be because I lived in the city that I don't know very much about my family." Another interviewee discussed his experience moving his family to Calgary and the difficulty they encountered with the lack of family support. His description is noteworthy, as he outlines the supportive role of his parents:

> The hardest thing was moving to Calgary and raising a family in Calgary. Coming from my background, even though I went to boarding school, I knew enough about families by the time I went to Calgary. Even though I was gone from my family and separated from them, I always knew I needed the connection. When we started a family, my mom would come up and visit, and that was important financially. As family, you want to count on your parents [financially] and also to come out and help raise the children. Or sometimes my mom would take them back to reserve. That type of family support is something you miss when you leave. That's how it was with me with my grandparents. Like that moving away, not having that type of support—especially back then—for us when we were raising our kids in Calgary. We never thought we should go on Welfare. It never occurred to us that there were places around to help you with your kids. Not having family was a pretty rugged life. There was no shortage of work. Calgary was booming at the time. But then I went back to the reserve and lived on the farm. I knew I had to go back. When the boom ran out in Calgary [and I returned home], I found the support I was missing all that time. It was like I'd never really gone.

These participants recognized that living in the city creates a distinct possibility of becoming alienated and isolated from relatives living on the reserve. For some, moving to the city made it easy to become anonymous and simply blend in with others. As one urban member explained, "It's very easy to just live like everybody else, and if you don't keep the connection with your family, it's pretty easy to isolate yourself and become mainstream." Another urban interviewee noticed that it was easy to lose track of her extended family: "Since I moved away and been here [Regina], other than my immediate family, having that extended, there's none of that here in the city. There isn't—that's just the honest truth of it." This participant spoke of the impact that living in the city may have on Cowessess people's sense of themselves:

> I really don't think they'll [her children] have any understanding [of family obligations that she has from living on the reserve], and I feel bad for myself. Someday I'm going to be an old woman. I'm going to be looking at my children around me, and my grandchildren and my great-grandchildren around me, who'll probably see things a lot differently than what my mom and dad saw, and what a lot of old people see. It's a very, very hard decision [to move to the city]. You do not know how much I struggled with moving home. That's a big one—and it's because of my children, not for me. It's for my children. They should be there. Every time I go back there, I know they should be growing up there. They should be there. They should feel that ground beneath their feet. They should be going to those community meetings, they should be part of that community. And that also means, though, taking on that same burden [dysfunction] as everybody that's there.

This respondent not only describes what she perceives as her children's lack of obligation to family because they live in the city, but she also alludes to what she expects her role to be when she is a grandmother. She acknowledges the dilemma of making the conscious decision to raise her children in the city as opposed to the reserve. Though there are numerous more educational and economic opportunities in the city than on the reserve, there is a cultural price for those opportunities. In addition, she believes that, in the city, her children will be better sheltered from the perceived dysfunction that exists on the reserve.

As will be shown later, the importance of family ties to connecting with one's past, present, and future is maintained in various ways and on many occasions. The views of these women about the importance of family were not isolated; every person interviewed, formally or informally, concurred. Even those who had raised the issue of dysfunction also stated the importance of family. Though there was acknowledgement that kinship relations have been altered due to residential school experiences, alcoholism, and social-economic situation, respondents maintained that they had strong bonds with their families, highlighting that kinship connections continue to be strong on Cowessess.

Maintenance of Family Connections

The way in which Cowessess people put into practice their belief in the importance of family ties is through the various means by which they maintain their family connections. Maintaining family connections was seen by many as fundamental to the preservation of an individual's identity as a First Nations person. All those interviewed linked maintaining family connection to fulfilling some sort of responsibility to family members and community. Here are some examples of the diverse ways that Cowessess people have fulfilled their responsibilities:

> I think that we continue to take care of the old people in our family. A case in point is my mother and father. My brothers and I continue to give what we can give. In my case, because I've been in management and done well financially the majority of my life, I was able to buy a second home and move them into that home. My older brother now lives in the basement and takes care of them, and so financially we're supporting them as they age. My brothers have taken responsibility for the family, as well. They have other aunts and uncles, cousins, [and] continue to provide support in different ways, whether it's a ride to the bank or the grocery store or whatever, to a wake on reserve. There's always that time after the reserve, so there's a lot of people around the old people that take care of them still.

> I don't know if there were responsibilities, but the one thing I know is that, from how I remembered my parents and grandparents, if there was a responsibility it is always with the children. There is always an instinctive internal notion. For me, because I am the oldest of fourteen kids and on my side of the family, I am the oldest on my mom's side of the family. I am the oldest of forty grandkids, so in that sense I was always the oldest for everything. I was always responsible for other people. It was something people did. There was always a whole bunch of kids, so at my grandmother's house she had a big day school where she kept the kids, and, literally, she had all the forty kids there as well as other kids she was keeping. So there was always a big group of kids there.

Our family, there's not too many elders left. On my mom's side, there's not too many left anymore. So it's my generation that's the next oldest, and when you look around, you need to teach your children well. You [we, the new generation of elders] need to slow down or you need to help [the next generations] do that. It's important to keep the family [ties]. It's like a big wheel, and you're in the centre of that wheel, and the spokes are your different relatives like this, and it just keeps it going. Some of my responsibilities or what I've learned is, I have to try to keep my children informed about our family, like my grandmother and all of those relatives, and try to keep close ties with all of them because there's really nobody left from my mother's side [of the family].

Well, when it comes to my sisters, you know, at the drop of a hat, if they need me I'll help them, because they've been there for me many times, you know? I've kind of messed up and fallen, and they were always there picking me up. Now that I'm in a better place myself, and I'm capable, if they were to come to me and ask me for anything, I'd gladly do it. It would be, like, my sister needs a babysitter, and I'd be, like, yeah. And it wouldn't be where I'd turn around and say, "Oh well, now you owe me a baby-sit, you watch my kids." 'Cause, you know, that's just not how we are. We help each other out a lot, you know. [If one of] my sisters needs me to go pick her kids up, and I'll go pick them up and come right back. … My niece gets dropped off in the city and she has nowhere to go, she'll phone me right away.

This respondent provides an example of the influential role the oldest sibling has on the family:

[My] family had been drinking since years ago, since after my dad died. My dad died in [the mid 1970s]. So, after that, it took about maybe five, six years, and my older sister started saying, well, this is it. We're spreading apart, all growing our own ways. I think it's time, as the older one, that we try and do something, so one by one, and the next thing you know we stopped drinking. I haven't drank for a while, now, you know—for quite a few years, now. So, this is what I try and tell my girls and my boy, but he doesn't drink anymore … but I'm happy, now, where I am and I'm proud of myself. I get that support from my family, 'cause there's about—out of seven of us, there's four of us they have their degrees in different areas, and one sister is going for her master's. So, we've all done well since we all quit that drinking thing.

For this respondent, maintaining connections was tied to a personal responsibility of giving back to the community:

It's our understanding of community [that makes First Nations people different than non-First Nations people]. Of being part of something bigger than ourselves and wanting to, to be responsible for being part of that bigger something. And that, I think, all comes back to why so many of us, when we're on the outside and get our education, and go on and do other great things, there's always, at the back of our minds, we have to give back. We have to give something back. It's not just for me to give this good job and to be able to buy a nice car. It's something else that's inside of me. I know I have to do that, because that's part of my responsibility and I don't feel good if I don't continue to do that.

The ability to carry out one's duties successfully was a source of pride because it signified that an individual was in a relatively strong social and economic situation. For most individuals, reaching their present situation meant that they had overcome many of their own personal challenges. The fact that relatives seek assistance is an acknowledgement of their status and their ability to fulfill their kinship obligations. Their status is won through fulfillment of their cultural role.

For many respondents, the role of elders was identified as central. The following responses were typical about the role of elders:

It's how you are taught [learning about your responsibilities]. It was how I was taught from my *kohkum*, and the way she was brought up, and so then she teaches those values and passes them on to me. … Then I turn around and pass them on to my daughter. [My grandmother] taught me patience, how to get through life a lot easier, you know. She taught me cooking, she taught me sewing, she taught me many different things like that. That I've passed on … hopefully I'll pass on some to her. It's just kind of like a binding, you know, a binding situation.

The thoughts and the ideas and the values that they [elders] have in life when you're close to them, they instill some of those in you. It's an ongoing process. It's hard to explain. It's values, you know. I mean, all people have values, but when you're close to people—relatives or kin—when you are close to them, you watch and you see, or maybe you do it subconsciously. I don't know, but you're around it and it instills something in you. Like the laughter, you know. Like, every year, Cowessess people get together and it's the laughter, and, I mean, it's deep-down meaningful.

You're taught different things by your siblings or your parents, your grandparents, your aunts and uncles, about who you are as a First Nations people without even talking about it. Like humour … there's a different level of humour in our communities, and a special kind of humour. In the streets, you often see Indian people solemn, and it's really a trait of an oppressed people. And I've done a little bit of talking with various people who have done research on the humour of oppressed people. On the surface we're stoic, don't show expression, we're silent, [but] you walk into our homes, there's laughter and there's a special humour that was always a part of our families. So, talking and listening to my grandparents, watching my grandparents [was important].

My grandfather used the herbs and the roots, and what we ate and what we used for medicine, and listening to my grandparents talk, and he would talk to me in Saulteaux and I would answer him in English, and culture really becomes a critical part of kinship, your relatives. And it just has a huge impact on who we are as First Nations or Métis people.

What becomes evident from the interviews is that a sense of responsibility is imparted to children through constant and consistent contact with extended family members, especially elders. Most identified elders as their role models. The elders usually taught by imitation, but also in direct ways, like how to act properly.

Many elders interviewed on the reserve had left at some point in their lives, but decided that in their retirement they preferred to return home. One elder had been away for nearly forty years before he decided to return:

> Well, my dad had passed away, and I thought, well, it would be a good place to retire. I'll go back home. What really started me thinking about coming home was when I had a dream of my grandmother. She spoke Cree with a little French in it in my dream. I was talking to her, and she told me that my home was over there [Cowessess] and I really started thinking that maybe I should go back home.... I liked it [moving back to Cowessess], because that was home. I didn't like the city. I was glad to get that house on the reserve. I felt good. I felt at home. I fulfilled what my grandmother told me [in my dream].

As adults, the necessity to earn and provide a living, combined with the lack of economic opportunities on the reserve, compelled many people to relocate to the city. In their elder years, however, free of economic obligations, they felt a metaphysical pull to return to their place of belonging. Individuals feel their connection to the reserve at a deep psychological level. Elders in their stage of life are free to respond to this imperative to fulfill their sense of well-being. Though not all elders were inspired to move back to the reserve because of a dream, they did all mention a desire to return. There have also been a number of younger members who have returned to take band-related jobs, usually in band administration or even as councillors. Most band members interviewed also said that they would relocate to the reserve if there were more employment opportunities. Most believed, or perhaps hoped, that a stronger economy would lead to a decrease in the social dysfunction.

Another consistent theme across all respondents was that family meant a connection to past, present, and future. One reserve woman, for example, stated that, for her, family meant "people that you hold close to you, it's all like just one big family. It's important for you because it's your connection to where you come from and maybe even where you're going to." This respondent linked family histories to her idea of the importance of family: "Probably kinship, to me, is my relatives, my past history, my growing up, the growing up of my children, and I guess, like, the histories of my family." Another woman was adamant that family was not based on government legislation: "It's [family/kinship is] all connections. It's nothing to do with the law or government policy or legislation, you know. Your family is your family. It could change a lot of things, but when there's a connection, there's a connection." An elder living in Regina explained in detail the importance of family to her:

That's a good one. Like the relatives, that means a lot to us. It's family and it's good to have a lot of relatives. We are related and we act as such. When we see a cousin there is a kind of bond, and we stick up for one another, and it's a good feeling to be among the relatives. It gives you a secure feeling when you are with family. Relatives, to me, are very precious. It's a reminder of security. We have the same ways because our parents lived together and they have those ways, and then it changes after you get married. They have their own little ... but relatives mean a lot.

Family gatherings are opportunities for individuals to be reminded of their family histories and their relatedness. Such gatherings also provide a time and a place, especially for the young, to be socialized about proper etiquette and community responsibility:

Learned it from my mom. I learned it from my dad. It's just the way they talked. It was just the way it was. It was just the way we treated people when you go to a wake or when you go to one of our family ... our community meetings, you know. The children served the elders, and it didn't matter [which family you were from]. I remember serving ... I was only, maybe six years old, and they sent all of us—five-, six-, seven-year-olds—out with trays of sandwiches. And we would have to go get the elders tea, and through that kinship your ... your community is built. You have to serve these old people and they get to know you and you grow up and you ... you bond with them because that's the way it was. So, kinship was not something no one told me about. It was just something that, from when you grow up on the reserve and your parents bring you to these community meetings to these, these, uh, social things, whether it was wakes or whether it was, uh, band meetings-type things. That's the way it was and it still happens today, you know. You still go to these events—even bingos—and a lot of younger ones are serving the older people with their sandwiches and the tea. And that's part of learning the kinship, I think, 'cause it connects [you] to who you are serving. You understand the meaning on a deeper level, I think—that this person's part of where you're from.

Community gatherings were places where children were socialized in acceptable community behaviour based on appropriate kinship roles. At these events, grandchildren are expected to serve the elders. In traditional feasts, even though women prepare the food, men serve the food—first to elders, then to the women and children.

Family reunions were another function mentioned as significant by interviewees. Members of the Lavallee, Stevenson, and Lerat families all stated that they hold regular family reunions on Cowessess. These reunions attract family members from across Canada and the United States. Some family members may not be band members, but members of other reserves. Some are not status Indians or even Aboriginal. Nonetheless, all are welcomed to the reunions as relatives. The reunions function to reacquaint family members with one another and to introduce those members who had never had contact with their families. The importance of these events is highlighted by the example of a middle-aged woman who had earlier raised concerns about the effects of residential school and alcoholism on kinship. She stated that, "there is no doubt in my mind, when we do get together as a family, like we did this last weekend in our family reunion, we are very close to each other and consider each other very much part of our family." Another man explained his responsibilities at family gatherings:

> Well, on my mom's side of the family, we would always have family gatherings when my grandmother was still alive. My grandmother ... she had seven children. We always had our family gatherings—and they are huge affairs—and so, not only would we have my first cousins, but also, as generations went on, we would have our second cousins there. And being the oldest, I was always the one who had to be the emcee. Part of what I do when I am with that side of the family, I tell them about our family—about our mothers, our sisters, and their parents. So, when it comes to family gatherings, I always tell them what our family background is. That's my responsibility.

The annual Cowessess First Nation Traditional Powwow, held in August, draws many urban members back to the reserve to rekindle family ties in much the same way as do family reunions. The Saskatchewan Indian Summer Games, an annual event first held in 1974, which attracts up to four thousand athletes and even more spectators, was hosted by Cowessess in 1998. Many band members traveled to the reserve for this event, thus facilitating family bonds. That the games were held only two years after Cowessess band members had ratified their TLE agreement inspired many urban members to attend the games, including those who had never been to the reserve. Many of these members were drawn to Cowessess because of the attention that the games and the TLE signing had drawn, and also as a result of the TLE committee's outreach efforts to connect with the urban membership. My late mother, who had made her third trip to Cowessess since 1995, reported on the Cowessess games for the *Eagle Feather News*, a local Aboriginal newspaper.[9]

Some interview participants' responses provided a contrast to the impact of the *Indian Act* on determining relatives and thereby challenged imposed legal or racial definitions. Unlike the earlier member who drew a distinction between status and non-status Indians in acknowledging relatives, these two respondents claimed that a relative does not necessarily have to be a First Nation person. This first urban woman states: "I had a cousin who married somebody not from Cowessess. Now he's passed on, but she's not. She is like part of the family. She's like an auntie. She married into the family, and yet he's no longer here, but she's still part of the family. Like, she'll call to check on us, she takes my mom for coffee and movies and supper at least once a month. [Not] a blood relative, but she's related by marriage. And so it's family, just like I said earlier. It's, like, the family, you know." That the woman was referred to as an auntie suggests that her cousin was from the same generation as her mother. This respondent, however, did not state whether her auntie's siblings were also considered relatives. Similarly, this woman outlined her experience as a member of an extended, blended family:

> I guess it's about how people adopt you. My aunt married a white guy [who] had kids from his previous marriage, and they all kind of blended together. And you know, to this day, I can see that's my cousin. I walk out and I'll see my cousin. People wonder, "well, he looks like a white person, how is he your cousin?" Or they think, "he's kind of white." How you are an Indian? I don't think I've paid attention to the *Indian Act*. I don't think I ever paid much attention to anything in general except for my little world, but I don't think I've paid too much attention to the *Indian Act*. I don't even know what's written in there. I just listen to what my sisters have to say about it.

For this respondent, the definitions of Indian found in the *Indian Act* had no bearing on how she and her family members defined their relatives.

That the city of Regina's Cowessess band membership has nearly twice the population of the reserve itself has meant that urban members have had to make some adjustments in order to maintain family connections. For those who live off-reserve, however, there was a sense of the added importance of ensuring family bonds. Some urban families had been able to maintain their connection by living near each other: "The families like my grandmother and her sisters and brothers always lived close together. So, there's always been that closeness with the families, like with the cousins and the aunties and uncles, and great aunties, great uncles, and it's always been that way." For some urban members, however, distance from the reserve increased the distance from relatives: "I found that living off the reserve distances us relatives. Like, even just knowing the relatives, like, I basically just know maybe ten percent of the reserve. Yeah, they were like strangers, but we did have gatherings, we did get together … but we also have a distance between each other." As the next example shows, in many cases these bonds were forged during times of need: "I haven't lived on the reserve for so many years, but we're still a close family, big family. We always try to get together. To me, that means a lot, because you need that support, you know, especially when we're all … if one of us is going through a personal crisis, we get together." Asked whether the sense of family responsibility changes when people move to the city, many offered this kind of response: "They are the same, but after you move off the reserve, it is a different life and you are not too much with those people, because a lot of those people have moved away and we have cousins all over. You miss the respect. When [my sister] dies, my kids will be lost [as she provides them with much support]. [My sister's] side, they don't know them because they were gone."

The next respondent mentioned that since she grew up in Regina she had not had much contact with her extended family, and therefore did not believe that she was raised with a sense of responsibility to her family. Nevertheless, she did help raise a nephew and two nieces:

> When I was growing up, no [she had no familial responsibilities]. But now, with this, with my generation, it seems that if your brothers and sisters need help with taking care of the children … it just seems like you just do it 'cause I brought up two nieces and one nephew, and I have one niece with me. One was my brother's

daughter, but he moved all over the country with his job. So we brought her up, and then my nephew [and] their mother moved around the city. And we wanted to keep them stable, so we kept them so they would only go to one school and one high school, so they wouldn't be uprooted all the time. Yeah, and I still have ... my niece is nine and she'll be with me 'til whenever she wants to be, 'til she wants to leave or whatever. I think when, with First Nations people, when someone can't take care of them, that [the] grandparents or the other aunts have to help bring them up. So it wasn't ... she [my niece] was just there and, okay, we have to take care of her, and it was no big deal.

She did acknowledge, however, that she had learned her sense of responsibility from her mother:

My mom helped bring up some of her aunt's children for a while ... for maybe a year or two, or something, or help provide, like, bought clothes for them because her sister couldn't afford to. She would buy clothes for them and stuff like that. You kinda just absorbed what they were doing, right? I think, also, if you help people, that it will come back to you. Like, if you help ... like, if someone needs something and you can provide it, and if it doesn't impose any hardship on you, that somehow it will come back to you if you give somewhere down the road.

Many who lived in Regina had been able to adapt to the urban environment, yet still learn the cultural values of kinship relationships and carry out their responsibilities. This woman, for example, described her relationship with her grandmother, and how the way she treats her grandmother is linked to how her grandmother treated her when she was a younger, less stable person:

Like, I know she [her grandmother] enjoys bingo. So, I'll give her money for that, and I'll take or drive [her] wherever she wants to go. Or, one day, I'll phone her up and I'll say, "Come over for supper, I'm making something special for supper. You come over." She'll be say,"Yeah, okay, I'll come." Or, I'll take them out to eat. Like, I know she loves liver. So I'll take her to the city hall and I'll take her out for liver, but I mean ... [I'll do these things] because

I know she enjoys it. I know she would enjoy an out-of-the-blue [surprise]. I'll just think of her and I'll tell her, "I'll come pick you up and we'll go for lunch." There were a couple times when I was ... I had bad luck, and I had to kind of depend on her, and she never, ever, you know, acted or treated me like I owed her anything.

Like many elders, her grandmother used indirect methods as a means to transmit the cultural values to guide kinship behaviour.

Some urban members who have never lived on the reserve have decided they should move back as a means to learn more about their family culture. This woman talked about her Regina-raised daughter's experience of moving to Cowessess:

One of [my] girls has lived on the reserve, but she didn't like it at all because of the conditions at that time—no jobs. So, she had to move into a little town, and she's been living there ever since, working in a little town. She talks to her aunties on the reserve. She goes to visit them, and they talk to her about stuff you know about [their family history], and that their uncle was the chief of the reserve for many years before he passed on, and [about] my dad, or their grandpa [who] died at such a young man. Well, he didn't have a high-school or elementary ... he was a farm labourer, so he died a farm labourer. So, they talk to the girls and tell them about our dad's side [of the family].

For her daughter, the economic conditions meant that she had to leave the reserve to obtain a job, but her relative proximity to the reserve allowed her to connect with her family and learn about her family history.

However, the contemporary social realities of urban living pose challenges to this indirect method of socialization, making it perhaps less effective than in previous generations. This particular respondent spoke about the difficulties that she faces in passing on her values to her children:

I want to teach my kids that responsibility, you know. I don't want to be handing them things and thinking they have to expect it. Because if they get something, they have to do something for me, you know. It's just ... just the way ... I don't want them to think I owe them this. So, I always tell them, "Nowhere does it state that

I have to buy you this. I'm doing it because I want to do it. So now you have to turn around and do something for me." ... "Okay, like what?" ... "Like, wash my walls, why don't you?" I want to teach them responsibility, and I talk to them. And, you know, there's this thing about the gangs. I was worried [my nephew] was in a gang, and so I turned around and I sat down with my son and I told him about gangs and how they'll approach you, and how they pressure you, and the fear of getting beaten up if you don't join. I didn't know. I thought because I kept ... kept my family out of, you know, the central—"the hood"—that my kids were sheltered. But I didn't know. My nephew joined a gang in our area, and I thought we were away from that stuff.

Indian gangs in the cities of Regina and Saskatoon, which have a combined Aboriginal population of approximately 40,000, have presented significant challenges to Aboriginal families.[10] For many gang members, the close-knit structure of gangs has provided an alternative to families mired in dysfunction. However, male youths from stable and functional families, as the example above shows, are also targets of gang recruitment.

Others, like the following person, were able to maintain their family ties with frequent visits to the reserve and by having relatives visit them:

I think that our connection to our reserve was never broken. The years that we spent, the fifteen years that I spent in [the United States], which was about a five-hour drive from [a Native American reservation] to Cowessess—we made that ... sort of that trek back and forth, maybe two to four times a year. And throughout the years that I was in high school, many of those of us who were dispersed from my family, the —— clan, who went to Calgary, Edmonton, and in our case [an American state], the children would come back and stay with the grandparents for the summers. So I had June, July, and August off coming from the [an American state] school system. And throughout all of my ... from the time I left until the time I was in grade ten, I spent all those three months back home on my home reserve with my grandparents. And they were the ones that taught me a lot as I grew up. So, our connection never was broken. We have lots of relatives that we continue to visit and who live on reserve. So, we may have been dispersed but we never, we've never really called Cowessess our home.

The previous speaker called his family a clan. Though Skinner, as noted in Chapter 2, identified two Saulteaux clans on Cowessess in the early twentieth century,[11] it is generally thought that the Plains Cree and Métis had no clans. Many people today, however, refer to families as clans. For example, this woman stated about her family, "Our clan is huge and expanding. My mom, she is a great-great-grandmother, and she's 77." The only function of the term "clan" appears to be that it helps explain how a person can belong to a certain clan—say, the Lavalee clan—without having the Lavalee surname, and is not used in the anthropological sense of the term.

This urban resident said she does not know her whole family, yet her family is a source of acceptance from relatives and non-relatives from Cowessess, as well as other First Nations communities:

> I know who my mom's sisters are—my cousins—but I don't know any distantly related to me. Over my lifetime I've been kind of adopted in by other families. You know how, with Aboriginal people, if you know them for a few years, they'll take you in and protect you like their own.... I don't know a lot of my relatives on my mom's side or my dad's side.... My dad is from Beardy's [Beardy's and Okemasis First Nation], up north. So, up there, I only know my like dad's sisters, my aunts, my cousins.... When we go down to funerals, I'll be introduced to other people or even asked if I know this person from Cowessess, and I would say that I don't know what family that is. They would ask me which family I was from, and I will tell them my *mosoom*'s name and they would know him.

Interestingly, she notes that she does not know her maternal and paternal family to a great extent. Nonetheless, she still knows her aunts and cousins. This construction of family stands in stark contrast to many non-Aboriginal families' notion of family.

Cowessess people placed heavy emphasis on family. Their views varied little, whether they were long-time reserve residents or urban residents. The urban members, however, especially if they were second-generation urban dwellers with little contact with the reserve, tended to place more emphasis on their immediate rather than extended family. Even those who had been raised on the reserve and later moved to the city also tended to concentrate their familial relations on immediate family. Clearly, for many, maintaining family connections, and thereby the connection to the reserve, was a struggle. Yet, most of the people whom I interviewed or spoke with informally made attempts to strengthen the notions of family. Though most of the attempts were at the immediate family level, larger events facilitated extended family bonds. Additionally, the large Cowessess presence in Regina has helped some to keep extended family members close. The band has recognized the need to address urban members' needs and use monies from the TLE to develop an urban reserve in Regina, including possible commercial property and—more significantly in terms of strengthening social relations among urban members—residential property.

During the course of my field research, the issue of kinship or family relations was a recurring topic of discussion among Cowessess people. Many times, when I was introduced to someone, I was asked about my kinship. Again and again, as with the elders in the focus group, the person would then talk about how I was related to them or how their family knew my grandfather. There were also many discussions between members explaining different family connections to each other. During the residential school program, participants were asked to complete their family tree. Ranging in age from their late teens to their seventies, there were about twenty-five people in the program, including the two facilitators and myself. It was discovered that everyone was related to one another to some degree. The conversation again turned to how each was related. The program participants came from a relatively diverse background. Some, especially the older participants, had lived away from the reserve for many years, some had married outside the reserve, including to non-Indians, some were children of those "mixed" marriages, and one was a member of another First Nation who had married into Cowessess. One of the common traits among those participants was that almost all claimed more than one Aboriginal ethnicity—usually but not exclusively Plains Cree, Saulteaux, Assiniboine, and Métis. Implicitly, what was deemed more important was not so much to which cultural group a person belonged, but rather to which family that person was related.

6

First Nations Response to Membership Codes of the Indian Act: Bill C-31 and Cowessess First Nation

In 1985, when Bill C-31 amended the *Indian Act* and altered band membership codes, many First Nations people voiced their displeasure. As reported in the media, these tensions were due to competition over resources and issues of authenticity and governance that were probably too complex to capture the attention of most Canadians. Bill C-31 and the complex set of policies and legislation implemented by the Canadian government to define federal Indian status and band membership engendered issues of authenticity and government funding for First Nations, and influenced individual and collective responses to the new members. Since the 1850s, colonial and Canadian governments had imposed legal definitions designed to delimit the government's wards and its responsibility to those wards. However, the government's legal definition of Indian and the levels of assistance that it afforded those individuals changed considerably over time. These changes were not only usually precipitated by a desire to reduce expenditures on First Nations, but were also modified due to other factors, such as the government's assimilation policy and its response to legal and political pressures. The government's definitions influenced how Canadians viewed those defined as Indians, but, more importantly, external definitions eventually impacted how First Nations people viewed themselves and those whom they considered to be Indian. These imposed definitions undermined aspects of the kinship patterns of Saskatchewan First Nations.

The legal, political, and social ramifications of the *Indian Act's* membership code drew greater scrutiny in the 1970s and 1980s, when a number of

First Nations women launched a court action to strike down its sexually discriminatory sections and ignited heated debate. The legal debate, couched in such terms as tradition, culture, self-government, and colonial oppression, made it clear that many First Nations people had either internalized the imposed definition of Indian, had employed these definitions for their own benefit, or had political reasons for supporting the continued, if temporary, use of the definition. Cowessess First Nation political leaders were not part of the national debate over Bill C-31, as the Federation of Saskatchewan Indian Nations (FSIN) represented them at the national level.

Interviews conducted for this book show that, in contrast to the position of most First Nations leaders, Cowessess band members had a relatively high tolerance for band members who regained their Indian status through Bill C-31. These feelings are consistent with the cultural values expressed by band members, which placed importance on maintaining family ties and which are consistent with the values of kinship found in the Law of the People. Many respondents mentioned that they felt that it was wrong that First Nations women had to lose their status when they married non-status Indians and believed that the women were entitled to be reinstated. Others stated that Bill C-31 did not go far enough, because there were still relatives not eligible for Indian status. This is not to say that all were in agreement that Bill C-31 was well conceived. Some had expressed resistance to the implementation of the bill, while some C-31s said that they had not received equal treatment from the band because of their legal status. However, there was an acknowledgement that Cowessess people had a more favourable view towards C-31s than other First Nations, and that this view was linked to their historical, social, and cultural values.

Entrenchment of Legal Criteria for "Indian"

The *Indian Act* underwent many extensive amendments through to 1927, with minor amendments in the 1930s and a major revision in 1951 that sought primarily to accelerate the assimilation process, but was also used to control and punish those First Nations individuals who were perceived as undermining federal goals. One section that was repeatedly amended concerned the enfranchisement of status Indians. By the early 1900s, enfranchisement figures were dismal. Between 1857 and 1920, only 250 people had voluntarily enfranchised.[1] The federal government decided that adjustments were necessary in order to increase enfranchisement numbers. First, in 1917, the government offered the franchise without property requirements to First Nations individuals who lived off reserve, leading to nearly five hundred enfranchisements within two years.[2] The government also instituted compulsory enfranchisement for any individual over the age of twenty-one who had received an education, had served in the armed forces, or had left the reserve to obtain employment. These stipulations were subsequently redrawn in 1922.[3]

In the end, the *Indian Act* definitions changed kinship patterns. For example, the traditional kinship practice, for most First Nations, of incorporating non-First Nations men into the bands became illegal. In addition, the women who married non-Indians and their children were legally excluded from band membership and Indian status, a clear violation of traditionally kinship systems. Section 12(1)(b) of the amended *Indian Act* of 1952 reinforced the attack on kinship patterns as it stated that a "woman who is married to a person who is not an Indian was not entitled to be registered as an Indian."[4] For the most part, the sexual discrimination of the *Indian Act* that targeted and stripped women and their children of their Indian status remained a political non-issue until the 1970s, when some First Nations women challenged this membership criterion and sparked a response from on-reserve band members and First Nations leadership.

Challenges to the Indian Act's Membership Code

In the early 1970s, two First Nations women launched court actions that claimed that section 12(1)(b) violated the Canadian Bill of Rights based on sexual discrimination. The Royal Commission on the Status of Women report highlights the result of this discrimination, noting that between 1858 and 1968, 4,605 women lost their status due to the marrying-out clause, compared to only 185 men and women who voluntarily enfranchised over the same period.[5] In 1973, the Supreme Court of Canada ruled against them. Of great significance was that all of the national and provincial political First Nations organizations sided with the government in this court case. In 1981, however, the United Nations Human Rights Commission ruled that Canada had contravened Section 27 of the International Covenant on Civil and Political Rights that it had signed a few years earlier, which compelled the Canadian government to make changes to the *Indian Act*. An amendment was finally implemented on 28 June 1985.

The last three decades of the century were tumultuous times for Canada's Aboriginal people. In 1969, for example, the government unveiled its new Indian policy intentions, which spurred widespread demonstrations by First Nations people protesting both old and new proposed Indian policies. The Supreme Court of Canada also began handing down significant court decisions that furthered the cause of Aboriginal rights. A greater understanding of these events will better contextualize the arguments of both the proponents and opponents of the *Indian Act*'s membership provisions.

In 1971, two First Nations women initiated discrimination court cases. Jeanette Corbiere Lavell, an Ojibwe originally from Wikwemikong First Nation on Manitoulin Island in Ontario, was living in Toronto when she lost her status after marrying a non-status Indian in 1970. Her lawyer argued that, because section 12(1)(b) discriminated against Lavell due to her gender, it contravened the Canadian Bill of Rights. She initially lost her case, but was successful on appeal. Meanwhile, another woman, Yvonne Bedard from the Six Nations Reserve in southern Ontario, who had lost her status after marrying a non-status Indian, filed suit in an attempt to continue to live on her reserve. Buttressed by Lavell's appeal, Bedard won her case. The minister of justice (and future prime minister), John Turner, however, appealed both decisions to the Supreme Court because of their "far-reaching" consequences.[6]

In *Attorney-General of Canada v. Lavell*,[7] First Nations political organizations sought and were allowed standing before the Supreme Court, where they argued against changing the *Indian Act*. Their opposition stemmed in part from the introduction of the 1969 *Statement of the Government of Canada on Indian Policy* (better known as the White Paper) by Prime Minister Trudeau's Liberal government. The White Paper sought to "enable Indian people to be free—free to develop Indian cultures in an environment of legal, social and economic equality with other Canadians."[8] The government viewed the *Indian Act*, the treaties, the reserves, and the special relationship with First Nations as obstacles to integrating First Nations into mainstream Canadian society. First Nations leaders viewed the White Paper as an attempt to implement a U.S.-style termination policy and vehemently disagreed with the government's view of the treaties as obstacles. The late Harold Cardinal, then the twenty-four-year-old president of the Association of Alberta Indians, wrote in his seminal 1969 book, *The Unjust Society*, that "the policy statement confuses the administrative aspects (which the government consistently mishandled) with the government's legal and moral responsibilities. The treaty rights and Aboriginal rights, which the policy paper calls discrimination, are rights that the government of Canada, not Indians, has yet to fulfill."[9] The minister of Indian Affairs and future prime minister, Jean Chrétien, dismissed First Nations criticisms of the policies as the result of some sort of cultural deficiency: "[I]t is possible that the lack of trust is a deep seated cultural trait dating from the pre-Columbian society."[10] In 1971, after much First Nations protest, the policy proposals of the White Paper were withdrawn.

After the controversy of the White Paper, the government became cautious about any further changes to the *Indian Act*,[11] including those that would eradicate sexual discrimination. Although First Nations leadership responded with indifference when the women initially launched their court cases, their response changed quickly when they realized the implications. According to Cardinal, when the case reached the Supreme Court, the First Nations leaders came to believe that if the women won their case, it would lead to abolishing the *Indian Act* (even though the Indian Act had not been abolished by the 1970 SCC that struck down section 94(b) of the act, which forbade status Indians being intoxicated off reserve).[12] Cardinal's views echoed the words of David Ahenakew, chief of the Federation of Saskatchewan Indians, who stated in 1973, shortly after the Court handed down the *Lavell* decision, "the Indian Act is the only act that will protect the treaties but in its present state, it is destroying the treaties." However, he did not indicate how exactly the *Indian Act* protected treaties or how abolishing the *Indian Act* would be detrimental to them. Ahenakew went on to say that the Court's decision in the *Lavell* case was "an encouraging indication and a finding for the Indian Act and the treaties."[13] Although there was much criticism of the *Indian Act*, First Nations leadership believed that, with the act still in place, they could still lobby for its modification with their special status intact.[14]

After the *Lavell* case, First Nations women's groups and other feminist organizations implemented a new strategy to address the discrimination of section 12(1)(b). In 1977, Sandra Lovelace, a Maliseet woman from the Tobique Reserve in New Brunswick, took her case to the United Nations Human Rights Commission, claiming that Canada had violated the International Covenant on Civil and Political Rights by preventing recognition of federal status when an Indian married a non-Indian.[15] In 1981, the Commission ruled against the denial of rights: "Whatever may be the merits of the Indian Act in other respects, it does not seem to the Committee that to deny Sandra Lovelace the right to reside on the reserve is reasonable, or necessary to preserve the identity of the tribe. The Committee therefore concludes that to prevent her recognition as belonging to the band is an unjustifiable denial of her rights under article 27 of the Covenant."[16] As a result of this decision, Canada was forced to reformulate the *Indian Act* to comply with the International Covenant on Civil and Political Rights.

In 1980, Minister of Indian Affairs, John Munro, introduced a policy whereby bands could apply to suspend sections 12(1)(b) and 12(1)(a)(iv), the so-called "double mother" clause (referring to a person whose mother and grandmother were both non-status Indians). As of August 1981, no band in Saskatchewan had applied for the exemption. According to the *Western Producer* newspaper, Doug Cuthand, the first vice-chief of the Federation of Saskatchewan Indians (FSI), advised Munro "to exempt the whole country from the Indian Act, which he [Cuthand] called a colonial document imposed on Indian people which was designed to get rid of Indian nations."[17] Cuthand was reported as saying that more people "have been lost from bands through adoption of children by non-Indians than through the marrying of non-Indians and losing their status."[18] Meanwhile, Sol Sanderson, then chief of the FSI, advised First Nations women who married non-Indians not to sign forms that struck them from band lists. He acknowledged that section 12(1)(b) was a government strategy to assimilate First Nations people, but stressed that the FSI wanted to address the question of membership "on a broader basis rather than from the sex point of view."[19]

In October 1981, the Lac la Ronge First Nation, located in northern Saskatchewan, planned to hold a band referendum on whether women who married non-status Indians should lose their status. If the referendum passed, the band would have requested to the Department of Indian Affairs that they be exempted from section 12(1)(b), the first band in Saskatchewan to submit such a request. Interestingly, according to a *Saskatoon Star-Phoenix* news article, by that time almost all the bands in Saskatchewan had requested exemption from the double mother clause. Although there is no indication of the referendum's results, both male and female adult band members had successfully lobbied the band council to hold the referendum. Many of the women who had married non-status Indians had married Métis men. Many of the Métis families were no doubt related to the status Indians, which may have influenced band members' attitudes. Nevertheless, the National Indian Brotherhood (NIB, the precursor to the Assembly of First Nations) was leery of eliminating sexual discrimination from the *Indian Act*. Del Riley, the NIB president, stated in October 1981 that, "overtaxed band government won't be able to handle the influx onto reserves with the conditions as bad as they are." He warned that there would be "confrontations because of the enormity of the problem."[20]

In 1983, the government introduced Bill C-47 to amend the membership code of the *Indian Act*. Of significance was that all reinstated people and their children would gain status and band membership, which meant that bands would be able to control their band membership. Grandchildren (second generation) of reinstated people would not gain status if only one parent had status, unless the children were born after the bill was implemented. The bill also proposed to institute a blood quantum requirement, set at one-quarter.[21]

The AFN vehemently opposed the notion of not having control of band members and residency, and the Native Women's Association of Canada (NWAC) expressed concern about the denial of rights to second-generation people. Accordingly, the two organizations issued the "Edmonton Consensus," marking one of the few times that the AFN and the NWAC were able to resolve some of their differences. Of the agreement, AFN Grand Chief Ahenakew stated, "They propose the removal of all discrimination, including section 12(1)(b), the reinstatement in the general band list of all generations who lost status or were never registered, the recognition of First Nations' control of jurisdiction over citizenship. Bands will then determine who gets on active band lists. Bands only will determine the residency of non-Indians and non-members."[22] In the end, however, all this mattered little because the Liberal government was defeated in the 1984 election before any new Indian legislation was passed. As Weaver stated, "After nearly fifteen years in power and many rhetorical affirmations of the values of sexual equality, the Liberal government had failed to eliminate sex discrimination against Indian women in the Indian Act."[23]

After the Progressive Conservatives formed government, it moved quickly to deal with sexual discrimination in the *Indian Act* by introducing Bill C-31. The major components of the bill included:

1. Sexually discriminatory rules for registration would no longer exist.

2. Marriage would no longer lead to loss or gaining of status.

3. Restoration of people who had lost status due to marriage, discrimination, or enfranchisement.

4. Allowed for children, including those born out of wedlock, or those people who had lost status, to be registered for the first time as status Indians, but were not automatically conferred band membership.

5. Grandchildren of people who had lost status would not be eligible for reinstatement.

6. Enfranchisement would be removed from the Act.

7. Bands, if they so chose, would have two years to develop and assume control of their own membership.

8. If bands did not choose to assume control of membership, then the Department of Indian Affairs and Northern Development would retain control of membership.

9. Status and band memberships would no longer be mutually inclusive.

The bill was heralded as ending sexual discrimination in the *Indian Act* and providing band control of membership. The first of the two major components of the bill was that Indian status and band membership were separated, meaning that a person could be considered a band member but not be entitled to any benefits of Indian status. Concerns over expenditures were factored into the inclusion of this provision.[24] The second component was that the children were not given band membership, meaning that they could be asked to leave the reserve once they became legal adults. Even though both the AFN and NWAC criticized Bill C-31, it became law on 28 June 1985, retroactive to 17 April 1985 so as to meet the requirements of section 15 of the Constitution. Prior to Crombie introducing his proposals for the changes, Ahenakew asserted that the bands, not the federal government, should decide band membership.[25]

The amended *Indian Act* replaced sections 11 (persons entitled to be registered) and 12 (persons not entitled to be registered) with sections 6 and 7 of Bill C-31. Section 6(1)(c) allowed for the reinstatement of status for persons who had lost their status either because their mother and grandmother had lost Indian status through marriage (formerly section 12[a][iv], the double mother clause), because they had married a non-status Indian (formerly section 12[1][b]), or because they had enfranchised (formerly section 12[1] [*a*][iii]). Section 6(1)(f) refers to a person whose parents are both status Indians and contrasts with section 6(2), which refers to a person with one parent who is a status Indian. Initially, when the act was passed, section 6(2) primarily applied to children of those people who were reinstated through section 6(1)(c). Consequently, children of mixed marriages can gain status, but are not able to pass on status if they enter mixed marriages.

Section 7(1)(a) referred to a woman who had gained status through marriage to a status Indian (formerly section 11(1)(f)), but who for whatever reason had her name deleted from the band list. Section 7(2)(a) provided for an exception to women who had gained status through marriage and maintained it up to the time of the amendment. In other words, non-status Indian spouses could no longer gain status through marriage, but those spouses who had gained status through marriage, primarily white women but also a significant number of Métis women, would not lose their status due to the amendment.

Section 10(1) allows bands to develop their own membership codes, but section 13(2) provides them only two years to develop their memberships codes or they would have to abide by codes set out within the *Indian Act*.

Since the 1850s, colonial and Canadian governments have regulated the definition of Indian. These definitions, for the most part, have had no input from First Nations nor have they reflected First Nations conceptions of kinship. Throughout the nineteenth and most of the twentieth century, First Nations' concerns with Indian Affairs were not heard or were simply ignored. By the time Bill C-31 passed, First Nations had endured 135 years of externally imposed definitions on their identity as Indians. During this time, while First Nations people resisted the various colonial regulations confronting them, including the membership criteria, many had various reasons to argue that the *Indian Act* definition be maintained. This division was especially pronounced in the reaction to the proposal and implementation of Bill C-31.

Reactions to Bill C-31

Between 7 March and 30 April 1985, the federal government invited Aboriginal groups to provide input into the proposed changes to the House of Commons Standing Committee on Indian Affairs and Northern Development. Testimony before the Standing Committee was heard from leaders of national and provincial Aboriginal political organizations, chief and council members from various individual First Nations, and from national and provincial Aboriginal women's organizations. The testimony from these various groups highlighted the pronounced divisiveness of the issue.

Of primary concern to the First Nations political leadership was the impact that the proposed bill would have on First Nations self-determination. The Union of New Brunswick Indians contended that the bill would have a far-reaching impact on "self-determination, and the tribal nation lands set aside for the use and benefit of the aboriginal inhabitants of the Indian First Nations of North America."[26] Gord Peters, president of the Association of Iroquois and Allied Indians, stated before the Standing Committee "that if the federal government wanted to confer status on people that the communities did not recognize, they could still do that. What we object to is that in conferring status they would have the ability to confer membership at the same time or suggest that when a person has status, they immediately become involved as functioning members and participating members within the community."[27]

First Nations women also expressed their displeasure with the government's infringement on First Nations self-determination. Representatives for the Indian Women of Treaty 6, 7, and 8 stated in no uncertain terms that they did not mind the reinstatement policy—"We support women in that area"—but they explicitly "reject[ed] your interference in our roles, our responsibilities for determining who our membership should be."[28] The Federation of Saskatchewan Indian Nations (FSIN) recommended that the regulations for band membership should fall within band law. Indian law, the FSIN maintained, arose "from the historical application of customary law which Chiefs and Headmen enforced. The law has endured the passage of time and government to culminate in Section 25 of the Canadian Charter of Rights and Freedoms."[29]

Although there was an acknowledgement that the government was attempting to reverse discriminatory legislation, there was nevertheless resentment toward the government's heavy-handedness in imposing any legislation on First Nations people. Sharon Venne, representing Treaty 6 chiefs, questioned the government's motivation to "right the wrongs as you have stated, to decolonized Indians." "You can use whatever justification you want," she asserted, "but the fact is that you, the Government of Canada are imposing your will upon our communities which we will not accept."[30]

According to Venne, the Treaty 6 chiefs did not view the bill as "discriminatory or status or as non-government versus government issues; we see it as whether or not Indian people in this country have a right to self-determine and whether or not the government of Canada is going to recognize that right. That is what we see as the issue."[31] Bill Traverse, representing Manitoba Indians, addressed the issue of collective versus individual rights: "Our collective rights—particularly concerning our land, our culture, our language and governing institutions—will be automatically eroded and ultimately destroyed. Our lands are already overcrowded. Our resources are very short to meet health, education, housing and services, employment infrastructure or our own people in their commitment to the Indian way of life, let alone extending those resources to non-members residing on our territory. Our collective rights will not survive."[32]

The Nishnawbe-Aski Nation (NAN), a political organization representing forty-six Ojibwe, Cree, and Oji-Cree First Nations in northern Ontario, were troubled that new members would be automatically placed on the band lists and the Indian register. As the NAN's Dan Cromartie stated, "In the case of status and reinstatement, the federal government has advanced its two priorities at the expense of the priorities of the First Nations."[33] Catherine Twinn, representing Treaty 8 chiefs, stated that they had concerns over the constitutional validity of the bill for imposing reinstated persons on the band lists.[34] Some First Nations leaders asserted that, if individuals were recognized as band members by the band, they should then be recognized as status Indians by the federal government. The AFN's Wally McKay, for example, stressed this point, noting that the "[a]cceptance of this point would do a great deal to assure the First Nations of the basic good faith of the Government of Canada."[35]

Many First Nations leaders raised concerns about the potential economic impact of the bill. McKay stated that, although he favoured reinstatement, the new members could have a drastic impact on current communities. The bill, he warned, "must meet our concerns to prevent a flood of people from suddenly descending on the reserves." Because of the economic situation, he asserted, "We will not accept any proposal which threatens the viability of our communities."[36] Twinn also raised the issue of the potential impact of new members on First Nations' economic and social gains. The Treaty 8 chiefs had created a council that, Twinn argued, had "contributed greatly to the economic, social and general welfare of the nine bands." For the Treaty 8 chiefs, according to Twinn, it was "critical to the continuation of our economic and social progress and development that the spiritual consensus and cooperation that constitutes the fabric of our communal life should not be disturbed by a sudden and uncontrolled influx of persons who may lack any real commitment to that community, its traditions, and its custom."[37]

A number of representatives testified that the influx of new members could threaten the cultural integrity of First Nations. For example, Gordon Godwa of the Treaty 6 Alliance from Alberta stated, "The legislation is in fact saying anyone who can claim Indian blood directly from their ancestors are entitled to live on the reserves. We reject this concept. We see indigenous peoples as a people identifying with a particular culture, a particular community, and a particular value system. For us, people left our community by choice. They may racially look like Indians, but are they Indians?"[38] Not only did some leaders argue that their people's cultural integrity was threatened by the reinstatement of those who had lost their status, some also believed that the bill contravened First Nations cultural protocols. Eric Robinson, from Manitoba, stated to the Standing Committee that

> I think that in the teachings of our elders and particularly in our nation which is the Cree nation, when a person married outside the nation it was the expectation of the elders and the parents, and so that whoever this woman was marrying and that person's family would take care of this individual. Therefore, we had no worries. It was the same when we brought a woman into our nation. As told by our elders, the people expected us to take care of that woman and to care for her. So among the nations we represent here, I think that had always been the understanding of the kind of question you had in mind there.[39]

Some First Nations leaders expressed support for certain aspects of the bill. The Council of Yukon Indians, for example, asserted that the new bill was commendable but did not go far enough, because the grandchildren of the reinstated people could be band members but not status Indians. This notion, according to the Council, "was not acceptable to the Yukon people."[40] The Dene of the Northwest Territories objected to the fact that the children of reinstated women were not eligible for the same status: "A reading of clause 6 would indicate that they are only now eligible for status if both their parents were also status; that is paragraph 6(1)(f). They are still discriminated against."[41] The Nishnawbe-Aski Nation questioned whether Bill C-31 dealt equitably with those individuals who had enfranchised because it assumed that all enfranchisement was voluntary: "We all know this exception is a travesty of justice. The presumption should run the other way, as it did in Bill-47. Also, many people were enfranchised unfairly in this situation not listed in proposed paragraph 6 [(a)(d)]."[42] In contrast, the Nuu-chah-nulth wanted all their people to be placed on the band membership list: "That is where we differ from other groups in the country. Other groups do not want anybody back on the list. We say the bill does not go far enough. We think you should have just placed everybody back on the band list."[43]

Although mostly in favour of the bill, Métis and non-status Indian and Native women's organizations had some major criticisms of Bill C-31. Louis Bruyere, of the Native Council of Canada, asserted that the new bill only ended some of the more obvious forms of sexual discrimination. He stated that the bill would still "perpetuate others [other forms of sexual discrimination] and will create some new ones, especially by passing on the current sexual discrimination imposed on Indian women to their children, thereby replacing overt sexual discrimination with a new blood quantum system based on a distance from one or more parents who registered."[44] At the same time, the Native Women's Association of Canada, which endorsed the bill, raised the same issue as the Yukon Council and the Nuu-chah-nulth, namely that many Aboriginal people were excluded from federal recognition: "The band may decide to reinstate second generation descendants, yet the government will continue to deny them status.... Another category of aboriginal Indian people will therefore be created by this bill."[45]

These examples of the testimony at the Standing Committee are representative of the tone of the presentations. A majority of organizations had at least some minimal criticisms of the bill's potential impact, but overall the First Nations organizations were mostly opposed to the bill. Similar to how the creation of the White Paper had been handled, the government invited Aboriginal input into the bill, but then ignored that input. Unlike the White Paper, however, Bill C-31 was passed and became law.

Though the passage of the bill was viewed as a victory for First Nations women's rights, there was continued opposition from First Nations leadership, including some First Nations women leaders. For example, Isabel McNab, president of the Saskatchewan Indian Women's Association (SIWA), expressed mixed feelings toward the Bill C-31 amendments at the band level:

"[Some] want to bring them in [the treaty women that have lost status] and others think it's going to create a problem according to land base.... I don't know if I'm prepared to bring that many people in. ... I have a waiting list so long, of my own people who've lived on this reserve all these years and made it what it is, and they don't have proper housing."[46]

By February 1986, AFN Grand Chief George Erasmus condemned the amendment, not because it eliminated sexual discrimination but because it introduced a blood quantum. Erasmus pointed out that status Indians were now considered to be one hundred percent Indian, which was a legal fiction, since many status Indians were less than one hundred percent (i.e., they had at least one non-Aboriginal ancestor). The children of those who married non-status Indians were considered to be fifty percent Indian. Erasmus stated that, "unless these 'quarter bloods' marry someone with greater percentage of Indian blood than they have, their children will not be considered status Indians."[47] Many women's groups asserted that, even with the amendment, sexual discrimination against First Nations women would continue because the children of reinstated women fell under section 6(2) and would therefore be unable to pass on their status to their children. Although they were correct in this assertion, Erasmus and other First Nations leaders pointed out that the newly amended *Indian Act* not only affected reinstated women and their children but all First Nations people. Now, people who had not lost their status prior to 1985 and fell under 6(1) of the *Indian Act* could see their children classified as a 6(2) if they married a non-status Indian. Further, if the 6(2) children married non-status Indians, the subsequent generation would not be eligible for status.

Meanwhile, in November 1985, the Saskatchewan chiefs requested more time and resources to implement the new amendments in order to avoid unnecessary conflicts among band members. The chiefs argued that the $7,000 grant that the federal government allowed each band to prepare for the new citizens was inadequate. They also stated that the $15,000 increase for bands to help cope with new members was insufficient. At the FSIN legislative assembly, the chiefs unanimously requested more time and money. Since the *Lavell* case, First Nations leaders who resisted the elimination of sexual discrimination from the *Indian Act* had been portrayed as male chauvinists. Some of these critics viewed these new requests as a delay tactic to avoid meeting sexual equality legislation. The chiefs, however, blamed the federal government for fueling such sentiments. According to Ray Ahenakew, the executive director of the Meadow Lake Tribal Council, the government was "presenting the Indian Chiefs as male chauvinists and itself as champion of women's rights."[48] The implication of Ahenakew's statement was that the chiefs' request was based on policy deficiencies, not the sexual biases of the chiefs.

By mid-1987, Saskatchewan chiefs voiced their objection to section 13(2) of the new act, which gave bands two years to develop their own membership codes. Bands were given till 28 June 1987 to submit their membership codes to the Department of Indian Affairs for approval. After that date, bands had to adhere to the membership code outlined in the *Indian Act*. According to an article in the *Saskatoon Star-Phoenix*, the "forced acceptance of former members is an unwelcome prospect to many Saskatchewan Chief, who say they're already burdened with overcrowding and insufficient budgets."[49] As the June deadline neared, tensions increased. There were fears that Bill C-31 members would launch court actions against First Nations governments if they were not admitted as band members after the deadline. By 15 May 1987, only two Saskatchewan First Nations had implemented their own membership codes.

In early June, Roland Crowe, chief of the FSIN, told the minister of Indian Affairs, Bill McKnight, that a majority of Saskatchewan First Nations would not abide by the new membership criteria of the *Indian Act*. McKnight's response was, "[I]f the deadline isn't met, then the department will have the responsibility of adding the returnees' names to band membership lists."[50] Vern Bellegarde, first vice-chief of the FSIN, highlighted the resistance to section 13(2), allegedly saying that he "would rather be jailed than abide by Bill C-31."[51] On 28 June 1987, David Ahenakew, who was by that point the former chief of the FSIN and AFN, and had recently been appointed to the FSIN Senate, advised First Nations who wanted to challenge the *Indian Act* membership codes to implement their own codes. He told the chiefs, in his characteristically no-nonsense and defiant tone, "You can reject Bill C-31 but by God, if you don't put your own Indian (band membership) law in place, you'll find yourself in contempt of court or fined. … If they are going to take us to court let them challenge us under our own laws. It is time you put on your frozen mukluks and started kicking."[52]

In 1988, the federal government again invited Aboriginal organizations to Ottawa to give presentations to the Standing Committee on Aboriginal Affairs. The Standing Committee sought to assess the effectiveness of the

1985 amendments to the *Indian Act*. This forum allowed the First Nations leadership to reiterate positions they had been voicing for many years. Concerns over the effects of new members on reserve cultures were more prominent than in the 1985 hearings.

An example of this can be found in a series of questions and answers between a committee member and a member of an Alberta First Nation. The context for this exchange was that a committee member posed a number of questions to an elder in an attempt to understand the link between an Indigenous worldview and different rights for women:

> Q: Is it an indigenous worldview that your sister or your daughter has different rights than your brother?

> A: It is not a case of different rights, it is a case of the way it has always been in our communities. This is the indigenous world-view that we are talking about. When a man, such as myself, is willing to take a wife, I am to provide for that woman. That is the way it has always been. In this case, when a lady from our community marries somebody from Saddle Lake, they go with that man. … This is the way it has always been.

> These people have been away from the community for so long they do not realize that they are going to hurt us. They do not think like we do anymore. We think as Indian people because we live in a community; we are a community. These people are not a community anymore.

> Q: The women in your community who were born in your community and raised in your community … you do not have women who feel they should have similar rights to the men in your communities as far as passing on status.… Is their view not of value? Would they not have that view?

> A: They would not have that view if they think like Indians do. If you don't understand the very simple example I gave you, I am not sure if I should … it is collective rights.

At the Standing Committee hearings, Native women's organizations leveled complaints about the reinstatement process and the negative impact of the Bill C-31. According to NWAC, the process established by the Department of Indian Affairs to approve applications for reinstatement had been extremely slow. Out of 95,987 applications for Indian status that the department had received in the three years after the amendment had been made, only 44,461 had been approved. For NWAC, the low decision rate was a concern. Jean Gleason, NWAC's acting president, stated to the *Star-Phoenix* that "the process is not going well here at all. Many people are confused about how to apply for reinstatement and, once they do apply, there are months and months of waiting."[53]

Members of Aboriginal women's organizations also expressed concern about the negative impact that the amendments had on new members. Many band members from various First Nations directed their frustrations with the amendments to Bill C-31 members. Lillian Sanderson, of the Aboriginal Women's Council of Saskatchewan, expressed this view: "I'm not sure what it's like in other bands but where I come from I know there is a lot of bad feelings about Bill C-31 Indians as a result of discrimination against non-status Indians or Indian women wanting to get reinstatement. I guess I understand the frustration at getting this influx of people all of a sudden as they have no resources. They don't have the land to build new houses for these people if that is what they want. So there are a lot of problems with the bands themselves, and I understand that."

In 1991, Rose-Ann Morris, president of NWAC, confirmed the stress felt by new members owing to bands' financial constraints. Although Morris agreed that Bill C-31 was a good tool to reverse "the blatant discrimination," she also noted that, "the government was not ready to implement it."[54] According to a newspaper report, a survey of fifty-five Saskatchewan bands found that over one-third had disputes over allocation of funds for housing that were causing tension between old and new band members. As a result, Morris stated that discrimination against First Nations women was "basically still splitting up families. It's [the discrimination] not blatant but its [*sic*] still there."[55]

The First Nations reaction to the proposals and subsequent changes to the membership codes of the *Indian Act* demonstrate considerable division within First Nations communities. Groups who were in favour of the bill saw the changes as righting the wrongs of sexual discrimination and looked to the United Nations ruling in the *Lovelace* case, section 15 of the Charter of Rights and Freedoms, and the primacy of individual rights as supporting their positions. These groups, primarily First Nations women and feminist groups, framed the issue around women, and more specifically as a First Nations women's issue. Others who favoured the bill simply saw the changes as a recognition of their Aboriginal rights as First Nations people. Those who opposed implementation of Bill C-31, primarily the male First Nations political leadership, saw it as another attempt by the federal government to impose its will on First Nations people, further undermining First Nations' goal of self-determination. There was concern that the bill would cause further economic stress to First Nations government and people. Also, many leaders and First Nations people feared a perceived threat to the cultural and ethnic integrity of First Nations communities brought about by the bill. These concerns were evident in newspaper accounts of Bill C-31, in presentations to hearing committees prior to and after the passage of the bill, and in various First Nations' legal analyses. Further highlighting the complexity of the issue was that some political leaders found the bill or aspects of it amenable, even as Aboriginal women's organizations were opposed to the bill or at least some aspects of it. Criticisms of the amendment were forthcoming from the academic community, which was as divided as the political leadership. The amendment, meanwhile, took place with thousands of people applying for and eventually gaining Indian status recognition. For Cowessess, while resistance existed to the bill and to the new band members it created, the level of resistance did not match the level expressed by those in the wider First Nations leadership. As will be shown, the level of resistance was tempered by the continued importance of kinship relations exhibited by Cowessess band members.

Cowessess Members' Views of Bill C-31

The federal government's amendment of the *Indian Act* allowed those who had lost their federally recognized status as Indians (and their children) to gain reinstatement. I asked participants about their views of Bill C-31, specifically whether they believed the new membership code to be beneficial for Cowessess. Most felt that allowing relatives to regain their Indian status and secure band membership was good for the band. None of the band members interviewed expressed the level of animosity toward any individual new member that occurred on other reserves. This is not, however, to say that all participants agreed with all aspects of Bill C-31. On the whole, the views of participants interviewed for the research correspond with customary kinship practices that Elder Brother teaches through his stories.

Many of those interviewed understood why others had lost their status. People either voluntarily enfranchised because they believed that they would be better able to provide for their family, or because women had married non-status Indians or non-Indians. Many recalled the factors that had led their family, or people they knew, to lose their status. One respondent outlined the circumstances surrounding his family becoming enfranchised:

> At one point, our Indian status was taken away from us because our dad thought that we would never, ever come back to what he thought was a racist [situation and a] lack of opportunity [in the reserve] area to live. And that's the reason—they were basically looking for other ways to live and to survive. And so they moved off the reserve. There's always been a policy of the Canadian government to assimilate us, to reduce our treaty rights, and all that kind of stuff. But back then, you know, there were a number of injustices being done that were very calculating and callous in the way the government treated us. Any women who married a non-Indian man lost her status. For $400 a head, you could sign your family off the reserve and all your rights and benefits as an Indian. And so, we did that. My dad did that to us. And so we became at the end of the process in '85, we were then reclassified Bill-C31s because we reapplied to become status Indians. The fact that they took our status away from us made our bodies no less Indian than we ever were. Our bloodline shows that we are very strongly attached to, to Cowessess, and that never changes. So, it's only the government and the way they, their policies, dictate who is and who isn't an Indian. That really is the legal side of how we view our people, but then there's the real view—that's our view—you can't take Indianness away from you, you know.

This long-time reserve resident, now living in the urban area, outlined the impact that Bill C-31 had on the band:

> Well, Cowessess, we always had a big membership. We always knew that we don't know most of our people. I guess we always knew it [Bill C-31] was going to inflate our population, but it probably increased by five to six hundred. The law came in '85, I think, but it wasn't until the beginning of the nineties that Cowessess membership starting increasing really fast. I think the Bill C-31 registrations are done, now—at least for what it was

intended. But our population probably increases about a hundred every year. We are probably 3,200 now [the Cowessess population was 4,019 as of July 2013]. When I started working for Cowessess eleven years ago [in 1993], it was probably 2,200, and then it just jumped. It was all of the applications from Bill C-31. They said it would increase the membership list, and then they said there would be less [funds available for the band from the federal government] going around. But there wasn't enough room for people to stay here [to move back to the reserve, due to chronic housing and land shortages] anyway.

The divisiveness of Bill C-31 was also reflected in the reaction of the Cowessess First Nation's band council to the implementation of the new amendment. During a band council meeting that I attended in 2003, one councillor proudly proclaimed, "We accepted all C-31s into the band." Another man who was a councillor when Bill C-31 was introduced said that he was originally against the bill because it meant that there might be more new members living on the reserve than "original" members. He also noted that "a lot of these people went out and came back, and a lot of them, I don't know how many, but there were a few who volunteered, than came back again, which I don't think is right." He was particularly against the idea of those who had voluntarily enfranchised being reinstated, rather than just those women who had lost their status through marriage. Twenty years after the passage of the bill, he seemed to have softened his position. When asked if he thought that allowing the Bill C-31s back into the band was a positive or negative experience, he stated, "I think that's a good thing, then you get to know the people." Then he added, perhaps half-jokingly because he was in his seventies and had been married for many years, "I could have married my cousin and never know it." The disagreement of the council over Bill C-31 reflected the opinions of the band as a whole. These feelings did not go unnoticed by some Bill C-31 members. One Bill C-31 member, who was quoted in a special online issue of *Windspeaker*, a national Aboriginal newspaper, concerning Bill C-31, noted that, "If it were up to the bands, I think they would be a bit more discriminatory, and I don't think I would have got my status if my band had the choice of choosing who would be a member." Though Cowessess accepted all their Bill C-31 members, it was not through an explicit endorsement of the bill. Cowessess, like most Saskatchewan First Nations, did not implement its own membership code, and therefore was compelled to follow the code of the *Indian Act*.

Though there were some notable disagreements, the responses of long-standing band members to C-31s were generally positive. However, it must be kept in mind that a significant number of participants had relatives who were C-31s, or were themselves C-31s. For example, one reserve resident related how her family was always a physically and emotionally close family. When she was young, her immediate and extended family lived in a cluster of homes close to one another. As they grew older, her family would "have lots of family gatherings. We lived together, we moved to the city together, but now that we are getting older we are settling down back at home and closer together." For her, Bill C-31 had positive ramifications for her relatives. Expressing her views about Bill C-31, she said, "Oh, it was a good thing for me, because I had a first cousin that signed off the reserve, and with Bill C-31 they got some of their treaty rights back." For this woman, Bill C-31 meant that her close relatives were able to access treaty benefits, including the right to reside on the reserve near her, therefore allowing her to maintain her close familial bonds.

The attitudes of several band members who were interviewed is reflected in the views of these two well-respected community members, who noted that Bill C-31 did not go far enough:

> I don't deny the women getting their status back, because I don't think it was right that they lost it when an Indian married a white man, and when an Indian married a white woman she gained status. It wasn't right for the woman to lose her status. They draw the line on Bill C-31, so when a woman got her status back she was a Bill C-31 and her children, but not her grandchildren would get their status. Which I don't think is right.

> I think it's unfair for the non-Indian women that married Indian men. They became band members and they enjoy benefits that Indian men have, but after '86, these white women, they can't acquire the status of their husbands anymore. So you have families on the reserve who enjoy all of the benefits from being a status Indian on the reserve, and then you have another family with a white woman who enjoys no status, so if something happened to her husband they have nothing.

This respondent refers to the fact that the children of those reinstated did not receive full status. That is, reinstated persons can pass status to their children, but the children cannot pass on their status to their own children, unless they marry another status Indian. The last comment by this interviewee refers to a situation where a white spouse, in this case a woman, marries a band member and resides on the reserve. According to the 1985 amendment to the *Indian Act*, she would not be entitled to any band membership benefits, no matter how long she lived on the reserve. This woman would have to leave the reserve if her husband should die before her. Housing issues, including inheritance of houses, fall under land management. Cowessess' *Lands Management Code*, which failed to be ratified, had planned to allow for non-member spouses to continue to live on reserve after the passing of their member spouse. That these two prominent band members expressed disappointment that all individuals who were considered relatives were not included in Bill C-31 suggests that Cowessess people have retained inclusive notions of kinship held by earlier generations of Cowessess people. It also counters the opposition to Bill C-31 put forth by many First Nations leaders.

The following respondent pointed out that Bill C-31 does not take into account all the possible ways in which people had lost their status:

> Well, I will tell you one thing—it almost creates an imbalance between who is Indian and who is not Indian. It upsets me because my ex, I knew her family before I knew her. I was raised with her family, but she was taken away and raised in the white world when she was very young. So, I didn't know her. We are not related. They had a big family, too, but a lot of their grandkids got taken away. Some of them lost their status. My ex and her sisters were all raised in different homes, and one of them lost her status. Some of her sister's kids have status and some don't. Her sister then passed away and orphaned her son. So now what I have is my kids and their first cousin. Their first cousin comes from the same background, an Indian mom and an Indian dad, but he doesn't have status. So now we have two kids, first cousins. My kids have status, but [the cousin] doesn't have status. So he can't count on the reserve when he goes up for school [post-secondary education funding]. My daughter is going to school with funding, but he can't.

I asked, "So, do they see each other differently?"

> No, I don't think so. Like, on the reserve there [are] a lot of kids that were raised on Cowessess that aren't Cowessess band members. And that's so unfair, especially when these are our kids [children of Cowessess band members]. I think that it is, in a sense, very unfair for families to have one [with status] and one not to have [status]. I think that they miss out on a lot of benefits that they could be entitled to. So, that is one way of breaking down the community, cutting them off, then they don't have the support of their community.

His explanation is noteworthy for a number of reasons. First, although it is unclear why his nephew was not eligible to be reinstated, he did highlight a perceived shortcoming of Bill C-31—that not all relatives are necessarily eligible to gain their Indian status. Second, the kinship relationship between him, his children, and his nephew was not altered, regardless of legal definitions of Indian. Additionally, his narrative pointed to the fact that his nephew's case is not an isolated one. As he noted, there were a number of children raised on the reserve who were not band members, which implies that he believed that there were many people who should be eligible for band membership and Indian status.

One person whom I interviewed was a C-31 who felt that he and other C-31s were discriminated against after regaining status. This person said that he had had a hard time gaining access to housing since he returned to the reserve. Moreover, he later said that the chief and council often favoured their own families, whereas his family was small, with few relatives on the reserve and no family members on the band council.

One person claimed that some band members were still not in favour of Bill C-31: "There were certain members that didn't like the C-31s. All it was, they were giving the Indian woman her rights back that lost her status and her first children. I didn't see anything wrong with that. Where people started to have a problem was where they started coming back and wanting land from other people. That's where there was a problem, because there wasn't very much land to be taken, and from a Bill C-31 who never knew very much about living on a reserve in the first place."

The notions held by some Cowessess members that Bill C-31 members did not have the requisite knowledge or experience about living on a reserve is somewhat perplexing. While it is true that there are many C-31s—especially the children of reinstated people, who never lived on the reserve—many C-31s were actually born and raised on the reserve. In addition, many who had lost their status continued for years to visit their relatives on the reserve. What really made this notion puzzling for Cowessess members, however, is that, because Cowessess people have been migrating to urban areas for more than fifty years, there are at least two generations of families whose members have never lived on the reserve. In effect, there are many C-31s who would have more knowledge and experience about living on the reserve than some long-standing members.

The following research participant explained the difference between Cowessess people's views about C-31s versus those of other First Nations:

> It never really made that much of a difference. … Other reserves were different than Cowessess [in their treatment of C-31s] where most of their members [the other reserves' band members] stay on the reserve, and for them, bringing in people who are Bill C-31s created quite a bit of jealousy. So, many [other bands] made a rule that Bill C-31s weren't band members. Cowessess did not do that, probably because we are more open than that—in that most of our people live off the reserve. Our people have been marrying other people for a long time, white people included, for generations by now. In that sense, it's [including Bill C-31s as band members] not anything new. We're a small reserve—they are all Indians. On our reserve, eighty percent of our people leave and marry other people. So in that sense, when Bill C-31 came along, you had almost two extremes where one was very strict about who were Indians, and the other extreme, maybe people wanted to be inclusive of who their members bring in. So, Cowessess would be more on the other extreme of being more accepting. There are some [Cowessess] people who have a hard view of membership, but not the majority.

His explanation acknowledged the historically exogamous marriage practice of Cowessess people, a practice that continues to the present day. It also recognized the fact that Cowessess people understand that this marriage practice is an accepted cultural trait.

Though there were some who viewed Bill C-31 as having had a negative impact on the band, most saw it as having been positive for the band. Many mentioned that they were happy that their relatives were able to regain their status. Many respondents, however, also stated that Bill C-31 did not go far enough, because there were C-31 band members who were unable to pass on their status to their children. Others felt it was important that those members who were alienated from the reserve be reunited. As for the Bill C-31 band members, many mentioned that since their reinstatement they felt a connection to their homeland—a place from where they or their ancestors originated. They also spoke about the importance of attending family reunions held on the reserve. In addition, many of the urban members talked about how they passed on family histories and genealogies to ensure that their children understood who they were and from where they came. Though most band members spoke positively about C-31s, it should be noted that the interviews took place nearly twenty years after the passage of Bill C-31, so time may have softened some Cowessess people's view on both the legislation and the people who had regained their status. However, these interviews demonstrate, in part, that the level of resistance to and the resentment of Bill C-31, as expressed by many First Nations leaders, was not as prevalent for most Cowessess First Nation members.

7

Implementing Treaty Obligations in Saskatchewan: Cowessess First Nation and Treaty Land Entitlement

In the 1970s, several major political and legal shifts occurred in relations between First Nations and the Canadian government. As the decade began, the attack on First Nations' special relations with the federal government was exemplified by the government's introduction of the 1969 White Paper. The response of First Nations' leadership and the level of First Nations people's protests, combined with public support for First Nations' grievances, forced the government to shelve the White Paper in 1971. Then, in 1973, the Supreme Court of Canada released its decision in the *Calder* case. The *Calder* decision, in which the Supreme Court addressed the source of Aboriginal rights, has been seen as a victory for First Nations' Aboriginal rights, compelling the government to adopt a new approach to First Nations affairs. Later in 1973, the federal government created the Indian Claims Commission to address a multitude of comprehensive land claims put forth by numerous First Nations. Two years later, in 1975, in order to compensate First Nations for shortfalls in lands promised to them under the terms of treaty, the federal and Saskatchewan governments entered into Treaty Land Entitlement (TLE) negotiations with Saskatchewan First Nations.

Although a few First Nations had their TLE claims fulfilled by the early 1970s, most had to wait nearly twenty years, until the signing of the Treaty Land Entitlement Framework Agreement (TLEFA) in 1992, to have their claims settled. The major stumbling blocks to a speedier settlement were the jurisdictional and political squabbles between the federal and provincial governments. The one catalyst for compelling both these levels of government to achieve an agreement was the various decisions by the Supreme Court of Canada that appeared to favour First Nations' Aboriginal rights.

Cowessess First Nation was not part of the 1992 TLEFA, but signed its own separate agreement in 1996, as its claim was not validated by the federal government until after the 1992 agreement was signed. Though its agreement was similar to the 1992 agreement, a key difference lay in how the agreement was reached. Cowessess negotiators successfully argued for a larger amount by using annuities pay lists (which some scholars have argued was not beneficial to some First Nations) to determine its original band population, and then linked the discrepancies in its historic population to Commissioner Dewdney's starvation policy. Also, due to its demographic makeup, Cowessess had to undertake a comprehensive search of its off-reserve members in order to demonstrate its contemporary population and to ensure that as many of its off-reserve members as possible voted in the band referendum to approve the TLE framework agreement with the Canadian and Saskatchewan governments.

As a result, the TLE process acted to strengthen kinship ties with Bill C-31 members and with members who had lived off the reserve for many years. For most Cowessess people, the social benefits of reconnecting with members was as important as the financial gain provided by the agreement. For many, in fact, the social gains yielded by the TLE had more of an immediate impact than the financial gains.

The Emergence of Treaty Land Entitlement

The fulfillment of treaty land entitlements for Saskatchewan First Nations was a negotiated component of Treaties 4 and 6 in the late 1870s, but many First Nations never received their full treaty land entitlements. Federal attempts to meet their treaty land commitments occurred sporadically and on an ad hoc basis. As a result of the *Calder* decision, the government entered into negotiations with Aboriginal people to resolve outstanding land claims disputes, including treaty land entitlements.[1] Because of the stipulations of the *National Resource Transfer Act* of 1930, the Saskatchewan government had an interest in settling outstanding TLEs, and thus became an active participant in negotiations. However, the addition of provincial interests to the process delayed settlement because the two levels of government became embroiled, ostensibly, in jurisdictional wrangling, though in reality the question of financial responsibility over TLEs fueled the squabble.

In order to curtail costs, both levels of government proposed to implement settlement procedures that would limit the compensation for eligible First Nations. Faced with the prospects of court challenges by Saskatchewan First Nations, combined with the tone and tenor of the Supreme Court's decisions in Aboriginal and treaty rights cases, both governments were forced to compromise their positions, thereby paving the way for the final Treaty Land Entitlement Framework Agreement (TLEFA) in 1992.

Following the signing of the treaties, surveying for reserves was to follow a formula of 640 acres per family of five, or 128 acres per person. Determining the amount of land to survey for a band was problematic in the 1880s, because band membership fluctuated, leading to errors in the band census.[2] Some First Nations people did not immediately want to settle on a reserve, preferring instead to follow the last of the buffalo. Others continued to move back and forth between bands to meet their social and economic needs. As a result, band population varied from year to year. In some cases, when the surveyor did not provide enough land in the initial survey, additional lands were surveyed. Peggy Martin-McGuire asserted that, although "the history of each reserve is unique, once bands and individuals completed migrating, relocating, and settling, most reserves fell short of the required size."[3]

In determining reserve sizes, some surveyors set aside extra land, knowing that the band's size would grow as people came in from the prairies. This is what happened at Cowessess First Nation in 1880. The Crooked Lake location was originally surveyed as O'Soup's reserve. The surveyor, however, set aside a sixty-square-mile reserve—enough for three hundred people (far more than the ninety-six people with O'Soup) on the expectation that the remainder of the band members who were at Cypress Hills would eventually relocate to Crooked Lake.[4] The amount of land set aside for the Cowessess band, however, was still well short of its entitlement, an issue that will be discussed in greater detail later in this chapter.

Prior to 1930, Indian Affairs made attempts to fulfill TLEs in Manitoba, Saskatchewan, and Alberta; but as time passed, the process became more complicated.[5] Whenever additional lands were added, another survey was required, resulting in multiple surveys; but in some cases shortfalls in acres remained. In order to provide the required lands, the authorities had to decide whether to use the population of the band at the date of the first survey (DOFS) or the population at the most recent survey. Pitsula provides examples of both of the formulas. The first multiplied the population at the date of first survey by 128 (the number of acres allowed by treaty per member), and then subtracted from that the actual amount of land that was originally received to determine the amount still owed the First Nation. For example, if the band population at DOFS was 100, and they originally received 9,800 acres, then the formula would be:

100 x 128 = 12,800 acres the First Nation should have received

12,800 − 9,800 = 3,000 acres owed the First Nation

The formula, based on the current population, meant multiplying the most recent official population by 128, and then subtracting that total from the actual amount of land originally received to arrive at the amount still owed the First Nation. For example, if the current population were 300 band members, the formula would be:

300 x 128 = 38,400 acres

38,400 − 9,800 = 28,600 acres owed the First Nation[6]

Indian Affairs used the current population formula from the late 1800s until the 1960s, when the provinces began to lobby against this formula.[7]

After 1930, the process was further complicated with the passage of the Natural Resources Transfer Act (NRTA), which transferred control of lands and resources to the three prairie provinces. Section 10 of the agreement acknowledged that the federal government had not fully met its TLE requirements, and ensured both that the provinces would have a role in TLE and that provincial Crown land would be needed to fulfill First Nations TLE. The provinces understood that the TLE in the northern portions of their respective jurisdictions had to be fulfilled, but were not overly concerned about expediting the process because these were not highly settled areas. The provinces also assumed that the TLE obligations for the southern First Nations had already been met.

In the early 1960s, the provinces began to assert their interests in the TLE process. Manitoba, and later Alberta and Saskatchewan, objected to the current population formula, instead arguing for the use of the DOFS formula. In response, the federal government proposed a compromise formula. This formula still used the current population as its base, but, in contrast to the current population formula, the acreage figure would not be subtracted from the amount of land originally assigned. Instead, that latter number was used to derive the percentage of land not received. Again using Pitsula's example, the First Nation cited above received seventy-seven percent of the land to which they were judged to be "entitled" (9,800 ÷ 12,800 = 76.5 percent), meaning that there was a twenty-three percent shortfall of acres. To make up the shortfall, the First Nation would receive twenty-three percent of 38,400, or 8,832 acres.[8] Research by the Federation of Saskatchewan Indians in the early 1970s demonstrated that there were five bands in northern Saskatchewan and ten in southern Saskatchewan that were owed nearly one million acres under TLE.[9] Using the compromise formula, the province of Saskatchewan set aside nearly 185,000 acres between 1968 and 1973 in northern Saskatchewan for TLE claims.[10]

Though progress on TLE in southern Saskatchewan had stalled after the election of the Trudeau government in 1968 and the introduction of the White Paper, the *Calder* decision brought changes to the federal government's Indian policy. Shortly after the decision was handed down, the federal government issued a "Statement on Claims of Indian and Inuit People," which defined two kinds of land claims. "Comprehensive claims" were those claims where Aboriginal people had never extinguished their Aboriginal title through treaty. "Specific claims" were those based on non-fulfillment of a treaty, the breach of an *Indian Act* or other statutory responsibility, the breach of an obligation arising out of government administration of First Nation funds or other assets, or an illegal sale or other disposition of First Nation land by government. Treaty Land Entitlements fall under the specific claims category. In 1973, the government established the Indian Claims Commission to deal with all Indian claims. These developments spurred much activity on the TLE front in Saskatchewan.

Over the next fourteen years, TLE negotiations were stymied by federal/provincial acrimony over jurisdictional issues. Still, Saskatchewan's First Nations were determined to push the governments to work toward a settlement. In 1973, the federal government informed the province that there were five southern First Nations in need of TLE. In 1975, the Federation of Saskatchewan Indians (FSI) identified twenty-three more First Nations with outstanding TLE claims. This surprised the provincial government, which had expected a much lower figure.[11] This led the FSI to request that the federal and provincial governments enter into discussions to reach settlements.[12] In August of that year, Minister of Indian Affairs, Judd Buchanan, wrote to all the provincial premiers to request their support in resolving the

TLE situation.[13] A year later, the Saskatchewan government responded by proposing a new formula for the settlement of the claims, under which entitlement would be based on band population as of 31 December 1976.[14] Additionally, if private lands were needed, the letter suggested that federal funds be used to purchase them (Bartlett 1990: 7). This was known as the "Saskatchewan Formula."

The Saskatchewan formula was praised and quickly agreed upon by FSI. This was not surprising, given that it was much more favourable than the previous compromise formula, and was similar to the current population formula.[15] The federal government, however, was not quick to respond to Saskatchewan's proposed formula. When the federal government did respond, its support was conditional, as it was not keen to use federal funds to purchase private lands. Even though the federal government publicly endorsed the Saskatchewan formula, they did not formally agree to implement it. As a result, the Saskatchewan formula fell into limbo. For the next three years, land transfers were few and proceeded slowly, with only six bands having their TLE completely fulfilled.[16]

In the May 1982 Saskatchewan election, the right-of-centre Progressive Conservatives defeated the New Democratic Party government. By that time, about ninety thousand acres—less than ten percent of the potential lands—had been transferred to Saskatchewan First Nations through the TLE process. In 1977, the FSI had identified twenty-five First Nations with TLE claims, of which the federal government had validated fifteen. By 1982, prior to the provincial election, the federal validation had increased to twenty-one First Nations TLE claims.[17] The 1982 change in provincial government further delayed settlement of outstanding TLEs.

The new provincial government quickly suspended all TLE negotiations and entered a period of review.[18] In June 1984, the provincial government announced its TLE policy, which contained four main points, as summarized by Bartlett:

1. Negotiations would be carried out on a band-by-band basis, resulting in different settlement packages for different bands.

2. The 1976 population base would be used as a guide for quantifying band entitlement (whether in land or land and add-on elements).

3. Financial compensation for third-party interests would be made by the federal government.

4. Tax exemptions, mineral rights, resource revenue sharing, and cash settlement were considered legitimate substitutes for land.[19]

The policy was based on an assumption that the Saskatchewan formula was legally binding and that the province could lose a court challenge if it deviated from it.

During this time, *Guerin* had made its way to the Supreme Court. This case revolved around whether the federal government acted irresponsibly by leasing Musqueam First Nation surrendered land for a golf course at far below the market value. Though the Court did not render its decision in this case until November 1984, the Musqueam First Nation's argument had been heard regarding the federal government's fiduciary responsibility for the surrender of reserve land. The court ruled that the *sui generis* nature of Aboriginal title placed a fiduciary responsibility on the federal government to make decisions that were in the best interest of First Nations people and a failure to do so would be a breach of its legal obligation.[20] In the shadow of the Court's decision, it is not surprising that, in March 1986, the federal government officially endorsed the province's proposal. It must be noted, however, that there is no direct or admitted link between the Court's decision (or the case in general) and the provincial and federal governments' new TLE policy. Nevertheless, given the political climate at the time, the fact that first ministers' meetings on Aboriginal constitutional amendments were about to take place, and that favourable Canadian public opinion on Aboriginal rights was at an all-time high (notwithstanding the concerns of some special-interest groups like the Saskatchewan Wildlife Federation), the two levels of government would have known of the *Guerin* decision and its potential implications. Clearly, it was in the interest of both levels of government to reach an agreement in the TLE claims of Saskatchewan First Nations that would be seen as fair and equitable.

Though the provincial and federal governments were pleased with the new TLE policy, the recently renamed Federation of Saskatchewan Indian Nations (FSIN) had serious misgivings. The FSIN directed criticism at both levels of government. In particular, the FSIN argued that settlements should not occur on a band-by-band basis, that bands should receive all the lands to which they were entitled, and that bands should have the authority to choose which lands are selected. The FSIN believed that the new policy effectively terminated the Saskatchewan formula and stated, echoing *Guerin* and foreshadowing *Sparrow*, that the province was "seriously jeopardizing the federal government's legal and trust obligations under the Constitution and the Treaties."[21]

In April 1986, the provincial and federal governments presented their agreed-upon "Draft Treaty Land Entitlement Criteria" to the Saskatchewan entitlement chiefs, who rejected it outright. The draft criteria restricted entitlement lands to a twenty-five-mile radius of existing reserves, offset improved lands (meaning fewer acres would be given), and encouraged bands to select lands contiguous to their reserves.[22] The entitlement chiefs' counter-proposal was not to federal officials' liking, and they subsequently broke off negotiations for a TLE policy agreement.[23]

In November 1987, however, Indian Affairs received legal advice that the federal government was legally obliged only for the shortfall acreage based on the population at the date of the first survey.[24] As a result, in 1988 the federal government publicly withdrew its support of the Saskatchewan formula,[25] though some TLE claims were still processed, like the 1988 Muskeg Lake First Nation claim, which created the first urban reserve in the city of Saskatoon as a result of the TLE process.[26] For all intents and purposes, however, the TLE process in Saskatchewan had ground to a halt.

The Saskatchewan TLE First Nations were clearly not pleased with the latest developments, and the chiefs of Muskowekwan, Ochapowace, Piapot, and Star Blanket First Nations (referred to as the MOPS bands) threatened to launch a court action if the federal government did not reinstate the Saskatchewan formula. To placate the chiefs and divert any potential court action, Indian Affairs agreed to appoint an independent third party to mediate a settlement process.[27] However, due to a lack of progress in appointing this independent third party, the FSIN, along with Star Blanket and Canoe Lake First Nations, filed a statement of claim against the federal government.[28] Under this threat, the federal government proved unwilling to take its chances in court.

In response to the statement of claim, in April and May 1989, the federal government quickly reached an agreement with the FSIN to create the Office of the Treaty Commissioner (OTC), and appointed former Saskatoon mayor, Cliff Wright, as treaty commissioner.[29] Wright, who had had a significant role in the creation of the Muskeg Lake urban reserve in that city, was charged with establishing a model to settle the outstanding TLE claims.

The treaty commissioner argued that a proportion of a band's current population based on a percentage of individuals or families for whom no land was surveyed—what he called the "equity formula"—was best suited to settle TLE claims in Saskatchewan.[30] The equity formula adhered to the government's treaty obligations, was consistent with recent legal interpretation of treaties, and adhered to the principles of treaty interpretation. Wright provides an example of how the equity formula should work:

> Band A had a reserve surveyed for it in 1890. The survey allotted 10,000 acres. However, the population of the Band at the time was 100, therefore the treaty land entitlement should have been 12,800 acres (100 x 128 acres). The per capita reserve allotment was therefore only 100 acres (10,000 divided by 100 people) instead of the 128 acres per capita as required by the provisions of Treaty. The percentage of per capita shortfall was thus 22%. This percentage of shortfall in relation to the total amount of land received by Band A would likewise be approximately 22%.
>
> The population in Band A in 1990 is 500. To calculate the treaty land entitlement due now, the following formula would apply:
>
> 500 people x 128 acres = 64,000 acres x 22% (percentage of shortfall expressed on either an individual or Band basis) = 14,800 acres.
>
> The quantum of entitlement would therefore be 14,800 acres in 1990.[31]

In other words, the band's shortfall acres would be 12,000, and its equity acres would be 14,800. In order to resolve land entitlement in the 1990s, the treaty commissioner proposed a willing buyer/willing seller system of acquiring land. Fears from rural municipalities of lost tax base (due to private rural lands converting to tax-free reserve status), the commissioner argued, would be alleviated by a one-time payment to municipalities that was large enough to generate interest to cover lost tax revenue.[32] The treaty commissioner argued that both levels of government should enter into a cost-sharing agreement to finance the purchase of land, and urged a swift settlement of TLEs, not only as a means of honouring the spirit and intent of the treaties, but also for the more pragmatic reason of curtailing increasing settlement costs.

The Treaty Land Entitlement Framework Agreement

In May 1990, the Supreme Court issued its decision in *Sparrow*, which likely impacted how the federal and provincial governments received the treaty commissioner's report and recommendations on TLE. In this case, Ronald Sparrow, also from Musequeam First Nation, argued that his arrest for using an oversized fishing net violated his Aboriginal right to fish as guaranteed under section 35 of the constitution. The Supreme Court ruled in Sparrow's favour. The Court's delineation of Aboriginal and treaty rights in section 35 of the Constitution highlighted government fears of allowing the MOPS bands to proceed with their court challenge. The Court ruled that, among other things, the federal government's fiduciary responsibility applied to section 35(1) Aboriginal and treaty rights, that a liberal interpretation be given to those rights, and that any infringement of those rights had to meet a strict justification test.[33] Although the decision was made within the context of the Musequeam First Nation's Aboriginal fishing rights, there can be little doubt that Saskatchewan's TLE First Nations would have had a strong case to argue that the failure of the federal and provincial governments to fulfill their TLE claims was a breach of their (the governments') section 35 fiduciary responsibilities without any justification. Both governments would have recognized the significance of *Sparrow* on any potential future suit. Indeed, the threat of the MOPS court challenge had spurred the federal government to create the OTC in the first place. The treaty commissioner's final recommendations called for a number of compromises by the two levels of government that would benefit the Saskatchewan First Nations. Even though the recommendations conceded much more to First Nations than either the federal and provincial governments had previously allowed, the two governments must have believed that a court challenge could have cost them even more.

After the release of the treaty commissioner's recommendations, both the federal government and TLE First Nations met amongst themselves to strategize how to proceed.[34] As Martin-McGuire pointed out, the recommendations were not a legally binding agreement, nor did they deal with all the issues, "but through the equity formula, the purchase policy and the creation of a mutually acceptable political climate, they formed a foundation for discussions on a framework agreement."[35] In January 1991, a protocol agreement was signed, which set out the process to be followed to achieve a TLE agreement. By September 1991, the federal and provincial governments agreed to terms for cost-sharing, though these were amended several times before becoming a part of the Treaty Land Entitlement Framework Agreement (TLEFA).[36] On 22 September 1992, twenty-six First Nations and the federal and provincial governments signed the TLEFA.[37] After the agreement was signed, each First Nation had to negotiate its own Band Specific and Band Trust Agreement with the federal government, and then ratify it through a band referendum. It was stipulated in the TLEFA that each First Nation had until 22 September 1995 to ratify its agreement. Failure to do so within that time would result in withdrawal of the settlement. On 31 August 1995, Keeseekoose First Nation became the last First Nation to ratify its agreement. Only one First Nation, Joseph Bighead, failed to ratify, choosing instead to opt out of the proposal.[38]

Management of TLE funds was strictly regulated. First Nations had to establish a TLE trust into which the funds would be deposited. TLE trustees were then charged with the responsibility for administering TLE funds. The amount of funds awarded to a First Nation was based on its equity acres (the equity acres were greater than the actual shortfall acres). Funds were to be deposited into TLE trusts over a twelve-year period and could only be used to purchase shortfall acres, though a small amount could be used for special projects, such as elders' payments or paying for a First Nation council and TLE trustee expenses. Interest from the TLE funds, however, could be used in any manner that a First Nation saw fit. Similarly, revenue generated from TLE lands could also be used at the First Nation's discretion. Once the short-fall acres had been purchased, First Nations could either purchase more lands, if they chose, or divert the funds into any other project.[39]

The TLEFA was hailed as very positive for both the First Nations and the province. At a news conference on 26 May 1992 announcing the agreement, Dan Bellegarde, the first vice-chief for the FSIN, noted that the First Nations' land base could double as a result of TLE. This was confirmed by the OTC, which noted that, prior to the TLE process, reserve land comprised about only one percent of the provincial land base, but upon completion it would account for just over two percent. Lloyd Barber, chief negotiator for the FSIN and former president of the University of Regina, pointed out that First Nations would not be restricted to acquiring Crown land, but would be able to buy land from anyone willing to sell. Toby Stewart, the OTC's executive director, stated that TLE "will certainly be a shot in the arm for everyone involved with the land purchases. The ripple effect will be felt in many sectors of our economy."[40] Certainly, the spin-off effects for provincial economic development made TLE more palatable for those who would have otherwise been opposed to the process. This might explain the endorsement of the process by the Association of Saskatchewan Taxpayers (AST), an organization critical of government spending generally, and of money spent on Indian Affairs specifically. Responding to the TLEFA, AST president, Kevin Ayram, said that, from a moral and economic perspective, using tax dollars to settle TLE was ultimately in the taxpayers' best interests. The Regina *Leader-Post* reported Ayram as saying that, "Native people can't build a sound economic future on government handouts. They must be allowed to control some of the economic levers to make them more independent and self-sufficient."[41]

The new TLE process, however, was not immune to criticism. As early as 1995, TLE First Nations were experiencing problems in getting their selections converted to reserve status. According to the FSIN newspaper, the *Saskatchewan Indian*, the FSIN and TLE First Nations had started to work with federal and provincial representatives to "streamline" the reserve creation process. This process has continued to be slow, with many First Nations still waiting years for their selected lands to be converted to reserve status.[42]

Brenda McLeod, in her thesis on Witchekan Lake First Nation's TLE, was critical of the TLEFA negotiations process. She argued that there was a problem in properly providing accurate documentation for the historical population, which was the basis for shortfall acreage, thereby limiting a more beneficial entitlement claim. McLeod also suggested that First Nations' oral history was not given enough credibility in comparison to written documents.[43] The use and type of written documents was also a concern. Tyler and McLeod both raised problems surrounding the use of annuity pay lists to document nineteenth century First Nations populations. Tyler asserted that "these pay sheets were not designed to keep track of the number of Indians. They were designed to keep track of the amount of money the Agent had doled out."[44] As McLeod pointed out, annuity pay lists recorded the names of individuals who received their five-dollar annuities in any given year. If a person did not receive their annuity payment, the annuities would be paid in arrears the next time that person appeared to receive his or her money. McLeod suggested that researchers for First Nations may have limited their research to the annuity pay list because they were "the most convenient and easily accessible" documents.[45] Specifically referring to Witchekan Lake First Nation, a band that had signed an adhesion to Treaty 6 in 1950, McLeod argued that available census records had not been used to crosscheck the data in the annuity pay lists. McLeod was also critical of the practice of handling all TLE First Nations as a single homogenous group, even though the FSIN and TLE chiefs were in favour of this strategy. According to McLeod, this approach ignored distinctions between bands and therefore lessened their potential benefits. She asserted that the lack of research stemmed from the fact that the federal and provincial governments and the FSIN were all faced with upcoming elections, and that the "motivation to settle TLE lay in potential election pressures that each side could exert. Given the many years this outstanding debt remained unresolved, its settlement would be somewhat of a political coup for those seeking re-election."[46]

A few First Nations have had some problems with the proper management of TLE funds. First Nations have to follow strict guidelines in the administration of TLE funds to ensure that mismanagement does not occur. However, a few First Nations have been able to locate loopholes in the regulations, which has allowed for misspending. There are only a few legitimate ways for First Nations to access TLE funds that are not used to purchase shortfall acres. First Nations are allowed to use TLE funds to pay for council members and TLE trustee expenses related to conducting TLE business. In some cases, trustees recorded unreasonable expenses, even completely draining the TLE funds. These First Nations not only lose out on purchasing their shortfall acres, they are also responsible for repaying that money to the federal government. Although these cases have received fairly broad media attention, they are, in fact, relatively few.

These criticisms notwithstanding, the overall impact of TLE has been positive for First Nations and the province. Much of the land purchased by TLE First Nations in southern Saskatchewan has been agricultural land. The First Nations have subsequently leased these lands to Aboriginal and non-Aboriginal farmers, generating significant revenues. A number of First Nations have used their TLE money to purchase lands in urban areas. On these "urban reserves," First Nations have bought or built office and/or retail buildings. These sites have been leased primarily to First Nations businesses and government agencies, employing thousands of people, mostly First Nations people. Urban First Nations have benefited not only from finding employment in urban areas, but also from not having to pay income tax, as status Indians working on reserve are exempt from that particular tax.

In 2004, the final installment of the TLE funds were deposited into the trust accounts of the original TLE First Nations. The total amount exceeded $500 million, with a potential to purchase over 1.5 million acres of land.[47] The original TLE First Nations are still purchasing and converting land to reserve status. There are also a number of First Nations who are still receiving their TLE installments. These First Nations were not part of the TLEFA in 1992 because their claims had not been validated by the federal government at the time of signing.

Though Saskatchewan's First Nations had been lobbying to have their TLE addressed since the 1880s, they met with little success until the Supreme Court began to rule on Aboriginal rights. After the government shelved the White Paper's termination policy, the Supreme Court ruled in *Calder* that Aboriginal rights could exist without an executive order. Shortly thereafter, the federal government instead terminated its responsibility to "Indians and lands reserved for Indians," and created the Office of Native Claims to facilitate settlement of outstanding Indian land claims. By 1975, the province of Saskatchewan had entered into TLE discussions, eventually introducing the Saskatchewan formula in 1977. Although Pitsula argued that responsibility for the lack of TLE settlements based on the Saskatchewan formula rested with the federal government's resistance to the formula, some blame also fell on the province. By the early 1980s, the province introduced new policies that in effect signaled its wish to distance itself from the Saskatchewan formula. There is no doubt that this new direction was influenced by growing public opposition to the Saskatchewan formula, and the upcoming provincial election. In 1982, the new Progressive Conservative government entered into a two-year TLE policy review. Its new TLE policy, which supported the Saskatchewan formula, was introduced the same year that the *Guerin* decision, which acknowledged the federal government's fiduciary responsibility to First Nations, was handed down. The new policy was introduced because the province was concerned that it would lose a court challenge for not adhering to the Saskatchewan formula. This policy spurred new tripartite discussions, which again stalled due to jurisdictional squabbles. By 1988, the federal government officially abandoned the Saskatchewan formula and then was faced with the threat of a court challenge by four TLE First Nations. To placate the First Nations, the federal government moved to establish the Office of the Treaty Commissioner and appointed a treaty commissioner to develop recommendations to settle the TLE claims. The treaty commissioner's recommendations were released the same month that the Supreme Court rendered its decision in *Sparrow*. This decision linked the federal fiduciary responsibility to Aboriginal and treaty rights found in section 35(1) of the Canadian Constitution. It is little wonder, then, that the federal and provincial governments accepted the recommendation of the treaty commissioner, even though those recommendations provided more benefits to First Nations than either government had previously accorded them. Had they not conceded, they might have stood to lose considerably more.

Cowessess First Nation and Treaty Land Entitlement

On 25 April 1995, Cowessess First Nation reached a tentative agreement with the Canadian and Saskatchewan governments for its TLE settlement, which was subsequently ratified by the band membership on 7 December 1995. Minister of Indian Affairs Ronald Irwin, Saskatchewan Minister of Indian and Métis Affairs Joanne Crofford, and Chief of Cowessess Lionel Sparvier signed the agreement in a public ceremony held on Cowessess First Nation on 14 March 1996. The agreement called for the federal and provincial governments to pay Cowessess more than $46.6 million in twelve installments, making it at the time the second-largest TLE settlement in the province and the largest in southern Saskatchewan. The first installment of $12.8 million was deposited into the Cowessess trust accounts in April 1996, and the final TLE payment of $1.1 million was paid in 2008. The TLE negotiation and ratification process was different for Cowessess than it had been for most of the other TLE First Nations. The difference was partially due to the advantageous bargaining position that Cowessess had enjoyed with the federal and provincial governments, as well as to the band's mixed city/reserve composition. These factors were directly tied to the historical circumstances of the Cowessess First Nation. For one thing, the TLE process was facilitated by the principles of kinship adhered to by Cowessess members. Because of these principles, Cowessess was able to use the TLE process to not only link historical ancestors to contemporary members, but as a means to include members—both new members and members who had relocated off reserve and lost touch with the band—in deciding the outcome of the land claim.

For Cowessess First Nation, the process of obtaining validation for a claim from the Department of Indian Affairs was long and complex. Cowessess leaders had long believed they had a TLE claim, but could not substantiate it. In the early 1970s, Lou Lockhart, a consultant hired by Cowessess, completed an initial count of Cowessess 1880s annuities pay lists and, according to his assessment, concluded that the First Nation had sufficient numbers to qualify for a TLE claim. Indian Affairs officials, however, believing that Cowessess would never be able to qualify for a claim, rejected Lockhart's assessment. But Lockhart would not be deterred, and continued his research. According to Terence Pelletier, Cowessess TLE coordinator and later chief, "It is important to remember, that when those INAC [Indian and Northern Affairs Canada] people said that, it made Lou Lockhart more determined to research and prove Cowessess' claim. He eventually did. So, he is kind of like the 'Luke Skywalker' of Cowessess."[48]

Cowessess' TLE claim was pursued by a number of long-term band councillors. Cowessess chiefs seldom had long-term involvement in the TLE claim. The chiefs, for their part, worked toward settling the TLE claim; as Pelletier stated, "as long as there is breath in their lungs, the chief's primary and only job would be to get treaty rights and land payments." The chiefs of Cowessess, however, unlike the councillors, are seldom re-elected to second or third terms of office. The work of Cowessess TLE, therefore, was primarily carried out by the councillors. The councillors who worked on the claim in the 1970s and 1980s were Edwin Pelletier, Harold Lerat, Henry Delorme, and Howard Young. In the 1980s and early 1990s, Councillor Hubert Gunn, in particular, worked on the claim, participating in the actual negotiations and the initial ratification process. Gunn died in 1996, and so he was unable to "benefit from the land claim he spent so many years lobbying for."[49]

Even with these men working on the claim, validation moved slowly. By the late 1980s, there was some acknowledgement from Indian Affairs that Cowessess had a shortfall; but in order to be eligible for validation, the band had to meet certain criteria. As Pelletier noted, "It was not enough to find 10, 20 or 50 persons. It had to be a significant shortfall to qualify for a validated claim."[50]

Indian Affairs used the annuity pay lists to substantiate the TLE claims. These pay lists, developed during the 1880s, were the means by which the government kept track of who had been paid their annuities, and contained certain information on each individual, such as year of payment, the individual's name, location of payment, and the band to which the individual belonged. In the Cowessess TLE claim, a problem arose regarding which years were to be used to substantiate populations. Pelletier explained, "There was a condition that made Cowessess' TLE questionable from Indian Affairs point of view. It had to do with the date of the treaty pay lists that were used to determine the acreage from the date of first survey of the reserve. Whatever year the reserve was surveyed (DOFS), that was the year the pay lists were counted against the acres surveyed."[51] The problem for Cowessess was that there were multiple surveys for the reserve. The first was completed in 1878, when Louis O'Soup led a splinter group to Crooked Lake. A second was conducted in 1881, when Chief Cowessess brought the reminder of his band from Cypress Hills and joined O'Soup's group at Crooked Lake. This issue was part of the stumbling block that prevented Cowessess from gaining validation in 1992, along with the other First Nations.

The validation of Cowessess' claim in October 1993 did not translate into a quick TLE agreement. The federal government agreed that Cowessess had a significant shortfall. The reserve was surveyed in 1881 for 480 people, but based on evidence that Indian Affairs possessed, Cowessess band membership was actually 680. Using the equity formula, Cowessess was entitled to receive $27 million from the federal government to settle the outstanding claim. But Cowessess rejected this offer. The band argued that, in fact, there were considerably more original members than the 680 that the federal government maintained. Indian Affairs disagreed, and wanted Cowessess to substantiate its claim with the annuity pay lists. In contrast to the argument made by McLeod and Tyler, described in the previous section—that pay lists may not have been the most reliable source to document First Nations TLE claims—using pay lists proved to be beneficial for Cowessess.

Cowessess' negotiators had noticed that there were many people who had accepted annuities for one year, but who then never again appeared on the pay lists. One of the stipulations of the TLE claim was that an individual had to appear on a band's annuity pay lists in two consecutive years to be counted towards the claim. Cowessess argued that these people did not appear the second time because they had died. Indian Affairs argued that the people might have gone to other bands, taken scrip, or left Canada entirely to join relatives on American reservations in Montana or North Dakota. Cowessess researchers determined that the people in question did not appear on any other band list in Canada or the United States, nor in the scrip records. They also found no trace of them in the records of the Hudson's Bay Company, which would have been an important source of income. Cowessess then argued that those people be included in their claim by linking their "disappearance" from the historical records to Edgar Dewdney's 1880s starvation policy, detailed earlier in Chapter 3. Pelletier linked Cowessess' position regarding the pay lists to Dewdney's policies: "Cowessess claimed that these persons died on the prairies during the year between treaty payments. It was a federal government policy at the time to withhold food or rations to certain Indians and Cowessess claim was that the Indians starved on the plains because of it. We argued that the federal government should not benefit in that case because it was their own policy that killed them and they can't benefit now by not paying Cowessess land benefits because Cowessess band members were dead and couldn't show up for the pay list counts."[52]

As mentioned previously, the federal government has never acknowledged the starvation policy or its devastating effects on Saskatchewan's First Nations people.[53] The government may have been reluctant for a discussion of this issue to enter the public realm. It is worth noting that, since the late 1990s, over one thousand Aboriginal human remains have been re-interred in Saskatchewan. In 1990, a number of stakeholders, including the Saskatchewan Indian Cultural Centre (SICC, an FSIN institution) agreed to establish a provincial burial ground north of the city of Saskatoon. By 1999, nearly five hundred Aboriginal human remains were reburied in that location. These human remains were found in farmers' fields, during road construction, and other seemingly random places. In 2001, another five hundred human remains were re-interred in the Cypress Hills. Between 1969 and 1973, 305 human remains were excavated from a cemetery in the Cypress Hills region and housed at the University of Saskatchewan.[54]

The facts surrounding the reasons for the re-interment of this latter group are not readily known. There was no news coverage, no press releases, and no public discussion whatsoever of the reburials. There is only a passing reference in an academic journal article discussing how Aboriginal people and museum professionals had been able to develop a working relationship.[55] Regarding the more recent reburials, a small group of elders from the SICC apparently wanted to keep the ceremonies quiet as a measure to ensure that the remains would not again be disturbed, being concerned that the reinterred remains not fall prey to grave robbers. Saskatchewan, however, does not have a substantial history of grave robbing. It is not clear whether the elders had been made aware of the low frequency of grave robbing in Saskatchewan. If the elders had not been made aware of this fact, the question that then begs to be asked is why not? The secrecy of the reburials is in contrast to burials conducted in the United States.[56] Cowessess First Nation, which had demonstrated that a significant number of its ancestors had starved to death at or near Cypress Hills, did not have a representative on the SICC elders' council.

Whatever the case, Indian Affairs decided not to challenge Cowessess on this issue and agreed to include those people who Cowessess claimed had died because of the government's starvation policy. Each name was to be reviewed separately by Indian Affairs to determine the merit of their inclusion in the Cowessess numbers. Finally, with close to three hundred additional names being added through this time-consuming process, the government's chief negotiator decided to strike a deal with Cowessess. The negotiator suggested that the government would accept half of the remaining names on Cowessess' list without a review process. The benefit for Cowessess was that it would fast-track the agreement and guarantee them a large settlement. Cowessess agreed. Pelletier concluded, "In that sense, Cowessess negotiated the TLE deal as opposed to hard numbers being the formula."[57] Cowessess' TLE settlement, then, was based on a negotiated band population of 804, though band officials estimated that the population was closer to nine hundred, and possibly as high as a thousand. Where other First Nations may have limited their claims by using the pay lists, as McLeod and Tyler asserted, the pay lists combined with the starvation policy argument was a crucial component to Cowessess' settlement. It is not certain, however, whether other First Nations could have negotiated better settlements had they employed the starvation policy argument.

In total, Cowessess' settlement entitled it to purchase up to 189,367 acres (equity acres) and a minimum of 53,312 acres (actual shortfall acres). Cowessess' TLE agreement adhered to the same principles found in the original TLEFA. As Cowessess was not a part of that agreement, it was able to negotiate other concessions not found in the TLEFA. Chief Lionel Sparvier outlined these concessions in a letter addressed to his band members:

> 7. The ability to withdraw from the Trust funds an amount not exceeding $1,147,000, of which $800,000 may be utilized for Band development purposes, and $347,000 for the providing of one time lump sum payment to elders of the Band over the age of 65.[58]

The $800,000 could be used for any project deemed suitable to the First Nation without being subject to the constraints of the TLE agreement. Money was set aside for elders, because it was believed that they would have the least to gain from the long-term benefits derived from TLE:

8. The ability to establish Trusts in the areas of Band development, education, culture and recreation for the use of all band members living on and off the reserve.[59]

The funds for these projects could come from one of two sources. The first was from interest income generated from trust property, but it would require prior approval from TLE trustees. The second source was from the actual principal of the TLE fund. The use of this source could be problematic, as it could lead to a draining of the TLE accounts. Using this money would therefore need approval of the band membership through a band-wide ratification vote:

9. The inclusion of an amendment clause that allows the Band Council and its Trustees the ability to address any future changes in the tax system that may put in jeopardy the taxability of income generated from the Trust property.[60]

Other First Nations are required to conduct a ratification vote to amend their trust agreements, but Cowessess was able to negotiate a more time-effective measure. As Chief Sparvier explained to his membership, this was "a substantial concession, and one which will allow the Band and Trustees the ability to react quickly to any changes in the current tax system":

10. The inclusion of a floating upper limit on the purchase price of land.

11. The ability to purchase lands, prior to acquisition of the shortfall acres, without the purchase of underlying mines and minerals up to maximum of 4,000.[61]

Both of these concessions are of great importance in purchasing urban lands. The upper limit is the maximum amount of money that a band can spend to purchase a piece of property. A floating upper limit takes into consideration the amount of money that Cowessess has already received and the amount that it has spent to purchase land throughout the land acquisition process; as a result, the upper limit will change as purchases are made. As Chief Sparvier noted, these new clauses were important because "it will allow the Band greater flexibility in the structuring of land acquisition arrangements, particularly as they relate to the acquisition of urban land."[62] This is significant, considering the large number of band members that reside in urban areas, especially in Regina and Saskatoon.

According to the equity formula, the band's present population figure was as important as the historical population. First Nations children are not automatically given Indian status at birth; their parents have to fill out a form and register them through Indian Affairs. It was common for parents not to register their children, because status Indians benefits could still be accessed until the child reached eighteen years of age. For the TLE, however, only those registered, including children, would count toward the claim. During the period of negotiations, then, Cowessess sent out numerous letters to band members to remind them to register their children for Indian status. In addition, the band leadership, relying on family connections, instructed its members to encourage any relatives to apply whom they believed were eligible for Indian status through Bill C-31. The band even offered assistance to help in the application process. In contrast to many other bands, TLE was a mechanism for Cowessess to incorporate its Bill C-31 members into the band in an important way. Though Cowessess gained financially from this, TLE thus also served as a vehicle to reconnect with members.

After Cowessess and Indian Affairs had reached an agreement on the TLE settlement, Cowessess then had to ratify it through a band-wide referendum. Like the other TLE First Nations, Cowessess needed the consent of a majority of band members to ratify the agreement. The composition of Cowessess, combined with Indian Affairs ratification regulations, made the process very arduous. At the time of the agreement, Cowessess' population exceeded 2,500, with nearly eighty percent living off reserve. In 1993, however, Cowessess only had addresses for approximately three hundred people. There were two crucial regulations to which Cowessess had to adhere for the ratification vote to be valid. First, every non-vote was counted as a "no," for the purposes of the TLE agreement. Second, the First Nation was required to have eighty percent of the eligible voters' addresses, which represented about 1,400 addresses. Clearly, it was incumbent upon Cowessess to locate as many members as possible.

The band embarked on an intensive campaign to ascertain the whereabouts of its membership. Many lived in various communities in the province, with a large number in the city of Regina and a smaller number in Saskatoon. Significant numbers were also found in Vancouver, Calgary, Edmonton, and Winnipeg, as well as throughout Canada, and in foreign countries like Australia, Russia, and the United States.

Once Cowessess began compiling the addresses of its membership, it then had to tackle the time-consuming and costly endeavour of informing and explaining the TLE agreement. Members were sent copies of the agreement, along with a summary prepared by the band's lawyers. The actual agreement was comprised of two documents: the *Cowessess Treaty Land Entitlement Agreement* and the *Cowessess Treaty Land Entitlement Trust Agreement.* These documents comprised nearly two hundred pages of densely legalistic language that most non-lawyers would find difficult to understand. To help explain the documents, Cowessess scheduled on- and off-reserve informational meetings. At first, the off-reserve meetings were only scheduled for major western cities, but later included cities in Ontario.

These meetings were not only a means for TLE officials from the First Nation to explain the agreement better, they also served as a way to meet and connect with the urban membership, many of whom had never lived on Cowessess. At these urban meetings, the TLE officials, Terrence Pelletier and Hubert Gunn, encouraged urban members to visit and reconnect with their relatives and homeland. Indian Affairs covered the meeting costs. It had also agreed to fund the ratification process, for which it used a formula that paid Cowessess a certain amount for each member who lived in Saskatchewan, more for those who lived outside the province, and more still for those living abroad. The band, however, was unable to arrange for meetings outside the country.

It took nearly three years from the time that the TLE settlement was reached until the ratification vote. Cowessess band members had a number of options for how to cast their votes. They could vote on the reserve, or in a number of urban voting stations located throughout western Canada. Members not living near such stations could vote by mail. One member, for example, was serving in the navy in an undisclosed duty aboard a Canadian warship. His ballot was forwarded by the military and received for the final count. Cowessess TLE officials spent much time, energy, and resources—in all, over $300,000—but their efforts were rewarded when, on 7 December 1995, the membership voted overwhelmingly in favour of the agreement.

The time and resources spent on traveling to the various urban centres and meeting urban members was crucial to the final vote total. The significance of the urban vote can be observed in the failed ratification vote, in 2001, of the *Cowessess First Nation Lands Management Act.* In 1996, Cowessess First Nation became one of fourteen First Nations nationwide who signed the

Framework Agreement on First Nations Land Management, which was later passed by Parliament as the *First Nations Land Management Act*. The framework agreement provided these First Nations "with the option to manage their reserve lands outside the *Indian Act*."[63] Each First Nation had to develop its own land management act, which then had to pass a simple majority ratification vote. However, Cowessess' land management act ratification vote did not pass, even though a majority of those who did vote supported the new act. The problem was that non-votes outnumbered yes votes. Those non-votes were primarily from the urban membership. Cowessess is attempting to hold another ratification vote on its land management act, and will no doubt be seeking a higher participation rate from its urban membership.

On 14 March 1996, the signing ceremony for the TLE agreement was held at the Cowessess First Nation community hall, which was packed with off-reserve and on-reserve community members, as well as officials from the FSIN and the provincial and federal governments. Gifts and appreciation were given to the TLE committee and the volunteers who worked at the various voting stations. Minister Irwin told the gathering, "This agreement confirms my government's commitment to resolving Aboriginal land claims and fulfills its treaty obligation to the people of Cowessess First Nations. ... With the purchase of new land, the Cowessess First Nation will forge a link with the past and create an opportunity for the future. This settlement will provide an economic base which will benefit current community members as well as future generations."[64] Minister Crofford noted that the "agreement fulfills provincial obligations and provides Cowessess First Nations with the resources necessary for future economic development that will benefit all of Saskatchewan."[65] And Chief Lionel Sparvier told the crowd that, "Treaty 4 contained an obligation to provide land to our people. ... This agreement settles our people's right to receive land as a reserve. It is my hope that the resources acquired by the settlement of this outstanding promise will promote the well-being of our people."[66] At the end of the signing ceremony, Cowessess officially became a TLE First Nation.

Cowessess' TLE process is noteworthy on a number of fronts. First, the negotiations demonstrated Cowessess' perseverance in obtaining the best possible deal for all its band members. Their goal was to extract as much money from the federal and provincial governments as possible, and clearly the use of the starvation policy argument achieved this goal. Though money was one motivating factor in the Cowessess negotiation strategy, another underlying motivation was enforcing recognition of the federal government's treaty responsibilities to those people who had died, if not an acknowledgement of the government's complicity in their deaths. As a result of this recognition, the ancestors have been able to leave a tangible legacy to the present-day Cowessess band members. The efforts to enumerate as many people as possible as contemporary band members has also enabled Cowessess not only to gain more money, it has maximized the number of descendants of the original Cowessess band who can benefit from the treaty. Another important aspect of the TLE process was that Cowessess has strengthened its financial and social capabilities. Financially, the band has been and will continue to be able to enter into economic development ventures that benefit not only on-reserve but also off-reserve members. Socially, because the First Nation had to make contact with many long-lost members, either indirectly through the many mailouts or directly through informational meetings. The TLE was a community effort that (re)ignited its kinship relations with off-reserve members and increased its nation-building capacity.

Cowessess Members' View of the Impact of TLE

The $46 million injection that Cowessess received from its Treaty Land Entitlement settlement has continued and will continue to have monumental repercussions for the First Nation and its members. Aside from the obvious financial benefits of the settlement, the band may also reap a number of social benefits. Because Cowessess had to locate and contact off-reserve members to ratify the agreement, many members became involved in band activities and have since reconnected with the band and with relatives. The TLE has also spawned new projects that may also increase off-reserve members' involvement with the band. When asked to provide their views of TLE and its social impact on the band, many thought that the TLE provided a way for off-reserve members to reconnect with the band in a meaningful way and that it would have positive future ramifications. Still, others were apprehensive about the inclusion of members who had long been disconnected from both the band and their on-reserve relatives.

Many of those interviewed were able to discuss the circumstances of Cowessess' TLE. One participant outlined what he believed to be the reasons why Cowessess did not receive full land entitlement. Though some of the details he provided are not accurate, his testimony nevertheless illustrates how some band members have understood their entitlement. His description is also significant for the oral history that it contains:

Beginning with the Treaty Land Entitlement process, they had to validate all those claims. So, it took years of research and historical archival looking to, to come up with, I guess, justification and authorizing, validating a true claim. So, I did a little bit of research, and I went, I looked at what [Chief] Cowessess, where [Chief] Cowessess was. [I found out that] he lived in the southwest with a band of Indians, his people. But the North West Mounted Police, there was a number of chiefs or headmen with their people that were sort of all migrating to the Fort Walsh area there. And the RCMP, the government, they thought they were gonna start attacking, because the buffalo were drying up. I think Sitting Bull had just been sent back south and Riel's rebellion had happened.[67] And there were a lot of scared people on the prairies at that time. So, to disperse them out of that region and to open up settlement … for the settlers to come in, they decided to sign the treaties.[68] And there was maybe a forest, but there was a migration of all those bands that were in the, the Maple Creek area to the reserve from that region. And I think Cowessess and his people, they had come down with Cowessess and his people. But the problem was a lot of his people were not there when the heads were counted [referring, presumably, to the survey at Crooked Lake, not Cypress Hills]. They were out hunting and trapping or doing stuff outside of that group that was counted. And then, when they got to the reserve, there were some more people already there. They decided they weren't going to move, so the reserve started small to begin with, and then, through devious ways of reducing that land, the Indian agent, you know, sold off some to the [white farmers] over here. And so the reserve started to shrink very fast. And we ended up with almost half of the reserve within those first few years. That was after survey, 'cause my grandfather used to tell me that the reserve line, you know, when you come from Broadview and you make that big turn. There's a big turn there, where the reserve starts, and then you go into the reserve. I don't know if you know that one. Well, that line was not, that was on the other side of the highway [Highway #1, the Trans-Canada Highway] when

> Cowessess was surveyed. So, it was all that land that was included
> in our Treaty Land Entitlement settlement. So, now we have all
> those white farmers. I don't know all their names, but the ——s
> were a big farm family. It would be interesting to know how they
> got their land.

This participant alluded to what he believed was the original boundary of the
reserve. According to what his grandfather had told him, the reserve's southern border pushed south of the town of Broadview. Other band members
repeated this assertion. One member mentioned that the southern boundary
ended at a creek just south of Broadview. This would mean that the northern
boundary was the Qu'Appelle River and the southern boundary was the
creek. Use of both waterways does suggest a logical and natural place for
leaders to demarcate boundaries.

The following participant reflected the views of some band members who
did not know exactly what TLE meant:

> Just by working for the [band] I'm learning a lot of stuff. Like,
> everything is so foreign to me, you know, like about TLE. ... Well,
> I didn't even know what that stood for ... that it meant, you know,
> TLE. I didn't even know that. And I was asking my co-worker,
> and she didn't even know what it meant, either. So, she asked the
> head guy, here, and he told us what it was. ... Treaty land entitle-
> ment, oh, you know, being so urbanized ... and everything seems
> to be so foreign, like learning everything all over or it's new.

Although she attributed her lack of knowledge of TLE to her being an urban
band member, most other urban members interviewed understood TLE.

When asked if they thought that it was a good thing that the band employed many strategies, including traveling all over the country in an attempt
to contact as many members as possible, some participants were not as certain
of the positive effect of the TLE process in connecting people. For example,
this woman expressed her ambivalence:

> I really can see either way. I mean, I think it was probably an
> important thing that we had to do, from an administrative point
> of view. When you look at it in terms of reconnecting with band
> members who were lost, say, to the rest of us, I think that was prob-
> ably a good thing. That was a positive thing about it, because then

it made those people reconnect with their roots. So, you know, that was a good thing for us to be able to bring our people back to understand where they're from, but would it make a big impact on many of them if they've never been to the reserve? Probably not for most of them, especially if they've been in the mainstream for a long time. I don't know if they would even understand [the reserve lifestyle]. It would be like putting something in front of someone that they don't see it, 'cause they've never experienced it. They have no understanding of what it is and whether it was important to them to have that connection. The people who probably came to the [urban TLE] meetings were the people who [were] probably curious enough about where they were from and wanting, part of themselves wanting to connect and be part of that membership. For the rest, the rest of the eighty-five percent in all those communities probably, didn't even, couldn't even be bothered to show up at the [TLE] meetings. 'Cause I'm sure there was a very small portion of the [urban] people that went to, that even bothered to come to the [TLE] meetings.

One respondent said that he believed Indian Affairs made the process much more complex and expensive than it should have been:

Well, my personal opinion is, I think it was a tremendous waste of money. To have to get the vote from those people who had lost the connection to the reserve at some point. Some of them were two, three generations down the line from ever having lived on the reserve. I know that our vote cost us hundreds of thousands of dollars because of all the travel that those people had to do. [They had to go] out and sell it. They really had nothing to sell [to the urban members]. Those members living in Toronto or Calgary, Edmonton, they say, "Well, we were getting all this money, we're going to put some of it aside for education. So you should be able to go to school." And that's all they could sell. But from the government's point of view, [the TLE process was a way of not having] the reserves from coming back [to] Indian Affairs and saying, "Well, our membership didn't say we could sign this off." Because Indian Affairs is saying, "Once you sign on the dotted line, our responsibility for that land that was illegally taken from you and we give you the money, after that our hands are washed." And so, they wanted the membership to vote fifty plus one percent. So that they could wash their hands with what they had done originally. But I don't see the benefit. You know, we had to go, we have twenty-four hundred members, three hundred and eighty-five at that point were living on reserve. Even if we just said within the province or whatever, but they [Indian Affairs] made them go out and find thirteen in Calgary and ten in Toronto.

Some clarification is needed with regard to this respondent's comments about the band setting aside money for education. Indian Affairs does not provide any funding directly to urban First Nations persons with the exception of support for post-secondary education. With the TLE, however, First Nations can divert interest from their trust accounts to address any needs, including those in urban areas. The reason for this is because, legally, the TLE money, unlike funds allocated for band administration, does not belong to the federal government. In addition, the TLE agreement allows Cowessess to purchase land in urban areas and convert that land to reserve status, though most of the land purchased to date by Saskatchewan TLE bands has been used for commercial purposes. Cowessess has purchased land on the outskirts of Saskatoon and in Regina, and in 2013 they built a four-storey, 35,000-square-foot office building in Regina, which was very exciting for the membership. Given the number of urban members living in Regina and Saskatoon, the band membership overall is in favour of urban developments. After all, if Cowessess established an urban residential reserve, it is conceivable that its members would be entitled to the same benefits that members residing on the home reserve currently receive, even though many issues would need to be ironed out, such as governance and residency requirements.

Interview participants generally responded that the TLE process had been positive for the band and its members:

> I think it was a good thing as a band member for locating everybody from Cowessess. This was a good thing 'cause that makes you realize, like, holy cow, why did some of these people move away that far? Like, some live over the ocean! ... You know, and I just shook my head. Oh my god, so why did these people move [far away], some for school, maybe, you know? Why did they do that? Maybe they wanted to do that. I don't know ... but I thought it

> was a good idea, 'cause then you know how many people there is
> and then some of them I'd like to get to know.

This participant suggested that the band contacted urban members only to
fulfill its obligation to the TLE: "That's the only time they contact them, is
when they want to use them, and then they forget about them." Though she
may have been skeptical about the band's motivation for contacting previously
disconnected members, she nonetheless clearly believed that the members
should have been contacted:

> Even if these people didn't live on the reserve, they are still con-
> sidered band members. And they're entitled to everything from
> the reserve, and if at any point they want to go back to the reserve,
> they should be able to go back to the reserve—they're band mem-
> bers. They have a share in that reserve. It belongs to everyone. It
> doesn't belong to any individual according to the treaties. So, yes,
> I believe they should have been counted, because the more people,
> the more you were entitled to.

To the question, "Do you think there is any kind of connection between
the TLE and the importance of family?" this next participant responded by
tying the TLE to treaty rights, maintenance of family, and the social dislocation of band members:

> Yeah. You look at what we didn't have. We were entitled to this
> [certain amount of land] and we didn't get it. What did we miss
> because of a result of that? We had three thousand people with
> eighty percent of the people living off the reserve. Well, could
> it be because we didn't have half of our land? Could it be the
> half that we did get, we lost a quarter of it [through government
> fraud]? What happens when people leave? They no longer have
> the support of their community. They have to take their children
> somewhere else, and they raise their families without the support
> of back home, without the support of the reserve. If you don't have
> the reserve to live on, where are you going to go? I guess that is
> why Cowessess has such a big membership that has left. So, to
> me, that is what TLE means. When you look at it from a treaty
> right point of view, and it wasn't until we got the forty-six million,
> it was only then that I realized how valuable our treaty right was.

And the TLE is a treaty right and that treaty right was supposed to somehow guarantee the security of Cowessess people. And if we never got that, then that's what happened, our people lost their security. So that's what happens to Indians when they don't have their land. Indians lost their status of their reserve. Indians without land are nothing. So, that is what TLE is. It represents what happened historically. It answers why there are so many off the reserve. It answers why the social conditions are like that. It also offers some kind of hope for the future, now that we can reconnect with the land. We know what the land represents to us. How we can use that to our benefit. I think we have a hell of future. Maybe I won't see it, but I know my family will. So TLE, in terms of land, I think we just don't know how important it is to us. To me, that's what I think. If that treaty right to land had, can be fulfilled, think what would happen if all of the other treaty rights were fulfilled. We don't know what we are missing. When you get forty-six million, you now know what you were missing before, and you know what the treaty right was that you were fighting for. Nobody knew that, I don't think. We had our [past] leaders that understood the importance. If they didn't fight for it, what would we have?

This last participant saw the lack of land, and loss of land, as having a negative impact on band members' ability to increase their economic opportunities, and therefore to maintain their social and economic security. The lack of economic opportunities available on Cowessess has fueled social dysfunction or urban migration or both. The significant and prolonged urban migration served to increase social dislocation among band members. He identified land and band members' security as treaty rights, because without the land there can be no security. Cowessess' ability to purchase land and implement economic projects is therefore seen as a fulfillment of a treaty right to achieve band members' wellbeing.

As I listened and watched people interact, I sensed that welcoming attitude, which Pelletier and Gunn had shown toward those of us who attended the TLE informational session in Toronto. This was another example of Cowessess residents' desire to connect with other Cowessess people, even those of us who had had little contact with the reserve.

Conclusion

In the early 2000s, I attended a Federation of Saskatchewan Indian Nations legislative assembly in Saskatoon. There, I met and talked briefly to a Cowessess band councillor. Upon hearing that I was an urban band member, he happily expressed his feelings about off-reserve members: "we have members everywhere and we are proud of all of them." This, of course, could have simply been politician talk. Many Cowessess people, however, whether they are politicians, bureaucrats, or grassroots people, express this kind of sentiment regarding members who have left the reserve to pursue opportunities far from the home community—some who maintained their connections to the band, others who became disconnected. This book has attempted to explain the basis for the way in which contemporary Cowessess kinship practices are played out. The underlying assumption is that these practices were rooted in the cultural values of pre-reserve people. While acknowledging that colonial forces have had an impact on cultural practices of Aboriginal people, this study shows they have not passively forsaken their culture. For Cowessess people, this has meant that some cultural practices have been abandoned, some have been altered, while others have been maintained intact. No matter the extent of the cultural change, the cultural values informing those practices have remained virtually unchanged. In the case of Cowessess, the values encoded in the Elder Brother stories form the basis of their current kinship practices.

This book has sought to show how historical, scholarly, and legal perceptions have impacted Aboriginal people in Canada, and to contrast this with how members of Cowessess First Nation view themselves based on the stories of Elder Brother and the Law of the People. Nevertheless, this book is by no stretch of the imagination definitive. Whether or not the kind of views on kinship found in Cowessess may also be found in other Aboriginal groups in Saskatchewan, elsewhere in Canada, or in the United States is a question that must be left to others. So, too, is a consideration of other possible values contained in the Law of the People, which may also have been carried over into modern times. For example, what do the stories say about gender relations or governance, and to what degree are Aboriginal people adhering to such values? This study has focused only upon Elder Brother stories, and not the other stories found within Cree and Saulteaux/Ojibwe tradition. Hopefully, others will explore those stories in some detail. By examining traditional stories, Native Studies scholars not only assist us in expanding our understanding of contemporary Aboriginal cultures, they will themselves also be contributing to cultural persistence, preservation, and revitalization.

Conducting this kind of research allows for a more thorough understanding of a particular community. There is a tendency on the part of scholars and policy makers to make generalizations about Aboriginal communities that have little basis, and then develop theories or policies based on those generalizations. Research into the histories and experiences of First Nations and other Aboriginal communities provides the necessary context better to understand contemporary issues from local Aboriginal cultural perspectives. This can help to dispel the notion of a monolithic Aboriginal culture by highlighting the complexities and diversity that exists in Aboriginal Canada. This study has shown the cultural kinship practices particular to Cowessess First Nation. Other communities' kinship practices will invariably differ, based upon their own paths through the colonial minefield of Canadian history.

Even though many Cowessess members may not have heard any Elder Brother stories, this book has shown that the stories continue to have importance. Cowessess members have, for the most part, continued to place an emphasis on kinship connections, something that was evident throughout my field study. The formal interviews with study participants and informal conversations with several band members showed that a majority of Cowessess people had positive attitudes about C-31s and the reconnection of band members through the TLE process. Many also spoke with pride of the various family reunions that took place on the reserve. These attitudes were shaped within the context of family/kinship connections, not within tribal or ethnic affiliations. This is further illustrated by the fact that, when two Cowessess members meet for the first time, they ask, "Who are you related to?" or "Who's your family?" not "Which tribe do you belong to?" A person's family name places that person within the familial reserve context. This is not to say that ethnicity is totally ignored, but that it is not the primary identifier that connects people, not in the way that family/kinship does.

In the focus group discussions held with the elders, the elders were highly consistent in their responses to questions about the social impact on Cowessess of Bill C-31 and TLE. For these particular elders, maintaining family connections took precedence over all other concerns; therefore, they saw Bill C-31 and TLE as strengthening Cowessess First Nation. Though a majority of interviewees echoed these views, they were far from unanimous in their assessment of Bill C-31 and TLE. Cowessess people, generally speaking, were genuinely open to Bill C-31s and urban members. However, this book should not be interpreted to suggest that Bill C-31 was a flawless piece of legislation that Cowessess people completely endorsed. In fact, some interview participants recognized the limitations of the new membership codes. In addition, this book should not be seen as presenting Cowessess as some kind of ideal community. Like all communities, it has its tensions. There are certain issues that strain relations, including housing, which is in short supply on the reserve, and urban/reserve tensions over band support and band politics, which can be very divisive, as demonstrated by the fact that chiefs are not usually re-elected to a second term. Band political power is usually drawn along family lines. There has also been some animosity toward allowing new members into the band. Some have also expressed reservations regarding the band's obligations under the TLE agreement to contact members who have had little or no understanding of, or contact with, the home community. Nevertheless, the band and band members have in general continued the cultural practice of inclusion from pre-reserve and early reserve times. As one interview participant stated of the inclusive attitude held by many band members: "I mean, it's, it's a value that's instilled from people of Cowessess." This principle of inclusion is linked to pre-reserve kinship patterns found in the Law of the People. The laws outlined ways to incorporate people into a band based on kinship roles and responsibilities. This provided an important survival mechanism that allowed multicultural groups to flourish. In the contemporary context, for Cowessess people, while these patterns have adapted and changed, they continue to serve as a mechanism for physical, mental, and emotional survival.

In addition, contemporary kinship patterns ensure that band members' collective identity as Cowessess people survives. Such enduring notions inform the ways in which the Cowessess First Nation and Cowessess band members have responded to Bill C-31 and treaty land entitlement.

Notes

Introduction

[1] Mosom and Kohkom are Cree terms for grandfather and grandmother, respectively. These terms are often used not only for a person's biological grandparents but also for any relative of a person's grandparents' generation. In this case, Edwin Pelletier was my grandfather's cousin. It should also be noted that Mosom and Kohkom can be applied to any person considered an elder.

[2] DeMallie, "Kinship: The Foundation."

[3] Ibid., 350.

[4] Métis are generally described as people of mixed First Nations and French ancestry who developed a culture different from both. Halfbreeds are people of First Nations and British, predominantly Scottish, ancestry. One trait that has been used to distinguish the two groups was the European language spoken. Therefore, even though the Halfbreeds were primarily Scottish, they often referred to as English Halfbreeds. More recently, due to the pejorative connotation of the term "halfbreed," English Halfbreeds have increasingly preferred the term Métis. In this book, except when discussing Halfbreed people specifically, the term Métis will be used.

[5] Johnston, "Ojibway Heritage," 7.

[6] Binnema, Common and Contested Ground; Bishop, Northern Ojibwa; Bishop, "The Emergences of the Northern Ojibwa"; Bishop, "The Indian Inhabitants of Northern Ontario"; Bishop, "Northern Ojibwa Emergence"; Bishop and Smith, "Early Historic Population in Northwestern Ontario"; Dawson, "Historic Populations of Northwestern Ontario"; Denny, "The Algonquian Migration From Plateau to Midwest"; Dunning, "Social and Economic Change"; Evans, "Prehistoric Blackduck–Historic Assiniboine"; Greenberg and Morrison, "Group Identities in the Boreal Forest"; Hodge, "Handbook of Indians of Canada"; MacNeish, "An Introduction"; Meyer, "Time-depth of the Western Woods Cree"; Leo Pettipas, "Aboriginal Migrations"; Ray, "Indians in the Fur Trade"; Russell, "Eighteenth-Century Western Cree"; Smith, "Leadership Among the Southwestern Ojibwa"; Smith, "Western Wood Cree"; Smith, "The Western Cree"; Wilford, "A Revised Classification"; Wright, "Cree Culture History."

[7] Brizinski, "Knots in a String"; Milloy, "The Plains Cree"; Peers, "Changing Resource-Use Patterns of Saulteaux Trading"; Peers, "The Ojibwa of Western Canada." The anthropological term "tribe" refers to a type of society that developed institutions that function to govern or organize a number of bands or villages as one entity.

8 Albers, "Symbiosis, Merger, and War"; Bishop, "The Northern Ojibwa and The Fur Trade"; Dunning, "Social and Economic Change"; Innis, "The Fur Trade in Canada"; Mandelbaum, "The Plains Cree"; Milloy, "The Plains Cree"; Peers, "The Ojibwa of Western Canada"; Stanley, "The Birth of Western Canada."

9 Brown, "Metis, Halfbreeds, and Other Real People."

10 Wilson, "Prehistoric Man"; Giraud, "The Métis in the Canadian West"; Stanley, "The Birth of Western Canada"; Morton, "Manitoba, A History."

11 Tallbear, "DNA, Blood and Racializing the Tribe," 81.

12 Comeau and Santin, "The First Canadians," 33.

13 Ibid.

14 Ibid.

15 Morris, "The Treaties of Canada," 331.

16 Hakansson, "The Detachability of Women."

17 Birth, "'Most of Us Are Family Some of the Time.'"

18 Kammerer, "Descent, Alliance, and Political Order Among Akha," 659.

19 Lowe, "A Widow, a Child, and Two Lineages."

20 Choi, "Land Is Thicker Than Blood."

21 Jones, "Group Nepotism and Human Kinship," 779.

22 Austin-Broos, "Places, Practices, and Things," 118.

23 Fowler, "Shared Symbols, Contested Meanings"; Harmon, "Indians in the Making"; Knack, "Boundaries Between"; Berndt, "Kinship as Strategic Political Action."

24 Berndt, "Kinship as Strategic Political Action," 4.

25 St-Onge, "Uncertain Margins"; Macdougall, "One of the Family."

26 Innes, "Oral History Methods in Native Studies," 70–71.

27 Cruikshank, "Life Lived Like a Story," 19.

28 For a discussion that places this research within the insider/outsider context, see: Innes, "'Wait a Second. Who Are You Anyways?'"

29 Ibid., 456.

Chapter 1
Elder Brother as Cultural Hero: The Law of the People and Contemporary Customary Kinship

1 Recent examples include: Martin, *Stories in a New Skin*; Doerfler, Stark, and Sinclair, eds., *Centering Anishinaabeg Studies*.

2 Fagan, "What's the Trouble with the Trickster?," 4.

3 Ibid., 5.

4 McLeod, *Cree Narrative Memory*, 97.

5 Skinner, "Plains Cree Tale," 351.

6 Radin, *The Trickster*.

7 Ballinger, *Living Sideways*, 21.

8 Ibid., ix.

9 Ibid., 155.

10 Ibid., x.

11 Ricketts, "The North American Indian Trickster," 343.

12 Radin, *The Trickster*, 162.

13 Ibid., 164.

14 Sinclair, "Trickster Reflections: Part I," 25.

15 Ballinger, *Living Sideways*, 21.

16 Ibid., 53.

17 Ibid., 54.

18 Johnston, "Tribal Language," 95.

19 Sinclair, "Trickster Reflections," 34.

20 Ballinger, *Living Sideways*, 68.

21 Teuton, "The Callout," 115–116.

22 Ballinger, *Living Sideways*, 67–68.

23 Johnston, "Is That All There Is?," 100.

24 Johnston, *The Manitous*, 60–69.

25 For example, see Brightman, *Acaoohkiwina and Acimonwina*, 13. In some versions, like the one presented below from Cowessess, he finds his younger brother. However, this version is not clear whether the wolf is his biological or fictive brother.

26 Ballinger, *Living Sideways*, 74.

27 Ibid.

28 Ibid., 168n62.

29 Morra, "A Preface: Ruminations About *Troubling Tricksters*," xii.

30 Sinclair, "Trickster Reflections," 42.

31 Brightman, *Acaoohkiwina and Acimonwina*, 6.

32 Linklater, "The Footprints of Wasahkacahk," 32.

33 Ibid., 67–68.

34 Ibid., 63.

35 Brightman, *Acaoohkiwina and Acimonwina*, 7.

36 Wheeler, "Reflection," 202.

37 Brightman, *Acaoohkiwina and Acimonwina*, 7.

38 Wheeler, "Reflection," 202.

39 Brightman, *Acaoohkiwina and Acimonwina*, 7.

40 McLeod, *Cree Narrative Memory*, 17.

41 Cuthand, "On Nelson's Text," 197.

42 Ibid., 195; Carlson, "Reviving Witiko," 359.

43 Carlson, "Reviving Witiko," 386.

44 McLeod, *Cree Narrative Memory*, 97–98.

45 Hallowell, "Ojibwa Ontology, Behavior and World View," 150.

46 Smith, *The Island of the Anishnaabeg*: 83–86.

47 Wheeler, "Reflection," 202.

48 McLeod, *Cree Narrative Memory*, 97.

49 Smith, *The Island of the Anishnabeg*, 175.

50 Brightman, *Acaoohkiwina and Acimonwina*, 61.

51 For example, in the index of Smith's *The Island of the Anishnabeg*, under "Great Rabbit" it says "*see* Nanabush," 228.

52 Ahenakew, "Cree Trickster Tales," 333.

53 Brightman, Acaoohkiwina and Acimonwina, 64.

54 Ibid.

55 Zion, "Harmony among the People," 265.

56 Williams, *The American Indian in Western Legal Thought*: 84.

57 Johnston, *Ojibway Heritage*, 20.

58 Sinclair: 23.

59 Zion and Yazzie, "Indigenous Law in North America in the Wake of Conquest," 74.

60 Auger, "The Northern Ojibwe"; Cruz, "Tribal Law"; Williams, *Discourses of Conquest*; Yazzie, "Life Comes Among the People."

61 Williams, *Discourses of Conquest*, 84.

62 Borrows, *Recovering Canada*, 14.

63 Auger, 124.

64 Cover, "Forward," 10.

65 Ibid., 3–4.

66 Johnston, "Is That All There Is?," 103.

67 Skinner, "Plains Cree Tales," 344–346. This story is a part of a larger story. Since I wanted to focus on this portion of the story, this version is slightly modified and shortened from Skinner's original text, as parts of it refer to other stories that would not make sense out of context.

68 Ibid., 350–351.

69 Mandelbuam, *The Plains Cree*, 126.

Chapter 2
A Historical View of the Iron Alliance

1 James E.G. Smith, "On the Territorial Distribution," 415.

2 Mackenzie, cited in James E.G. Smith, "The Western Cree," 437.

3 Russell, *Eighteenth-century Western Cree*, 42.

4 Hyde, *Indians of the High Plains*; Innis, *The Fur Trade in Canada*; Jenness, *Indians of Canada*; Lowie, *Indians of the Plains*; Mandelbuam, *The Plains Cree*; Morton, *A History of the Canadian West*.

5 Mandelbuam, *The Plains Cree*, 45–46.

6 Bishop, "Territorial Groups Before 1821"; Dickason, *Canada's First Nations*; Milloy, *The Plains Cree*; Ray, "Fur Trade History"; Ray, *Indians in the Fur Trade*; Sharrock, "Cree, Cree-Assiniboine, and Assiniboines"; Sharrock and Sharrock, "A History."

7   Bishop, "Territorial Groups Before 1821," 160.

8   Gillespie, "Territorial Expansion"; Gillespie, "Territorial Groups Before 1821"; Russell, *Eighteenth-century Western Cree*; James E.G. Smith, "On the Territorial Distribution"; James E.G. Smith, "The Western Cree."

9   Gillespie, "Territorial Expansion," 163.

10 James E.G. Smith, "On the Territorial Distribution," 415.

11 Russell, *Eighteenth-century Western Cree*, 26.

12 Ibid., 12.

13 Smith, "Western Wood Cree," 257.

14 Russell, *Eighteenth-century Western Cree*; Miller, "Montana Assiniboine Identity."

15 Miller, "Montana Assiniboine Identity"; Ray et al., "Statement of Treaty Issues"; Russell, *Eighteenth-century Western Cree*; DeMallie and Miller, "The Assiniboine."

16 Bishop and Smith, "Early Historic Population"; Denig, *The Assiniboine*: 3–4; Greenberg and Morrison, "Group Identities in the Boreal Forest"; Hodge, *Handbook of Indians of Canada*; Jenness, *Indians of Canada*; Lowie, *The Assiniboine*; Mandelbaum, *The Plains Cree*; Peers, *The Ojibwa of Western Canada*; Sharrock and Sharrock, "A History"; Sharrock, "Cree, Cree-Assiniboine, and Assiniboines."

17 Russell, *Eighteenth-century Western Cree*, 172.

18 DeMallie and Miller, "The Assiniboine"; Denig, *The Assiniboine*; Dickason, *Canada's First Nations*; Lowie, *The Assiniboine*; Ray, *Indians in the Fur Trade*.

19 DeMallie and Miller, "The Assiniboine."

20 DeMallie and Miller, "The Assiniboine"; Ray, *Indians in the Fur Trade*.

21 Bishop and Smith, "Early Historic Population"; Hlady, "Indian Migrations"; Jenness, *Indians of Canada*; Ray, *Indians in the Fur Trade*.

22 Andersen, "Alberta Stoney"; Bishop and Smith, "Early Historic Population"; DeMallie and Miller, "The Assiniboine"; Denig, *The Assiniboine*; Hlady, "Indian Migrations"; Hodge, *Handbook of Indians of Canada*; Jenness, *Indians of Canada*; Lowie, *The Assiniboine*; Miller"Montana Assiniboine Identity"; Ray, *Indians in the Fur Trade*.

23 Russell, *Eighteenth-century Western Cree*, 173.

24 Dawson, "Historic Populations of Northwestern Ontario"; Innis, *The Fur Trade in Canada*; Russell, *Eighteenth-century Western Cree*; C.J. Wheeler, "The Historic Assiniboine."

25 Russell, *Eighteenth-century Western Cree*, 173.

26 C.J. Wheeler, "The Historic Assiniboine," 120.

27 Bishop, "Northern Ojibwa Emergence," 43.

28 Hickerson, "The Genesis of a Trading Post Band."

29 Ibid.

30 Hickerson, *The Chippewa and their Neighbors*, 188.

31 Hamilton, "Competition and Warfare," 112; Cox, "Debating the 'debatable zone.'"

32 Hamilton, "Competition and Warfare," 111.

33 Fred Eggan, *Social Anthropology*, 533.

34 Hickerson, "Some Implications."

35 Smith, "On the Territorial Distribution."
36 Bishop, "The Emergences of the Northern Ojibwa"; Dunning, *Social and Economic Change*; Speck, "Family Hunting Territories."
37 Bishop, "The Emergences of the Northern Ojibwa," 51.
38 Ibid.
39 Bishop and Smith, "Early Historic Population," 56.
40 Binnema, *Common and Contested Ground*; Bishop and Smith, "Early Historic Population"; Hickerson, "Some Implications"; Milloy, *The Plains Cree*; Ray, "Statement of Treaty Issues."
41 Greenberg and Morrison, "Group Identities"; Schenck, *Voice of the Crane*.
42 Greenberg and Morrison, "Group Identities," 75–76.
43 Bishop, "Northern Ojibwa Emergence," 15.
44 Ibid., 22.
45 Denny, "The Algonquian Migration," 113.
46 Binnema, *Common and Contested Ground*, 74.
47 Ibid., 76.
48 Wright, "Prehistory of the Canadian Shield," 95.
49 Ibid.
50 Binnema, *Common and Contested Ground*, 77.
51 Wilford, "A Revised Classification"; MacNeish, "An Introduction."
52 Wright, *Cree Culture History*, 94.
53 Dawson, "Historic Populations," 169.
54 Evans, "Prehistoric Blackduck–Historic Assiniboine"; Pettipas, Aboriginal Migrations; Denny, "The Algonquian Migration."
55 Binnema, *Common and Contested Ground*, 78.
56 Bishop and Smith, "Early Historic Population"; Bishop, "The Indian Inhabitants."
57 Bishop, "Northern Ojibwa Emergence."
58 Bishop and Smith, "Early Historic Population," 57.
59 Ibid., 59.
60 Bishop, "The Indian Inhabitants," 254.
61 Ibid., 253–254.
62 Ibid., 267.
63 Giraud, *The Métis in the Canadian West*; Joseph Howard, *Strange Empire*; Innis, *The Fur Trade in Canada*; Arthur S. Morton, *A History*; W.L. Morton, *Manitoba, A History*; Stanley, *The Birth of Western Canada*.
64 Stanley, *The Birth of Western Canada*, vii.
65 Ibid.
66 Morton, "The Battle of Grand Coteau."
67 Pannekoek, *Snug Little Flock*; Irene Spry, "The Metis and Mixed Bloods."
68 Brown, *Strangers in Blood*; Brown, "Woman as Centre"; Olive Dickason, "From 'One Nation' in the Northeast"; John Foster, *Some Questions*; John Foster, "Wintering";

Gorham, "Families of Mixed Descent"; Peterson, "Ethnogenesis"; Peterson, "Many Roads to Red River"; Peterson, "Prelude to Red River"; Van Kirk, *Many Tender Ties*.

69 Ray, *Indians in the Fur Trade*.

70 Brown, "Woman as Centre."

71 Foster, "Some Questions"; Foster, "Wintering."

72 Foster, "Wintering," 9.

73 Miller, "From Riel to the Métis."

74 Foster "We know who we are"; Thorne, *Many Hands*; Widder, *Battles for the Souls*.

75 Devine, "Les Desjarlais"; Devine, *The People Who Own Themselves*; Macdougall, "Socio-cultural Development"; Swan, "The Crucible."

76 Devine, *The People Who Own Themselves*, 13

77 Ibid., 107.

78 Ibid., 139–140.

79 Swan, "The Crucible," 341.

80 Macdougall, "Socio-cultural Development," 4.

81 Ibid., 6–7.

82 Ibid., 28.

83 Ibid.

84 Devine, *The People Who Own Themselves*; Peers, *The Ojibwa of Western Canada*; Mandelbaum, *The Plains Cree*; Ritterbush, "Culture, Change and Continuity"; Rodnick, "Political Structure."

85 Katherine Pettipas, "Severing the Ties That Bind," 50.

86 Denig, *The Assiniboine*; Lowie, *The Assiniboine*; Rodnick, "Political Structure."

87 Mandelbaum, *The Plains Cree*, 106.

88 Ray, *Indians in the Fur Trade*.

89 Ibid.

90 Ibid.

91 Peers, *The Ojibwa of Western Canada*, 28.

92 Ray, *Indians in the Fur Trade*.

93 Devine, *The People Who Own Themselves*; Swan, "The Crucible."

94 Ray, *Indians in the Fur Trade*.

95 Ibid.

96 Stonechild et al., *Survival of a People*.

97 Milloy, *The Plains Cree*.

98 Fowler, *Shared Symbols, Contested Meanings*.

99 Ibid., 46–47.

100 Milloy, *The Plains Cree*.

101 David Smyth, "Review Essay: Missed Opportunity," 346.

102 Morton, "The Battle of Grand Coteau."

103 Smyth, "Review Essay: Missed Opportunity."

104 Welsh, *The Last Buffalo Hunter*.

[105] Cowie, *The Company of Adventurers*, 301–302.

[106] Milloy, *The Plains Cree*.

[107] Johnston, *The Battle at the Belly River*.

[108] Ibid.

[109] Milloy, *The Plains Cree*, 117.

[110] Owram, *Promise of Eden*.

[111] Milloy, *The Plains Cree*; Tobias, "Canada's Subjugation."

[112] Hildebrandt and Huber, *The Cypress Hills*; Kennedy, *The Whiskey Trade*.

[113] Dempsey, "Alberta's Indians."

[114] Tobias, "Canada's Subjugation."

[115] Friesen, "'Magificent Gifts'"; Tobias, "Protection, Civilization, Assimilation."

[116] Innes, "I do not keep the lands"; Tobias, "Protection, Civilization, Assimilation."

[117] Morris, *The Treaties of Canada*, 97.

[118] Ahenakew and Wolfart, *Ana-ka-pemwewehahk*; Taylor, "Two Views."

[119] Ray et al., "Statement of Treaty Issues," 201.

[120] Ray et al., *Bounty and Benevolence*; White, "'Give Us a Little Milk.'"

[121] Friesen, "Magnificent Gifts," 49.

[122] Morris, *The Treaties of Canada*, 98.

[123] Innes, "'I do not keep the lands.'"

[124] Tobias, "Canada's Subjugation."

[125] Hildebrandt and Huber, *The Cypress Hills*, 93.

[126] Hildebrandt and Huber, *The Cypress Hills*; Walker, "Nez Perce."

[127] Dempsey, "Alberta's Indians."

[128] Hogue, "Disputing the Medicine Line."

[129] Tobias, "Canada's Subjugation."

[130] Ibid.; Tyler, "A History of Cowessess Band."

[131] Christiansen, *Ahtahkakoop*.

[132] Tobias, "Canada's Subjugation"; St. Germain, "'Feed or Fight.'"

[133] Tobias, "Canada's Subjugation."

[134] Ibid.

[135] Ibid.

[136] Hogue, "Disputing the Medicine Line," 10.

[137] Ibid.

[138] Ibid.

[139] Tobias, "Canada's Subjugation."

[140] Hogue, "Disputing the Medicine Line," 14.

[141] James Dempsey, "Alberta's Indians," 114.

[142] Indian Affairs *Annual Report*, 1883, 98.

Chapter 3
Multicultural Bands on the Northern Plains and the Notion of "Tribal" Histories

[1] Albers, "Symbiosis, Merger, and War"; Albers, "Changing Patterns"; and Sharrock, "Crees, Cree-Assiniboines, and Assiniboines."

[2] Sharrock, "Crees, Cree-Assiniboines, and Assiniboines," 95.

[3] McLeod, "Plains Cree Identity."

[4] Ibid., 441.

[5] Skinner, "The Cultural Position of the Plains Ojibway."

[6] Skinner, "Plains Cree Tale."

[7] Miller, "From Riel to the Metis," 19.

[8] Sharrock, "Cree, Cree-Assiniboine, and Assiniboines," 97.

[9] Ibid.

[10] Albers, "Changing Patterns," 91.

[11] Fogelson, "Perspectives," 51.

[12] Ibid., 51.

[13] Darnell, "Rethinking the Concepts," 93.

[14] Binnema, *Common Contested Ground*, 12.

[15] Berndt, "Kinship as Strategic Political Action," 25–26.

[16] Ibid., 31.

[17] Ibid., 34–51.

[18] Ibid., 36.

[19] Devine, *The People Who Own Themselves*; Mandelbaum, *The Plains Cree*; Peers, *The Ojibwa of Western Canada*; Rodnick, "Political Structure"; Ritterbush, "Culture Change And Continuity."

[20] Rodnick, "Political Structure," 408.

[21] See for example Albers, "The Plains Ojibwa"; DeMallie and Miller, "The Assiniboine"; Lowie, "The Assiniboine"; Mandelbaum, *The Plains Cree*; Peers, *The Ojibwa of Western Canada*; Peers and Brown, "There is No End."

[22] Peers and Brown, "There is No End," 533.

[23] Ibid.

[24] DeMallie, "Kinship and Biology in Sioux Culture."

[25] Albers, "Symbiosis, Merger, and War"; Brown, *Strangers in Blood*; Sharrock, "Cree, Cree-Assiniboine, and Assiniboines"; Van Kirk, *Many Tender Ties*; White, "'Give Us a Little Milk'"; White, "The Woman Who Married a Beaver."

[26] Albers, "Changing Patterns on Ethnicity," 114.

[27] Van Kirk, "'Marrying-In' to 'Marrying-Out,'" 4.

[28] See, for example, Mandelbaum, *The Plains Cree*; and Peers and Brown, "No End to Relationships."

[29] Mandelbaum, *The Plains Cree*, 105–106.

[30] Ibid., 106.

[31] Peers, *The Ojibwa of Western Canada*; Hickerson, "The Genesis of a Trading Post Band."

32 Tanner, *The Falcon*, 38.

33 Ibid., 44.

34 Hickerson, "The Genesis of a Trading Post Band," 310.

35 Moulton, ed., *The Lewis and Clark Journals*: 441–443 (emphasis in original).

36 Ibid., 305, 317.

37 Tanner, *The Falcon*, 31.

38 Peers, *The Western Ojibwa*, 9.

39 Ibid., 132.

40 Ibid., 79.

41 Rodnick, "Political Structure," 409.

42 For example, see Carter, *Lost Harvests*; Tobias, "Canada's Subjugation"; Hogue, "Disputing the Medicine Line"; and Pettipas, *Severing the Ties That Bind*. Although the focus of the articles by Tobias and Hogue is Plains Cree and Pettipas's book examines prairie First Nations' responses to government religious suppression, many of the bands and individuals whom they discuss were of mixed ancestry. For example, Petitipas's second chapter, "The Ties That Bind: The Plains Cree," places the Plains Cree at the centre of her examination.

43 Carter, *Lost Harvest*, 45.

44 Tobias, "Payipwat."

45 Hugh Dempsey, "Pǒtikwahanapiwǒyin (Poundmaker)."

46 Hugh Dempsey, *Big Bear*.

47 Tobias, "Payipwat."

48 Cuthand, *Askiwina*; Turner, "Wikaskokiseyin."

49 Tyler, "PASKWÜW."

50 Milloy, *Plains Cree*, 107.

51 Peers, *The Western Ojibwa*, 186.

52 Ibid., 187.

53 Camp, "The Turtle Mountain Plains-Chippewa and Métis," 42.

54 Ibid., 75.

55 Sharrock, "Cree, Cree-Assiniboine, and Assiniboines," 113.

56 Ibid., 114.

57 Cited in Sharrock, "Cree, Cree-Assiniboine, and Assiniboines," 113.

58 Devine, *The People Who Own Themselves*, 120.

59 Tobias, cited in Barkwell and Longclaws, *History of the Plains-Ojibway*, 95–96.

60 Devine, *The People Who Own Themselves*, 132.

61 Carter, "O'Soup, Louis."

62 Morris, *The Treaties of Canada*, 119.

63 Ibid., 222.

64 Hogue, "Disputing the Medicine Line," 10.

65 Carter, "O'Soup, Louis."

66 See, for example, Brown, *Strangers in Blood*; Brown, "Woman as Centre"; Dickason, "From 'One Nation' in the Northeast"; John Foster, "Some Questions"; John Foster,

"The Origins of the Mixed Bloods"; Gorham, "Families of Mixed Descent"; Peterson, "Prelude to Red River"; Peterson, "Ethnogenesis"; Peterson, "Many Roads to Red River"; and Van Kirk, *Many Tender Ties.*

67 Innes, "Beyond Red River."

68 Macdougall, "*Wahkootowin,*" 439.

69 Swan, "The Crucible." Swan's use of the term "Indianized Frenchmen" is in reference to individual French Canadian traders who lived among First Nations groups and adopted their customs and culture rather than those freemen who formed their own bands.

70 Macdougall, "*Wahkootowin,*" 437–438.

71 Ibid., 456.

72 St-Onge, "Uncertain Margins," 2–10.

73 Ibid., 3.

74 Ibid., 9.

75 Ibid.

76 Ibid., 10.

77 Gibson, "When is a Metis an Indian?"

78 Stonechild and Waiser, *Loyal Till Death.*

79 Lagimodiere, "Historians Chided for Misinformation."

80 Darnell, "Rethinking the Concepts of Band and Tribe," 97. See also Dawson, "Historic Populations"; Gillespie, "Territorial Expansion"; Greenberg and Morrison, "Group Identities in the Boreal Forest"; Russell, *Eighteenth-Century Western Cree*; Schenck, *Voice of the Crane*; Smith, "On the Territorial Distribution of the Western Woods Cree"; and Wheeler, "The Historic Assiniboine."

Chapter 4
The Multicultural Composition of Cowessess First Nation

1 Mandelbaum, *The Plains Cree.*

2 Tyler, "A History," 1.

3 Lerat, *Treaty Promises*, 56.

4 Devine, *The People Who Own Themselves*, 276.

5 Ibid., 120–1.

6 Carter, "O'Soup, Louis."

7 Neufeld, "Keeseekoowewin."

8 Lerat, *Treaty Promises*, 106.

9 Carter, "O'Soup, Louis"; Lerat, *Treaty Promises*; Tyler, "A History."

10 Tyler, "A History."

11 Ibid.

12 Carter, "O'Soup, Louis"; Tyler, "A History."

13 Tyler, "A History"; Lerat, *Treaty Promises*: 29.

14 Carter, "O'Soup, Louis."

15 Tyler, "A History."

16 Lerat, *Treaty Promises*, 12.

17 Ibid.

18 Tyler, "A History."

19 Lerat, *Treaty Promises*, 41.

20 Ibid.; Tyler, "A History."

21 Indian Affairs *Annual Report*, 1883, 71.

22 Tyler, "A History"; Andrews, "Indian Protest Against Starvation."

23 Tyler, "A History," 28.

24 Ibid.

25 Lerat, *Treaty Promises*, 54.

26 Andrews, "Indian Protest Against Starvation," 44.

27 Cowie, *Company of Adventurers*, 417.

28 Tyler, "A History," 32.

29 Carter, *Lost Harvest*, 121.

30 Ibid.

31 Tyler, "A History"; Carter, *Lost Harvest*.

32 Tyler, "A History"; Andrews, "Indian Protest Against Starvation."

33 Andrews, "Indian Protest Against Starvation," 46.

34 Wolfe, *Earth Elder Stories*, 59.

35 Andrews, "Indian Protest Against Starvation," 50.

36 Carter, "O'Soup, Louis."

37 Cited in Lerat, *Treaty Promises*, 49.

38 Tyler, "A History"; Lerat, *Treaty Promises*.

39 Stonechild and Waiser, *Loyal till death*.

40 Tyler, "A History," 38–41.

41 Lerat, *Treaty Promises*, 90.

42 Carter, "O'Soup, Louis"; Tyler, "A History"; Christensen, *Ahtahkakoop*; Lerat, *Treaty Promises*.

43 Cited in Christensen, *Ahtahkakoop*, 579.

44 Carter, "O'Soup, Louis."

45 Carter, *Lost Harvest*.

46 Tyler, "A History"; Carter, "O'Soup, Louis."

47 Carter, "We Must Farm"; Carter, *Lost Harvest*; Tyler, "A History"; Christensen, *Ahtahkakoop*.

48 Cited in Carter, *Lost Harvest*: 213.

49 Carter, *Lost Harvest*: 213.

50 Carter, *Lost Harvest*; Carter, "We Must Farm"; Barron, "The Indian Pass System."

51 Pettipas, *Severing the Ties That Bind*.

52 Miller, *Shingwauk's Vision*.

53 Lerat, *Treaty Promises*.

54 Innes, et al., "Saskatchewan Indian Reserves."

[55] Carter, *Lost Harvest*; Tyler, "A History"; Lerat, *Treaty Promises.*

[56] Lerat, *Treaty Promises.*

[57] Tyler, "A History."

[58] Carter, *Lost Harvest.*

[59] Tyler, "A History."

[60] Beal, "Money, Markets and Economic Development."

[61] Tyler, "A History."

[62] Ibid.

[63] Lerat, *Treaty Promises.*

[64] Tyler, "A History."

[65] Ibid., 50.

[66] Carter, *Lost Harvest.*

[67] Lerat, *Treaty Promises.*

[68] Ibid., 61, 98–107. In 1981, the Cowessess First Nation submitted a specific claim to the Department of Indian Affairs, alleging that the surrender was invalid under the *Indian Act.* In March 1994, the federal government rejected the claim, and in August 1996 Cowessess requested that the Indian Claims Commission (ICC) begin an inquiry into the rejected claim. The inquiry was split into two phases. The panel for Phase I determined that the surrender vote was not valid, and recommended that Canada accept Cowessess' claim. In March 2002, the federal government rejected this recommendation. In October 2002, Cowessess requested that the ICC proceed with Phase II of the inquiry to determine whether the federal government had breached its fiduciary duty. On 6 October 2006, two of the three ICC commissioners found that the government did not breach its fiduciary obligation to Cowessess, and recommended that Canada should not accept the claim for negotiation (Indian Claims Commission, 2006). The impact of the commissioners' recommendations has yet to be determined.

[69] Carter, *Lost Harvest*, 48.

[70] Carter, "O'Soup, Louis."

[71] Acoose, *Iskwewak–kah'ki yaw ni wahkomakanak.*

[72] Zieman, "Run for Acoose."

[73] Lerat, *Treaty Promises.*

[74] Ibid.

[75] Ibid., 91.

[76] Carter, "O'Soup, Louis."

[77] Lerat, *Treaty Promises.*

[78] Ibid., 95–96.

[79] Opekokew, *The First Nations*, 31.

[80] Carter, *Lost Harvest*, 256.

[81] Carter, "O'Soup, Louis"; Opekokew, *The First Nations*, 32.

[82] Carter, *Lost Harvest*, 256.

[83] Carter, "O'Soup, Louis."

[84] Opekokew, *The First Nations.*

[85]   Carter, *Lost Harvest*, 257.

[86]   Quoted in Carter, "O'Soup, Louis."

[87]   Opekokew, *The First Nations*, 33.

[88]   Ibid., 34.

[89]   Lerat, *Treaty Promises*, 129.

[90]   Johnston, *Indian School Days*.

[91]   Lomawaima, *They Called It Prairie Light*.

[92]   Lerat, *Treaty Promises*, 128.

[93]   Cited in Ibid., 125.

[94]   Cited in Ibid., 133–134.

[95]   Cited in Ibid., 133.

[96]   Barron, "The Indian Pass System"; Barron, "Walking in Indian Moccasins."

[97]   Innes, "The Socio-political Influence of the Second World War."

[98]   Robin, *Shades of Right*; Sher, *White Hoods*.

[99]   Lerat, *Treaty Promises*.

[100]   Ibid.

[101]   Canada, *Looking Forward, Looking Back*, 570.

[102]   Innes, "I do not keep the lands."

[103]   *Whitewood History*.

[104]   Davidson, "We Shall Remember"; Dempsey, "Alberta's Indians"; Innes, "The Socio-political Influence of the Second World War"; Innes, "'On home ground now.'"

[105]   Cited in Innes, "The Socio-political Influence of the Second World War," 83.

[106]   Lerat, *Treaty Promises*, 145.

Chapter 5
Cowessess Band Members and the Importance of Family Ties

[1]   Brown and Peers state that, "parallel cousins are the children of one's father's brother or mother's sister (i.e., of same-sex siblings); cross-cousins are the children of one's father's sister and mother's brother (i.e. of siblings of different sex). Concomitantly, all relatives of one's own generation were grouped either as sibling/parallel cousins (for whom the term was the same); or else they were cross-cousins, and potential sweethearts and mates" (Peers and Brown, "'There Is No End,'" 533). Though cross-cousins were potential marriage partners, people were not limited to choosing their cross-cousins.

[2]   Cuthand, "Protect women through tradition," A7.

[3]   Peers and Brown, "'There Is No End.'"

[4]   Ibid., 533.

[5]   Albers, "Changing Patterns."

[6]   Fishman, *Reversing Language Shift*.

[7]   Mandelbaum, *The Plains Cree*.

[8]   Peers and Brown, "There Is No End."

[9]   Muriel Innes, "My Trip to the 1998 Saskatchewan Indian Games."

[10] According to Statistics Canada, in 2001 there were 15,685 Aboriginal people living in Regina and 20,275 living in Saskatoon, compared to 1981 when 6,390 and 4,205 Aboriginal people lived in those cities, respectively, highlighting the trend in the urbanization of Saskatchewan Aboriginal people (Siggner and Costa, *Aboriginal Conditions*, 35). According to the Criminal Intelligence Service Saskatchewan (2005), in 2002 Saskatchewan had the largest per capita ratio of Aboriginal gang members in Canada, with approximately 1,315 gang members.

[11] Skinner, "The Cultural Position of the Plains Ojibway."

Chapter 6
First Nations Response to Membership Codes of the Indian Act: Bill C-31 and Cowessess First Nation

[1] Lawrence, "Real' Indians and Others."

[2] Dickason, *Canada's First Nations*.

[3] Lawrence, "Real' Indians and Others"; Jamieson, "Sex Discrimination and the Indian Act."

[4] Venne, *Indian Acts and Amendments*: 361–362.

[5] Royal Commission on the Status of Women, 1970, 238.

[6] Weaver, "First Nations Women," 98.

[7] [1974] S.C.R. 1349.

[8] Canada, *Statement of the Government of Canada on Indian Policy*.

[9] Harold Cardinal, *The Unjust Society*, 134.

[10] Chretien, "Indian policy—a reply," 9.

[11] Cardinal, *The Rebirth of Canada's Indians*: 107.

[12] *R v. Drybones* [1970] S.C.R. 282.

[13] Lisac, "Indian Act Claimed Only Treaty Protection."

[14] Cardinal, *The Rebirth of Canada's Indians*.

[15] *Sandra Lovelace v. Canada* [1981] No. R.6/24, U.N. Doc. Supp. No. 40 (A/36/40) at 166.

[16] Ibid.

[17] "Discrimination still faces women."

[18] Ibid., 39.

[19] Earl Fowler, "FSI opposes marriage law," A3.

[20] Canadian Press, "Indian Leaders Warn Gov't," A14.

[21] Weaver, "First Nations Women," 112.

[22] Cited in ibid., 113.

[23] Ibid., 115.

[24] Ibid., 116.

[25] Fowler, "Legislation would restore rights," A3.

[26] Canada, Parliament, House of Commons Standing Committee on Indian Affairs and Northern Development, *Minutes of Proceeding and Evidence*, 1st Session, 33rd Parliament, 1985, no. 17, p. 13.

27 Ibid., no. 21, p. 29.

28 Ibid., no. 21, p. 11.

29 Wuttenee, "Indian Act Amendments."

30 Canada, Parliament, House of Commons Standing Committee on Indian Affairs and Northern Development, *Minutes of Proceeding and Evidence*, 1st Session, 33rd Parliament, 1985, no. 17, p. 24.

31 Ibid., no. 17, p. 25.

32 Ibid., no. 13, p. 34.

33 Ibid., no. 27, p. 21.

34 Ibid., no. 25, p. 6.

35 Ibid., no. 16, p. 16.

36 Ibid., no. 16, p. 8.

37 Ibid., no. 26, p. 7.

38 Ibid., no. 17, p. 15.

39 Ibid., no. 17, pp. 21–22.

40 Ibid., no. 29, p. 6.

41 Ibid., no. 29, p. 24.

42 Ibid., no. 27, p. 23.

43 Ibid., no. 13, p. 20.

44 Ibid., no. 18, pp. 9–10.

45 Ibid., no. 28, p. 57.

46 Wuttunee, "Indian Act Amendments," 13.

47 Earl Fowler, "Indian Act changes," A3.

48 Earl Fowler, "Indian Chiefs," A6.

49 Earl Fowler, "Indian will fight band status issue," A8).

50 Earl Fowler, "Most Indian bands," A7.

51 Ibid.

52 Canadian Press, "Sask. Bands Must Enact Laws," A7.

53 Ommenney, "Bureaucracy thwarts native women's rights," A8.

54 Schuettler, "Indian Act Changes," 51.

55 Ibid.

Chapter 7
Implementing Treaty Obligations in Saskatchewan: Cowessess First Nation and Treaty Land Entitlement

1 Macklem, Indigenous Difference.

2 Brenda McLeod, "Treaty Land Entitlement."

3 Martin-McGuire, "The Importance of the Land," 275.

4 Tyler, "A History of Cowessess Band."

5 Pitsula, "The Blakeney Government."

6 Ibid., 193.

7   Ibid.
8   Ibid., 193.
9   Dyck, "The Negotiation of Indian Treaties."
10   Bartlett, "Native Land Claims."
11   Ibid.
12   Martin-McGuire, "Treaty Land Entitlement."
13   Knoll, "Unfinished Business."
14   Wright, "Report and Recommendations," 5. Bartlett, "Native Land Claims," 7.
15   Pitsula, "The Blakeney Government."
16   Martin-McGuire, "Treaty Land Entitlement," 63.
17   Ibid., 63, 67.
18   Bartlett, "Native Land Claims," 142; Martin-McGuire, "Treaty Land Entitlement," 66.
19   Bartlett, "Native Land Claims," 143.
20   Elliot, *Law and Aboriginal Peoples in Canada*, 41–42.
21   Ibid., 144.
22   Bartlett, "Native Land Claims"; Martin-McGuire, "Treaty Land Entitlement."
23   Martin-McGuire, "Treaty Land Entitlement."
24   Bartlett, "Native Land Claims."
25   Martin-McGuire, "Treaty Land Entitlement."
26   Lafond, "Creation, Governance and Management."
27   Bartlett, "Native Land Claims," 146.
28   Bartlett, "Native Land Claims"; Wright, "Report and Recommendations on Treaty Land Entitlement."
29   Bartlett, "Native Land Claims"; Martin-McGuire, "The Importance of the Land."
30   Clifford Wright, "Report and Recommendations."
31   Ibid., 39.
32   Ibid., 57.
33   Elliot, *Law and Aboriginal Peoples in Canada*, 80.
34   Martin-McGuire, "Treaty Land Entitlement."
35   Ibid., 71.
36   Ibid.
37   Gordon-Murdoch, "Treaty land entitlement," 22.
38   Ibid.
39   Martin-McGuire, "Treaty Land Entitlement."
40   Sutter, "Land Entitlements," A3.
41   Ibid.
42   Gordon-Murdoch, "Treaty land entitlement," 22.
43   Brenda McLeod, "Treaty Land Entitlement," 209.
44   Cited in Brenda McLeod, "Treaty Land Entitlement," 210.

45 Brenda McLeod, "Treaty Land Entitlement," 201.

46 Ibid., 225.

47 Knoll, "Unfinished Business," 75.

48 Terrence Pelletier, personal communication.

49 Ibid.

50 Ibid.

51 Ibid.

52 Ibid.

53 In fact, historians have not given the starvation policies much attention. However, a recently published book does explore the use of starvation on First Nations people on the prairie. See Daschuk, *Clearing the Plains.*

54 Miller, *The Gray Site.*

55 Hanna, "A Time to Choose."

56 For example, according to James Riding In, the Pawnee nation had up to 1996 reburied over one thousand of their ancestors' remains in public events. Riding In describes the significance of these public events: "Reinterment ceremonies, along with funeral feasts, evoke a gamut of emotional expressions, ranging from sorrow to joy. When conducting reburials, people rejoice at the fact that the repatriated remains are finally being returned to Mother Earth, but, like modern funerals, an air of sadness pervades the ceremonies. In particular, reinterring the remains of young children causes grieving and weeping. Mourning is part of the healing process in that reburials seek to restore harmony between the living and dead by putting restless spirits to rest. At another level, reburials bring closure to bitterly contested struggles" (Riding In, "Repatriation," 243).

57 Terrence Pelletier, personal communication.

58 Sparvier, "Cowesses First Nations."

59 Ibid.

60 Ibid.

61 Ibid.

62 Ibid., 3.

63 First Nations Land Management Agreement website, http://www.aadnc-aandc. gc.ca/eng/1317228777116/1317228814521 (accessed 2006).

64 Canada, "Cowessess First Nations Signs Treaty Land Entitlement Agreement," 1.

65 Ibid.

66 Ibid.

67 The "Red River Uprising" occurred in 1870 in Manitoba, and the "Rebellion" occurred in 1885 at Batoche, just north of the city of Saskatoon.

68 Chief Cowessess signed Treaty 4 in 1874.

Bibliography

Acoose, Janice. *Iskwewak-kah'ki yaw ni wahkomakanak: Neither Indian Princesses Nor Easy Squaws.* Toronto: Women's Press, 1995.

Ahenakew, Edward. "Cree Trickster Tales." *Journal of American Folk-Lore* 42, 166 (1929): 309–353.

Ahenakew, Freda and H.C. Wolfart, eds. and trans. *Ana-ka-pemwewehahk okakeskih-kemowina/The Counseling Speeches of Jim Ka-Nipitehtew.* Winnipeg: University of Manitoba Press, 1998.

Albers, Patricia. "Symbiosis, Merger, and War: Contrasting Forms Of Intertribal Relationship Among Historic Plains Indians." In *The Political Economy of North American Indians.* Edited by John H. Moore. Norman, OK: University Of Oklahoma Press, 1993.

_____. "Changing Patterns on Ethnicity in The Northeastern Plains." In *History, Power, and Identity: Ethnogenesis in the Americas, 1492–1992.* Edited by Jonathon Hill. Iowa City: University of Iowa Press, 1996.

_____. "The Plains Ojibwa." In *Handbook of North American Indians*, vol. 13, part 1. Edited by Raymond J. DeMallie. Washington, DC: Smithsonian Institute, 2001.

Andersen, Raoul R. "Alberta Stoney (Assiniboine) Origins and Adaptations: A Case for Reappraisal." *Ethnohistory* 17, 1–2 (1970): 49–61.

Andrews, Isabel Anne. "The Crooked Lakes Reserves: A Study of Indian Policy in Practice from the Qu'Appelle Treaty to 1900." MA thesis, University of Saskatchewan, 1972.

_____. "Indian Protest Against Starvation: The Yellow Calf Incident of 1884." *Saskatchewan History* 28, no. 2 (1975): 41–51.

Asch, Michael and Patrick Macklem. "Aboriginal Rights and Canadian Sovereignty: An Essay on *R. v. Sparrow.*" *Alberta Law Review* 29, 2 (1991): 498–517.

Asch, Michael and Norman Zlotkin. "Affirming Aboriginal Title: A New Basis for Comprehensive Claims Negotiations." In *Aboriginal and Treaty Rights in Canada: Essays on Law, Equality, and Respect For Difference.* Edited by Michael Asch. Vancouver: University of British Columbia Press, 1997.

Auger, Donald. "The Northern Ojibwe and Their Family Law." DJur diss., Osgoode Hall, York University, 2001.

Austin-Broos, Diane. "Places, Practices, and Things: The Articulation of Arrente Kinship With Welfare and Work." *American Ethnologist* 30, 1 (2003): 118–135.

Ballinger, Franchot. *Living Sideways: Tricksters in American Oral Traditions*. Norman, OK: University of Oklahoma Press, 2004.

Barkwell, Lawrence and Longclaws, Lyle N. *History of the Plains-Ojibway and the Waywayseecapo First Nation*. Unpublished manuscript, 1996.

Barron, F. Laurie. "The Indian Pass System in the Canadian West, 1882–1935." *Prairie Forum* 13, 1 (1988): 25–42.

_____. "The CCF and the Development of Metis Colonies in Southern Saskatchewan During the Premiership of T.C. Douglas, 1944–1961." *Canadian Journal of Native Studies* 10, 2 (1990): 244–269.

_____. *Walking in Indian Moccasins: The Native Policy of Tommy Douglas and the CCF.* Vancouver: University of British Columbia Press, 1997.

Bartlett, Richard. "Native Land Claims: Outstanding Treaty Land Entitlements in Saskatchewan, 1982–89." In *Devine Rule In Saskatchewan: A Decade of Hope and Hardship*. Edited by Leslie Biggs and Mark Stobbe. Saskatoon: Purich Publishing, 1990.

Beal, Carl. "Money, Markets and Economic Development in Saskatchewan Indian Reserve Communities, 1870 to 1930s." PhD diss., University of Manitoba, 1995.

Bell, Catherine and Michael Asch. "Challenging Assumptions: The Impact of Precedent in Aboriginal Rights Litigation." In *Aboriginal and Treaty Rights in Canada: Essays on Law, Equality, and Respect for Difference*. Edited by Michael Asch. Vancouver: University of British Columbia Press, 1997.

Benson, Jayme. "Different Visions: The Government Response to Native and Non-Native Submissions on Education Presented to the 1946–68 Special Joint Committee on The Senate and House of Commons." MA thesis, University of Ottawa, 1991.

Berndt, Christina Gish. "Kinship as Strategic Political Action: The Northern Cheyenne Response to the Imposition of the Nation-State." PhD diss., University of Minnesota, 2008.

Binnema, Theodore. *Common and Contested Ground: A Human and Environmental History of the Northwestern Plains*. Toronto: University of Toronto Press, 2004.

Birth, Kevin. "Most of Us Are Family Some of The Time: Interracial Unions and Transracial Kinship in Eastern Trinidad." *American Ethologist* 24, 3 (1997): 585 601.

Bishop, Charles A. *The Northern Ojibwa and The Fur Trade: An Historical and Ecological Study*. Toronto: Holt, Rinehart and Winston, 1974.

_____. "The Emergences of the Northern Ojibwa: Social and Economic Consequences." *American Ethnologist* 3, 1 (1976): 39–54.

_____. "Territorial Groups Before 1821: Cree and Ojibwa." In *Handbook of North American Indians*, vol. 13, part 1. Edited by June Helm. Washington, DC: Smithsonian Institute, 1981.

_____. "The Indian Inhabitants of Northern Ontario at the Time of Contact: Socio-Territorial Considerations." In *Approaches to Algonquian Archaeology: Proceedings of the Thirteenth Annual Conference.* Edited by Margaret G. Hanna and Brian Kooyman. Calgary: The Archaeology Association of the University of Calgary, 1982.

_____. "The question of Ojibway Clans." *Actes du 20ieme Ccongres des algonquinistes.* Edited by William Cowan. Ottawa: Carleton University Press, 1989.

_____. "Northern Ojibwa Emergence: The Migration." *Papers of the thirty-third Algonquian conference.* Winnipeg: University of Manitoba Press, 2002.

Bishop, Charles and Estelle Smith. "Early Historic Population in Northwestern Ontario: Archaeological and Ethnohistorical Interpretations." *American Antiquity* 40, 1 (1975): 54–63.

Borrows, John. *Recovering Canada: The Resurgence of Indigenous Law.* Toronto: University of Toronto Press, 2002.

Brightman, Robert A. *Acaoohkiwina and Acimonwina: Traditional Narratives of the Rock Cree Indians.* Ottawa: Canadian Museum of Civilization, 1989.

Brizinski, Peggy. *Knots in a String: An Introduction to Native Studies in Canada.* Saskatoon: University Extension Press, 1993.

Brown, Jennifer. *Strangers in Blood: Fur Trade Company Families in Indian Country.* Vancouver: University of British Columbia Press, 1980.

_____. "Woman as Centre And Symbol in the Emergence of Metis Communities." *Canadian Journal of Native Studies* 3 (1983): 39–46.

_____. "Metis, Halfbreeds, and Other Real People: Challenging Cultures and Categories." *History Teacher* 27, 1 (1993): 19–26.

Brown, Jennifer and Laura Peers. "Chippewa and Their Neighbors: A Critical Review." In *Chippewa and Their Neighbors: A Study in Ethnohistory.* Edited by Harold Hickerson. Prospect Heights, IL: Waveland Press, 1988.

_____. "There Is No End to Relationship Among the Indians: Ojibwa Families and Kinship in Historical Perspective." *History of the Family* 4, 4 (1999): 529–555.

Canada. *Session Papers. Annual Reports of the Department of Indian Affairs.* Ottawa: Kings Press, 1880-1890.

Canada. Parliament. Special Joint Committee of the Senate and House of Commons Appointed to Examine and Consider the Indian Act. *Minutes and Proceedings and Evidence.* 1946 and 1947.

Canada. *Statement of the Government of Canada on Indian Policy.* Ottawa, 1969.

Canada. Standing Committee on Indian Affairs and Northern Development. Bill C-31, *An Act to amend The Indian Act Minutes of Proceedings and Evidence.* Ottawa, 1985.

Canada. Standing Committee on Aboriginal Affairs and Northern Development. *C-31 Fifth Report.* Ottawa: House of Commons, 1988.

Canada. Parliament. Senate. *The Aboriginal Soldier After the War: Report of the Senate of Committee on Aboriginal Peoples.* Ottawa, 1995.

Canada. "Cowessess First Nations Signs Treaty Land Entitlement Agreement." News Release, 1996.

Canada. *Looking Forward, Looking Back: Report of The Royal Commission of Aboriginal Peoples, volume 1*. Ottawa: Communication Group, 1996.

Canadian Press. "Indian Leaders Warn Gov't That Plan Will Meet Resistance." *Regina Leader Post*. 20 October, 1985: A14.

_____. "Sask. Bands Must Enact Laws to Fight Bill C-31: Ahenakew." *Saskatoon Star Phoenix*, 28 January 1988: A7.

Cardinal, Harold. *The Unjust Society: The Tragedy of Canada's Indians*. Edmonton: Hurtig Publishers, 1969.

_____. *The Rebirth of Canada's Indians*. Edmonton: Hurtig Publishers, 1977.

Carlson, Nathan D. "Reviving Witiko (Wendigo): An Ethnohistory of Cannibal Monsters in the Athabasca District of Northern Alberta, 1878–1910." *Ethnohistory* 56, 3 (2009): 359.

Carter, Sarah. *Lost Harvest: Prairie Indian Reserve Farmers and Government Policy*. Montreal: McGill-Queen's University Press, 1990.

_____. "O'Soup, Louis." In *Dictionary of Canadian Biography Online*, 2000, http://www.biographi.ca/EN/ShowBio.asp?BioId=41754&query=cowessess.

_____. "We Must Farm to Enable Us to Live: The Plains Cree and Agriculture to 1900." In *Native Peoples: The Canadian Experience*. Edited by R. Bruce Morrison and Roderick Wilson. Toronto: Oxford University Press, 2004.

Choi, Soo Ho. "Land is Thicker Than Blood: Revisiting 'Kinship Paternalism' in a Peasant Village in South Korea." *Journal of Anthropological Research* 56 (2000): 349–363.

Chretien, Jean. "Indian policy—a reply." *Canadian Forum* 281 (March 1970): 279–280.

Christensen, Deanna. *Ahtahkakoop: The Epic Account of a Plains Cree Head Chief, His People, and Their Vision For Survival, 1816–1896*. Shell Lake, SK: Ahtahkakoop Publishing, 2000.

Comeau, Pauline and Aldo Santin. *The First Canadians: A Profile of Canada's Native People Today*. Toronto: James Lorimer, 1990.

Cottam, S. Barry. "Indian titles as a 'celestial institution': David Mills and the St. Catherine's Millings Case." In *Aboriginal Resource Use in Canada: Historical and Legal Aspects*. Edited by Kerry Able and Jean Friesen. Winnipeg: University of Manitoba Press, 1991.

Cowie, Issac. *The Company of Adventurers: A Narrative of Seven Years in the Service of the Hudson's Bay Company during 1867–1874*. Toronto: William Briggs, 1913.

Cover, Robert. "Forward: Nomos and Narratives." *Harvard Law Review* 97, 4 (1983): 10.

Cox, Bruce Alden. "Debating the 'Debatable Zone': A Re-examination of Explanations of the Dakota-Algonquian Conflict." Departmental Working Paper, Department of Anthropology, Carleton University, 1986: 86–87.

Cruikshank, Julie. *Life Lived Like a Story: Life Stories of Three Yukon Elders*. Lincoln, NE: University of Nebraska Press, 1990.

Cruz, Christina. "Tribal Law as Indigenous Social Reality and Separate Consciousness: [Re]incorporating Customs and Traditions into the Law." *Tribal Law Journal* 1 (2001): 1–27.

Cude, Daniel G. "Identifying the Ojibway of Northern Lake Superior and the Boundary Water Region, 1650–1750." *Papers of the Algonquian Conference*. Winnipeg: University of Manitoba, 2001.

Cuthand, Doug. "Protect Women Through Tradition, Not Politics." *Saskatoon Star Phoenix*. 13 October 2006: A7.

Cuthand, Stan. "The Native Peoples of the Prairie Provinces in the 1920s And 1930s." In *One Century Later: Western Canadian Reserve Indians Since Treaty 7*. Edited by A.L. Getty and Donald B. Smith. Vancouver: University of British Columbia Press, 1978.

_____. "On Nelson's Text," in *'The Orders of the Dreamed': George Nelson on Cree and Northern Ojibwa Religion and Myth, 1823*. Edited by Jennifer S.H. Brown and Robert Brightman. Winnipeg: University of Manitoba Press, 1988.

Darnell, Regna. "Rethinking the Concepts of Band and Tribe, Community and Nation: An Accordion Model of Nomadic Native American Social Organization." In *Papers of the Twenty-Ninth Algonquian Conference*. Winnipeg: University of Manitoba Press, 1998.

Daugherty, Wayne and Dennis Madill. *Indian Government under Indian Act Legislation, 1868–1951*. Ottawa: Department of Indian Affairs and Northern Development Policy, Research, and Evaluation Group Research Branch, 1980.

Daschuk, James. *Clearing the Plains: Disease, Politics of Starvation and the Loss of Aboriginal Life*. Regina: University of Regina Press, 2013.

Davidson, Janet. "We Shall Remember: Canada's Indians and World War Two." MA thesis, Trent University, 1992.

Dawson, K.A.C. "Historic Populations of Northwestern Ontario." In *Papers of the Seventeenth Algonquian Conference, 1975*. Ottawa: Carleton University, 1976.

DeMallie, Raymond J. "Kinship and Biology in Sioux Culture." In *North American Indian Anthropology: Essays on Society and Culture*. Edited by Raymond DeMallie and Alfonso Ortiz. Norman, OK: University of Oklahoma Press, 1994.

_____. "Kinship: The Foundation for Native American Society." In *Studying Native America: Problems and Prospects*. Edited by Russell Thornton. Madison: University of Wisconsin Press, 1998.

DeMallie, Raymond and David Reed Miller. "The Assiniboine." In *Handbook of North American Indians*, vol. 13, part 1. Edited by Raymond J. DeMallie. Washington, DC: Smithsonian Institute, 2001.

Dempsey, Hugh. *Big Bear: The End of Freedom*. Lincoln, NE: University of Nebraska Press: Vancouver: Douglas and McIntyre, 1984.

_____. "Maskepetoon." *Dictionary of Canadian Biography Online*. 2000. http://www.biographi.ca/EN/ShowBio.asp?BioId=38692&query=Maskepetoon.

_____. "Pŏtikwahanapiwŏyin (Poundmaker)." *Dictionary of Canadian Biography Online*. 2000. http://www.biographi.ca/EN/ShowBio.asp?BioId=39905&query=Poundmaker.

Dempsey, James. "Alberta's Indians and the Second World War." In *For King and Country: Alberta in the Second World War*. Edited by Ken Tingley. Edmonton Provincial Museum of Alberta, 1995.

Denig, Edwin Thompson. *The Assiniboine: Forty-Sixth Annual Report of The Bureau of American Ethnology to the Secretary of Smithsonian Institution*. Edited by J.N.B. Hewitt. Regina: Canadian Plains Research Centre, 2000.

Denny, Peter J. "The Algonquian Migration from Plateau to Midwest: Linguistics and Archaeology." In *Papers of the Twenty-Second Algonquian Conference, 1990*. Ottawa: Carleton University, 1991.

Desmarais, Diedre A. "The Native Women's Association's struggle to secure gender equality rights within the Canadian Constitution." MA thesis, University of Regina, 1998.

Devine, Heather. "Les Desjarlais: Aboriginal ethnogenesis and diaspora in a Canadien Family." PhD diss., University of Alberta, 2001.

_____. *The People Who Own Themselves: Aboriginal Ethnogenesis in a Canadian Family, 1660–1900*. Calgary: University of Calgary Press, 2004.

Dickason, Olive. "From 'One Nation' in the Northeast to 'New Nation' in the Northwest: A Look at the Emergence of the Metis." In *The New Peoples: Being and Becoming Metis in North America*. Edited by Jacqueline Peterson and Jennifer S.H. Brown. Winnipeg: University of Manitoba Press, 1985.

_____. *Canada's First Nations: A History of Founding Peoples from Earliest Times*. Toronto: Oxford University Press, 2002.

"Discrimination still faces women marrying off reserve." *Western Producer*, 27 August 1981: 39.

Doerfler, Jill, Heidi Kiiwetinepinesiik Stark, and Niigaanwewidam James Sinclair, eds. *Centering Anishinaabeg Studies: Understanding the World Through Stories*. Winnipeg: University of Manitoba Press, 2013.

Dunning, Robert. *Social and Economic Change among the Northern Ojibwa*. Toronto: University of Toronto Press, 1959.

Dusenberry, Verne. "Waiting for the Day that Never Comes: The Dispossessed Metis of Montana." In *The New Peoples: Being and Becoming Metis in North America*. Edited by Jacqueline Peterson and Jennifer S.H. Brown. Winnipeg: University of Manitoba Press, 1985.

Dyck, Noel. "The Negotiation of Indian Treaties and Land Rights in Saskatchewan." In *Aborigine Land and Land Rights*. Edited by Nicolas Peterson and Marcia Langton. Canberra: Australian Institute of Aboriginal Studies, 1983.

Eggan, Fred. *Social Anthropology of North American Tribes*. Chicago: University of Chicago Press, 1955.

Elliott, David W. "Aboriginal Title." In *Aboriginal Peoples and the Law: Indian, Metis and Inuit Rights in Canada*. Edited by Bradford W. Morse. Ottawa: Carleton University Press, 1985.

_____. *Law and Aboriginal Peoples in Canada*. North York, ON: Captus Press, 2000.

Evans, Edward G. "Prehistoric Blackduck–Historic Assiniboine: A Reassessment." *Plains Anthropologist* 6 (1961): 271–275.

Fagan, Kristina. "What's the Trouble with the Trickster: An Introduction." In *Troubling Trickster: Revisioning Critical Conversation*. Edited by Deanna Reder and Linda M. Morra. Waterloo, ON: Wilfrid Laurier University Press, 2010.

Fishman, Joshua. *Reversing Language Shift: Theory and Practice of Assistance to Threatened Languages*. Philadelphia: Multilingual Matters, 1991.

Fogelson, Raymond D. "Perspectives on Native American Identity." In *Studying Native America: Problems and Prospects*. Edited by Russell Thornton. Madison: University of Wisconsin Press, 1998.

Foster, John. "The Origins of the Mixed Bloods in the Canadian West." In *Essays on Western History: In Honour of Lewis Gwynne Thomas*. Edited by Lewis H. Thomas. Edmonton: University of Alberta Press, 1976.

_____. "Some Questions and Perspectives on the Problem of Metis Roots." In *The New Peoples: Being and Becoming Metis in North America*. Edited by Jacqueline Peterson and Jennifer S.H. Brown. Winnipeg: University of Manitoba Press, 1985.

_____. "Wintering, the Outsider Adult Male and the Ethnogenesis of the Western Plains Métis." *Prairie Forum* 19, 1 (1994): 1–13.

Foster, Martha Harroun. "We know who we are: Multiethnic identity in a Montana Metis community." PhD diss., UCLA, 2000.

Fowler, Earl. "FSI Opposes Marriage Law." *Saskatoon Star Phoenix*, 14 September 1981: A3.

_____. "Legislation would restore rights of Indian women." *Saskatoon Star Phoenix*. 23 January 1984: A3.

_____. "Indian Chiefs: male chauvinist label unfair." *Saskatoon Star Phoenix*. 16 November 1985: A6.

_____. "Indian Act changes will deprive many of benefits: Eramus." *Saskatoon Star Phoenix*. 7 February 1987: A3.

_____. "Indian will fight band status issue." *Saskatoon Star Phoenix*. 14 May 1987: A8.

_____. "Most Indian bands will reject reinstated members. *Saskatoon Star Phoenix*. 18 June 1987: A7.

Fowler, Loretta. *Shared Symbols, Contested Meanings: Gros Ventre Culture and History, 1778–1984*. Ithaca and London: Cornell University Press, 1987.

Franklin, Robert and Pamela Bunte. "A Montana Metis Community Meets the Federal Acknowledgement Process." In *Proceedings of the International Conference on the Metis People of Canada and the United States*. Edited by William J. Furdell. Great Falls, MO: University of Great Falls, 1997.

Friesen, Jean. " 'Magificent Gifts': The Indian Treaties of the Northwest, 1869–1876." *Transactions of the Royal Society of Canada*, 1986: 41–51.

Furi, Megan and Jill Wherrett. "Indian Status and Band Membership Issues." Ottawa: Indian Affairs, 2003.

Gillespie, Beryl C. "Territorial Expansion of the Chipewyan in the 18th Century." In *Proceedings: The Northern Athapaskan Conference*. Mercury Series, Publications in Ethology, 27. National Museum of Canada, 1975.

_____. "Territorial Groups Before 1821: Athapaskans of the Shield and the Mackenzie Drainage." In *Handbook of North American Indians*, vol. 13, part 1. Edited by June Helm. Washington, DC: Smithsonian Institute, 1981.

Giraud, Marcel. *The Métis in the Canadian West*. Translated by George Woodcock. Lincoln, NE: University of Nebraska Press, 1986. Originally published as *Le Métis Canadien*. Paris: Institut d'ethnologie, 1945.

Gordon-Murdoch, Anita. "Treaty Land Entitlement." *Saskatchewan Indian*, July 1985: 4–27.

Gorham, Harriet. "Families of Mixed Descent in the Western Great Lakes Region." In *Native People, Native Lands: Canadian Indians, Inuit and Metis*. Edited by Brian A. Cox. Ottawa: Carleton University Press, 1988.

Green, Joyce. "Exploring identity and citizenship: Aboriginal women, Bill C-31 and the Sawridge case." PhD diss., University of Alberta, 1997.

_____. "Sexual Equality and Indian Governments: An Analysis of Bill C-31 Amendments to the Indian Act." *Native Studies Review* 1, 2 (1985): 81–95.

Greenberg, Adolph and James Morrison. "Group Identities in the Boreal Forest: The Origin of the Northern Ojibwa." *Ethnohistory* 29, 2 (1982): 75–102.

Hakansson, Tomas. "The Detachability of Women: Gender and Kinship in Processes of Socioeconomic Change among the Gusil of Kenya." *American Ethnologist* 21, 3 (1994): 516–538.

Hall, Anthony J. "The St. Catherine's Milling Company versus the Queen: Indian Land Rights as a Factor in Federal-Provincial Relations in Nineteenth Century Canada." In *Aboriginal Resource Use in Canada: Historical and Legal Aspects*. Edited by Kerry Abel and Jean Friesen. Winnipeg: University of Manitoba Press, 1991.

Hallowell, A. Irving. "Ojibwa Ontology, Behavior and World View." In *Teachings from the American Earth: Indian Religion and Philosophy*. Edited by Dennis Tedlock and Barbara Tedlock. New York: Liveright Publishing Corporation, 1975.

Hamilton, Scott. "Competition and Warfare: Functional versus Historical Explanations." *Canadian Journal of Native Studies* 5, 1 (1985): 93–113.

Hanna, Margaret. "A Time to Choose: 'Us' versus 'Them,' or 'All of Us Together.'" *Plains Anthropologist* 44, 1 (1999): 43–52.

Harmon, Alexandra. *Indians in the Making: Ethnic Relations and Indian Identities around Puget Sound*. Los Angeles: University of California Press, 1998.

Hickerson, Harold. "The Genesis of a Trading Post Band: The Pembina Chippewa." *Ethnohistory* 3, 4 (1956): 289–345.

_____. "Some Implications of the Theory of the Particularity, or 'Atomism,' of the Northern Algonkians." *Current Anthropology* 8, 4 (1967): 313–343.

_____. "The Red Lake and Pembina Chippewa." In *Chippewa Indians I*. New York and London: Garland Publishing, 1974.

_____. *The Chippewa and their Neighbors*. Prospect Heights, IL: Waveland Press, 1988.

Hildebrandt, Walter and Brian Huber. *The Cypress Hills: The Land and its People*. Saskatoon, SK: Purich Publishing, 1994.

Hlady, Walter. "Indian Migrations in Manitoba and the West." *Papers of the Historical and Scientific Society of Manitoba* 11, 17 (1964).

Hodge, F.W. *Handbook of Indians of Canada: Published as an Appendix to the Tenth Report of the Geographic Board of Canada*. Ottawa: C.H. Parmelee, 1913.

Hogue, Michel. "Disputing the Medicine Line: The Plains Cree and the Canadian-American Border, 1876–1885." *Montana: The Magazine of Western History* 52 (2002): 2–17.

Howard, James Henri. *The Plains-Ojibwa or Bungi: Hunters and Warriors of the Northern Prairies with Special Reference to the Turtle Mountain Band*. Lincoln, NE: J. and L. Reprint Co., 1977.

Howard, Joseph Kinsey. *Strange Empire: Louis Riel and the Métis People*. Toronto: J. Lewis and Samuel, 1974 (originally published: New York: Morrow, 1952).

Hyde, George E. *Indians of the High Plains: From the Prehistoric Period to Coming of Europeans*. Norman, OK: University of Oklahoma Press, 1959.

Indian Claims Commision. "ICC concludes its inquiry into phase II of the Cowessess First Nation 1907 surrender claim." News release, October 2006.

Innes, Muriel. "My Trip to the 1998 Saskatchewan Indian Games." *Eagle Feather News* 1, 6 (June 1998): 24–25.

Innes, Robert Alexander. " 'I do not keep the lands nor do I give them away': Did Canada and Plains Cree Come to a Meeting of the Minds in the Negotiations of Treaty Four and Six?" *Journal of Indigenous Thought* 2, 2 (1999). http://www.sifc.edu/inst/IndigenousThought/fall99/tocfall99.htm.

_____. "Oral History Methods in Native Studies: Saskatchewan Aboriginal World War Two Veterans." *Oral History Forum* 19–20 (1999/2000): 63–88.

_____. "The socio-political influence of the Second World War Saskatchewan Aboriginal veterans, 1945–1960." MA thesis, University of Saskatchewan, 2000.

_____. "American Indian Studies Research Is Ethical Research: A Discussion of Linda Smith and James Waldram's Approach to Aboriginal research." *Native Studies Review: Special Issue: Dialogue on Aboriginal Research Issues* 15, 2 (2004): 131–138.

_____. "'On home ground now. I'm safe': Saskatchewan Aboriginal Veterans in the Immediate Post-war Years, 1945–1946." *American Indian Quarterly* 28, 3–4 (2004): 685–718.

_____. "Beyond Red River: New Views of Metis History Symposium" (organizer and moderator). Michigan State University, 2006.

Innes, Robert, Brenda Macdougall, and Frank Tough. "Saskatchewan Indian Reserves." In *Atlas of Saskatchewan: Celebrating the Millennium*. Edited by Kai-iu Fung. Saskatoon, SK: University of Saskatchewan, 1999.

Innis, Harold A. *The Fur Trade in Canada: An Introduction to Canadian Economic History*. New Haven: Yale University Press, 1930.

Isaac, Thomas. *Aboriginal Law: Commentary, Cases and Materials*. Third edition. Saskatoon, SK: Purich Publishing, 2004.

Isfeld, Harpa K. "Who and what is a Canadian Indian? The impact of Bill C-31 upon demographic and epidemiologic measure of registered Indian population of

Manitoba." MA thesis, University of Manitoba, 1997.

Jamieson, Kathleen. "Sex Discrimination and the Indian Act." In *Arduous Journey: Canadian Indians and Decolonization*. Edited by J. Rick Ponting. Toronto: McClelland and Stewart, 1986.

Jenness, Diamond. *Indians of Canada*. Ottawa: National Museum of Canada, 1963.

Johnson, Ian V.B. *Helping Indians Help Themselves: A Committee to Investigate Itself, the 1951 Indian Act Consultation Process*. Ottawa: Treaties and Historical Research Centre, Indian and Northern Affairs Canada, 1984.

Johnston, A. *The Battle at the Belly River: Stories of the Last Great Indian Battle*. Lethbridge, AB: Historical Society of Alberta, 1966.

Johnston, Basil H. *Indian School Days*. Norman, OK: University of Oklahoma Press, 1989.

_____. *The Manitous: The Supernatural World of the Ojibway*. Toronto: Key Porter Books, 1995.

_____. "Is That All There Is? Tribal Literature." In *Anthology of Canadian Native Literature in English*. Third edition. Edited by Daniel David Moses and Terry Goldie. Toronto: University of Oxford Press, 2005.

_____. "Tribal Language," in *An Anthology of Canadian Native Literature in English*, ed. Daniel David Moses and Terry Goldie. Toronto: Oxford University Press, 2005.

Jones, Doug. "Group Nepotism and Human Kinship." *Current Anthropology* 41, 5: 2000), 779–809.

Kammerer, Cornelia Ann. "Descent, Alliance, and Political Order among Akha." *American Ethnologist* 25, 4 (1998): 659–674.

Kennedy, Margaret A. *The Whiskey Trade of the Northwestern Plains: A Multidisciplinary Approach*. New York: Peter Lang, 1997.

Knack, Martha. *Boundaries Between: Southern Paiutes, 1775–1995*. Lincoln, NE: University of Nebraska Press, 2001.

Knoll, David C. "Unfinished Business: Treaty Land Entitlement and Surrender Claims in Saskatchewan." Saskatoon, SK: Native Law Centre, 1987.

Kulchyski, Peter. *Unjust Relations: Aboriginal Rights in Canadian Courts*. Toronto: Oxford University Press, 1994.

_____. "What Is Native Studies?" In *Expression in Canadian Native Studies*. Edited by Ron F. Laliberte, et al. Saskatoon, SK: University of Saskatchewan Extension Press, 2000.

Lafond, Lester. "Creation, Governance and Management of the McKnight Commercial Centre in Saskatoon." In *Urban Indian Reserves: Forging New Relationships in Saskatchewan*. Edited by F. Laurie Barron and Joseph Garcea. Saskatoon, SK: Purich Publishing, 1999.

Lagimodiere, John. "Historians Chided for Misinformation." *Eagle Feather News* 10, no. 9 (2007): 6.

Lawrence, Bonita. " 'Real' Indians and Others: Mixed-Race Urban Native People, the Indian Act, and the Rebuilding of Indigenous Nations." PhD diss., Ontario Institute for Studies in Education, University of Toronto, 1999.

Lerat, Harold. *Treaty Promises, Indian Reality: Life on a Reserve*. Saskatoon: Purich Publishing, 2005.

Leslie, John and Robert Maguire, *The Historical Development of the Indian Act*. Ottawa: Treaties and Historical Research Centre, P.R.E. Group, Indian and Northern Affairs Canada, 1978.

Linklater, Eva Mary Mina. "The Footprints of Wasahkacahk: The Churchill River Diversion Project and Destruction of the Nelson House Cree Historical Landscape." MA thesis, Simon Fraser University, 1994.

Lisac, Mark. "Indian Act Claimed Only Treaty Protection." *Regina Leader Post*, 28 August 1973: A4.

Lomawaima, K. Tsianina. *They Called It Prairie Light: The Story of Chilocco Indian School*. Lincoln, NE: University of Nebraska Press, 1994.

Lowe, Edward. "A Widow, A Child, And Two Lineages: Exploring Kinship and Attachment in Chuuk." *American Anthropologist* 104, 1 (2002): 123–137.

Lowie, Robert. *The Assiniboine: Anthropological Papers of the American Museum of Natural History*, vol. IV, part 1. New York, 1909.

_____. *Indians of the Plains*. Lincoln, NE: University of Nebraska Press, 1982 (originally published by the American Museum of Natural History, 1954).

Macdougall, Brenda. "Socio-cultural Development and Identity Formation of Metis Communities in Northwestern Saskatchewan, 1776–1907." PhD diss., University of Saskatchewan, 2005.

Macklem, Patrick. *Indigenous Difference and the Constitution of Canada*. Toronto: University of Toronto Press, 2001.

MacNeish, Richard. "An Introduction to the Archaeology of Southwest Manitoba." *National Museum of Canada Bulletin* 157 (1958): 1–15.

Mandelbaum, David G. *The Plains Cree: An Ethnographic, Historical, and Comparative Study*. Regina, SK: Canadian Plains Research Centre, 1979.

Martin, Keavy. *Stories in a New Skin: Approaches to Inuit Literature*. Winnipeg, MB: University of Manitoba Press, 2012.

Martin-McGuire, Peggy. "The Importance of the Land: Treaty Land Entitlement and Self-Government in Saskatchewan." In *Aboriginal Self-Government in Canada: Current Trends*. Edited by John H. Hylton. Saskatoon, SK: Purich Publishing, 1999a.

_____. "Treaty Land Entitlement in Saskatchewan: A Context for the Creation of Urban Reserves." In *Urban Indian Reserves: Forging New Relationships in Saskatchewan*. Edited by F. Laurie Barron and Joseph Garcea. Saskatoon, SK: Purich Publishing, 1999b.

McCrady, David Grant. "Beyond Boundaries: Aboriginal Peoples and the Prairie West, 1850–1885." MA thesis, University of Victoria, 1992.

McLeod, Brenda. "Treaty Land Entitlement in Saskatchewan: Conflicts in Land Use and Occupancy in the Witchekan Lake Area." MA thesis, University of Saskatchewan, 2001.

McLeod, Neal. "Plains Cree Identity: Borderlands, Ambiguous Genealogies and Narrative Irony." *Canadian Journal of Native Studies* 20, 2 (2000): 437–454.

_____. *Cree Narrative Memory: From Treaties to Contemporary Times*. Saskatoon, SK: Purich Publishing, 2007.

McNeil, Kent. "The Meaning of Aboriginal Title." In *Aboriginal and Treaty Rights in Canada: Essays on Law, Equality, and Respect for Difference*. Edited by Michael Asch. Vancouver: University of British Columbia Press, 1997.

Meijer Drees, Laurie. *The Indian Association of Alberta: A History of Political Action*. Vancouver: University of British Columbia Press, 2002.

Meyer, David. "Time-Depth of the Western Woods Cree Occupation of Northern Ontario, Manitoba and Saskatchewan." In *Papers of the Eighteenth Algonquian Conference*. Edited by William Cowan. Ottawa: Carleton University, 1987: 187–200.

Miller, David Reed. "Montana Assiniboine Identity: A Cultural Account of an American Indian Ethnicity." PhD diss., Indiana University, 1987.

Miller, Harry B. *These Too Were Pioneers: The Story of the Key Indian Reserve #65 and the Centennial of the Church (1884–1984): With a Special Chapter on Fort Pelly and Other Forts of the Upper Assiniboine River*. Melville, SK: Seniors Consultant Service, 1988.

Miller, J.F.V. *The Gray Site: An Early Plains Burial Ground*. Ottawa: Parks Canada, 1978.

Miller, J.R. "From Riel to the Métis." *The Canadian Historical Review* 69, 1 (1988): 1–20.

_____. *Shingwauk's Vision: A History of Native Residential Schools*. Toronto: University of Toronto Press, 1996.

_____. *Skyscrapers Hide the Heaven: A History of Indian-White Relations in Canada*. Third edition. Toronto: University of Toronto Press, 2000.

Milloy, John. "The Early Indian Acts: Developmental Strategy and Constitutional Change." In *As Long as the Sun Shines and the Water Flows: A Reader in Canadian Native History*. Edited by Ian A.L. Getty and Antoine S. Lussier. Vancouver: University of British Columbia Press, 1983.

_____. *The Plains Cree: Trade, Diplomacy and War, 1790 to 1870*. Winnipeg: University of Manitoba Press, 1988.

Morra, Linda M. "A Preface: Ruminations About *Troubling Tricksters*." In *Troubling Trickster: Revisioning Critical Conversation*. Edited by Deanna Reder and Linda M. Morra. Waterloo, ON: Wilfrid Laurier Press, 2010.

Morris, Alexander. *The Treaties of Canada with the Indians of Manitoba and the North-west Territories Including the Negotiations on Which They Were Based*. Toronto: Prospero Books, 2000 (originally published: Toronto: Belfords, Clarke, 1880).

Morton, Arthur S. *A History of the Canadian West to 1870–1871*. Toronto: Thomas Nelson, 1939.

_____. "The new nation: The Metis." In *The Other Native: The/les Metis, Volume 1, 1700–1885*. Edited by Antoine S. Lussier and Bruce D. Sealey. Winnipeg: Manitoba Metis Federation Press, 1978.

Morton, William L. *Manitoba, A History*. Toronto: University of Toronto Press, 1957.

_____. "The Battle of Grand Coteau." In *The Other Native: The/les Metis, Volume 1, 1700–1885*. Edited by Antoine S. Lussier and Bruce D. Sealey. Winnipeg: Manitoba Metis Federation Press, 1978.

Moulton, Gary E., ed. *The Lewis and Clark Journals: An American Epic of Discovery: The Abridgment of the Definitive Nebraska Edition: Meriwether Lewis, William Clark, and Members of the Corps of Discovery.* Lincoln: University of Nebraska Press, 2003.

Murphy, Lucy Eldersveld. *A Gathering of Rivers: Indians, Métis, and Mining in the Western Great Lakes, 1737–1832.* Lincoln: University of Nebraska Press, 2000.

Neufeld, Peter Lorenz. "Keeseekoowewin." *Dictionary of Canadian Biography Online.* http://www.biographi.ca/EN/ShowBio.asp?BioId=40939&query=keeseekoow enin.

Nicks, Trudy and Kenneth Morgan. "Grande Cache: The Historic Development of an Indigenous Alberta Metis Population." In *The New Peoples: Being and Becoming Metis in North America.* Edited by Jacqueline Peterson and Jennifer S.H. Brown. Winnipeg: University of Manitoba Press, 1985.

Ommenney, Marg. "Bureaucracy thwarts native women's rights, groups says." *Saskatchewan Star Phoenix,* 27 February 1988: A8.

Opekokew, Delia. *The First Nations: Indian Government and the Canadian Confederation.* Saskatoon: Federation of Saskatchewan Indians, 1980.

Owram, Doug. *Promise of Eden: The Canadian Expansionist Movement and the Idea of the West, 1856–1900.* Toronto: University of Toronto Press, 1980.

Pannekoek, Frits. *Snug Little Flock: The Social Origins of the Riel Resistance of 1869–70.* Winnipeg: Watson and Dwyer, 1991.

Peers, Laura. "Changing Resource-Use Patterns of Saulteaux Trading at Fort Pelly, 1821–1870." In *Aboriginal Resource Use in Canada: Historical and Legal Aspects.* Edited by Kerry Abel and Jean Friesen. Winnipeg: University of Manitoba Press, 1991.

———. *The Ojibwa of Western Canada, 1780–1870.* Winnipeg: University of Manitoba Press, 1994.

Peers, Laura and Jennifer S.H. Brown. " 'There Is No End to Relationship among the Indians': Ojibwa Families and Kinship in Historical Perspective." *The History of the Family: An International Quarterly* 4, 4 (1999): 529–555.

Peterson, Jacqueline. "Prelude to Red River: A Social Portrait of the Great Lake Metis." *Ethnohistory* 25, 1 (1978): 41–67.

———. "Ethnogenesis: Settlement and Growth of a 'New People.'" *Journal of Indian Culture and Research* 6, 2 (1982): 23–64.

———. "Many Roads to Red River: Metis Genesis in the Great Lakes Region, 1680–1815." In *The New Peoples: Being and Becoming Metis in North America.* Edited by Jacqueline Peterson and Jennifer S.H. Brown. Winnipeg: University of Manitoba Press, 1985.

Pettipas, Katherine. *"Severing the Ties That Bind": Government Repression of Indigenous Religious Ceremonies on the Prairies.* Winnipeg: University of Manitoba Press, 1994.

Pettipas, Leo. *Aboriginal Migrations: A History of Movements in Southern Manitoba.* Winnipeg: Manitoba Museum of Man and Nature, 1996.

Pitsula, James. "The Blakeney Government and the Settlement of Treaty Indian Land Entitlements in Saskatchewan, 1975–1982." *Historical Papers: A Selection of the*

Papers Presented at the Annual Meeting held at Quebec, 1989. Ottawa: Canadian Historical Association, 1989.

_____. "The Saskatchewan CCF Government and Treaty Indians, 1944–1964." *Canadian Historical Review* 71, 1 (1994): 21–52.

Radin, Paul. *The Trickster: A Study in American Indian Mythology*. New York: Greenwood Press, 1975.

Ray, Arthur. *Indians in the Fur Trade: Their Roles as Trappers, Hunters and Middlemen in the Lands Southwest of Hudson Bay*. Toronto: University of Toronto Press, 1974.

_____. "Fur Trade History as an Aspect of Native History." In *Expressions in Canadian Native Studies*. Edited by Ron F. Laliberte, et al. Saskatoon, SK: University of Saskatchewan Extension Press, 2000.

Ray, Arthur J., Jim Miller, and Frank Tough. "Statement of Treaty Issues: Treaties as a Bridge to the Future." Presented to The Honourable Jane Stewart, Minister of Indian Affairs and Northern Development, and Chief Perry Belgarde, Federation of Saskatchewan Indian Nations, by The Honourable Judge David M. Arnot, Treaty Commissioner for Saskatchewan. 1998.

_____. *Bounty and Benevolence: A History of Saskatchewan Indian Treaties*. Montreal and Kingston: McGill-Queen's University Press, 2000.

Ricketts, Mac Linscott. "The North American Indian Trickster." *History of Religions* 5, 2 (1966): 343.

Riding In, James. "Repatriation: A Pawnee Perspective." *American Indian Quarterly* 20, 2 (1996): 238–250.

Ritterbush, Laren. "Culture Change And Continuity: Ethnohistoric Analysis Of Ojibwa And Ottawa Adjustment To The Prairies." Ph.D. diss., University of Kansas, 1990.

Robin, Martin. *Shades of Right: Nativist and Fascist Politics in Canada, 1920–1940*. Toronto: University of Toronto Press, 1992.

Rodnick, David. "Political Structure and Status among the Assiniboine Indians." *American Anthropologist* 39, 3 (1937): 408–416.

Royal Commission on the Status of Women in Canada. Report of the Royal Commission on the Status of Women in Canada. Ottawa: Information Canada, 1970.

Russell, Dale. *Eighteenth-century Western Cree and their Neighbours*. Ottawa: Canadian Museum of Civilization, Archaeological Survey of Canada, 1991.

Sandra Lovelace v. Canada, Communication No. R.6/24, U.N. Doc. Supp. No. 40 (A/36/40) at 166 (1981).

Schenck, Theresa M. "The Voice of the Crane Echoes Afar": The Sociopolitical Organization of the Lake Superior Ojibwa, 1640-1855. New York: Garland Publishing, 1997.

Schuettler, Darren. "Indian Act Changes Bring New Problems for Native Women." *Western Producer*, 14 January 1991: 51.

Shade, Jennifer Lynn. "Traditional Methods of Determining Tribal Membership." MA thesis, University of Victoria, 2002.

Sharrock, Floyd W. and Susan R. Sharrock. "A History of the Cree Indian Territorial Expansion from the Hudson Bay Area to the Interior Saskatchewan and Missouri Plains." *An Ethnological Report on the Chippewa Cree Tribe of the Rocky Boy Reservation and the Little Shell Band of Indians.* New York: Garland, 1974.

Sharrock, Susan R. "Cree, Cree-Assiniboine, and Assiniboines: Inter-ethnic Social Organization on the Far Northern Plains." *Ethnohistory* 21 (1974): 95–122.

Sheffield, R. Scott. *The Red Man's on the Warpath: The Image of the "Indian" and the Second World War.* Vancouver: University of British Columbia Press, 2004.

Sher, Julian. *White Hoods: Canada's Ku Klux Klan.* Vancouver: New Star Books, 1983.

Siggner, Andrew and Rosalinda Costa. *Aboriginal Conditions in Census Metropolitan Areas, 1981–2001: Trends and Conditions in Census Metropolitan Areas.* Ottawa: Minister of Industry, 2005.

Sinclair, Niigaanwedom James. "Trickster Reflections: Part I." In *Troubling Tricksters: Revisioning Critical Conversations.* Edited by Deanna Reder and Linda M. Morra. Waterloo, ON: Wilfrid Laurier Press, 2010.

Skinner, Alanson. "The Cultural Position of the Plains Ojibway." *American Anthropologist* 16, 2 (1914): 314–318.

_____. "Plains Cree Tale." *Journal of American Folktales* 29, 113 (1916): 351.

Slatterly, Brian. "Understanding Aboriginal Rights." *Canadian Bar Review* 66, 4 (1987).

Smith, Derek G. *Canadian Indians and the Law: Selected Documents, 1663–1972.* Toronto: McClelland and Stewart, 1975.

Smith, James E.G. *Leadership among the Southwestern Ojibwa: Publications in Ethnology* 7. Ottawa: National Museum of Canada, 1973.

_____. "Proscription of Cross-cousin Marriage among the Southwestern Ojibwa." *American Ethnologist* 1 (1974): 751–762.

_____. "On the Territorial Distribution of the Western Woods Cree." In *Papers of the Seventh Algonquian Conference, 1975.* Edited by William Cowan. Ottawa: Carleton University, 1976.

_____. "Western Wood Cree." In *Handbook of North American Indians.* Edited by June Helm. Washington, DC: Smithsonian Institute, 1981.

_____. "The Western Cree: Anthropological Myth and Historical Reality." *American Ethnologist* 14 (1987): 434–448.

Smith, Theresa S. *The Island of the Anishnaabeg: Thunderers and Water Monsters in the Traditional Ojibwe Life-World.* Moscow, ID: University of Idaho Press, 1995.

Smyth, David. "Review Essay: Missed Opportunity: John Milloy's *The Plains Cree.*" *Prairie Forum* 17, 2 (1992): 337–352.

Sparvier, Chief Lionel. "Cowessess First Nations—Treaty Land Entitlement." Cowessess Indian Reserve, Office of the Chief, 1995.

Speck, Frank. "Family Hunting Territories and Social Life of Various Algonkian Bands of the Ottawa Valley." *Geological Survey of Canada Memoir* 70 (1915): 1–30.

Spry, Irene. "The Metis and Mixed Bloods of Rupert's Land before 1870." In *The New Peoples: Being and Becoming Metis in North America.* Edited by Jacqueline Peterson and Jennifer S.H. Brown. Winnipeg: University of Manitoba Press, 1985.

Sodhi, Gurpreet Kaur. "Ignored Are the Wives and Children: Voices from Band Councils and Native Organizations during the Special Joint Committee of 1946–1948 and the Standing Committee on Bill C-31." PhD diss., Trent University, 1996.

St. Germain, Jill. "'Feed or Fight': Rationing the Sioux and the Cree, 1868–1885." *Native Studies Review* 16, 1 (2005): 71–90.

St-Onge, Nicole. "Uncertain Margins: Métis and Saulteaux in St-Paul des Saulteaux, Red River, 1821–1870," *Manitoba History* 53 (2006): 2–10.

Stanley, G.F.G. *The Birth of Western Canada: A History of the Riel Rebellion.* London: Longmans, Green, 1936.

Stonechild, Blair and Bill Wieser. *Loyal till death: Indians and the North-West Rebellion.* Calgary: Fifth House, 1997.

Stonechild, Blair, Neal McLeod, and Rob Nestor. *Survival of a People.* Regina, SK: Indian Studies Research Centre, First Nations University of Canada, 2003.

Sutter, Trevor. "Land Entitlements: Legal Wording and Few Hurdles Stand in Way." *Regina Leader Post* 26 May 1992: A3.

Swan, Ruth. "The Crucible: Pembina and the Origins of the Red River Valley Metis." PhD diss., University of Manitoba, 2003.

Tallbear, Kimberly. "DNA, Blood and Racializing the Tribe." *Wicazo Sa Review* 18, 1 (Spring 2003): 81–107.

Tanner, John. *The Falcon: A Narrative of the Captivity and Adventures of John Tanner.* New York: Penguin Books, 2000.

Tarasoff, Koozma J. *Persistent Ceremonialism: The Plains Cree and Saulteaux.* Ottawa: National Museums of Canada, 1980.

Taylor, John Leonard. "Two Views on the Meaning of Treaty Six and Seven." In *The Spirit of Alberta Indian Treaties.* Edited by Richard Price. Edmonton: Institute for Research on Public Policy and Indian Association of Alberta, 1980.

Teuton, Sean. "The Callout: Writing American Indian Politics." In *Reasoning Together: The Native Critics Collective.* Edited by Craig S. Womack, Daniel Heath Justice, and Christopher B. Teuton. Norman, OK: University of Oklahoma Press, 2008.

Thorne, Tanis. *Many Hands of My Relations: French and Indians on the Lower Missouri.* Columbia and London: University of Missouri Press, 1996.

Tobias, John. "Protection, Civilization, Assimilation: An Outline History of Canada's Indian Policy." In *As Long as the Sun Shines and Water Flows: A Reader in Canadian Native Studies.* Edited by Ian A.L. Getty and Antoine S. Lussier. Vancouver: University of British Columbia Press, 1983.

_____. "Canada's Subjugation of the Plains Cree, 1879–1885." In *Out of the Background: Readings on Canadian Native History.* Edited by Robin Fisher and Kenneth Coates. Toronto: Copp Clark Pitman, 1988.

_____. "Memey (Gabriel Cote)." *Dictionary of Canadian Biography Online.* 2000. http://www.biographi.ca/EN/ShowBio.asp?BioId=41111&query =Gabriel%20 AND%20CotÉ.

_____. "Payipwat." *Dictionary of Canadian Biography Online*. 2000. http://www.biogra-phi.ca/EN/ShowBio.asp?BioId=41111&query=Payipwat.

"Treaty Land Entitlement Ratifications Now Complete." *Saskatchewan Indian*, fall 1995: 22.

Turner, Allan R. "Wikaskokiseyin, also written Wee-kas-kookee-sey-yin, called Sweet Grass." *Dictionary of Canadian Biography Online*. 2000. http://www.biographi.ca/EN/ShowBio.asp?BioId=39439&query=Sweet%20AND%20Grass.

Turpel, Mary Ellen. "Aboriginal Peoples and the Canadian Charter of Rights and Freedoms: Contradictions and Challenges." *Canadian Woman's Studies* 10, 2 (1989): 149-157.

_____. "Patriarchy and Paternalism: The Legacy of the Canadian State for First Nations Women." In *Women and the Canadian State / Les femmes et l'État cana-dien*. Edited by Caroline Andrew and Sandra Rodgers. Montreal and Kingston: McGill-Queen's University Press, 1997.

Tyler, Kenneth. "A History of Cowessess Band." Unpublished paper prepared for the Federation of Saskatchewan Indians, 1975.

_____. "Kiwisance (Cowessess, Ka-we-zauce, Little Child)." In *Dictionary of Canadian Biography*. Edited by France Halpenny. Toronto: University of Toronto Press, 1982.

_____. "PASKWAW (Pasquah, Pisqua, The Plain)." *Dictionary of Canadian Biography Online*. 2000. http://www.biographi.ca/EN/ShowBio.asp?BioId=39874&query=PaskwŶw.

Van Kirk, Sylvia. *Many Tender Ties: Women in Fur-trade Society, 1670–1870*. Norman, OK: University of Oklahoma Press, 1983.

Venne, Sharon Helen. *Indian Acts and Amendments, 1868–1975: An Indexed Collection*. Saskatoon, SK: Native Law Centre, University of Saskatchewan, 1981.

Walker, Deward, Jr. "Nez Perce." In *Handbook of North American Indians*, vol. 12, part 1. Washington, D.C.: Smithsonian Institute, 1998.

Weaver, Sally. "First Nations Women and Government Policy, 1970–92: Discrimination and Conflict." In *Changing Patterns: Women in Canada*. Edited by Sandra Burt, Lorraine Code and Lindsey Dorney. Toronto: McClelland and Stewart, 1993.

_____. "The Status of Indian Women." In *Two Nations, Many Cultures: Ethnic Groups in Canada*. 2nd edition. Edited by Jean Leonard Elliott. Scarborough, ON: Prentice-Hall of Canada, 1993

Welsh, Norbert. *The Last Buffalo Hunter*. New York: T. Nelson, 1939.

Wheeler, C.J. "The Historic Assiniboine: A Territorial Dispute in the Ethnographic Literature." *Actes du 8e Congress des Algoquinists*, ed. William Cowan. Ottawa: Carleton University, 1977.

Wheeler, Winona. "Reflection on the Social Relations of Indigenous Oral History," in *Walking a Tightrope: Aboriginal People and Their Representations*, ed. Ute Lishcke and David T. McNab. Waterloo: Wilfrid Laurier University Press, 2005.

White, Bruce. " 'Give Us a Little Milk': The Social and Cultural Significance of Gift-giving in the Lake Superior Fur Trade." In *Rendezvous: Selected Papers of the*

Fourth North American Fur Trade Conference, ed. Thomas S. Buckley. St. Paul, MN: University of Minnesota, 1984.

_____. "The Woman Who Married a Beaver: Trade Patterns and Gender Roles in the Ojibwa Fur Trade." In *Expression in Canadian Native Studies*, eds. Ron. F. Laliberte, et al. University of Saskatchewan Extension Press, 2000.

Whitewood History. n.p., n. d.

Whyte, John D. "The Lavell Case and Equality in Canada." *Queen's Quarterly* 81, 1 (1975): 28–42.

Widder, Keith. *Battles for the Souls: Metis Children Encounter Evangelical Protestants at Makinaw Mission, 1823–1837*. East Lansing, MI: Michigan State University Press, 1999.

Wilford, Lloyd. "A Revised Classification of the Prehistoric Cultures of Minnesota." *American Antiquity* 21, 2 (1955): 130–142.

Williams, Robert A., Jr. *The American Indian in Western Legal Thought: The Discourses of Conquest*. New York: Oxford University Press, 1990.

_____. *Like a Loaded Weapon: The Rehnquist Court, Indian Rights, and the Legal History of Racism in America*. Minneapolis: University of Minnesota Press, 2005.

Wilson, Daniel. *Prehistoric Man: Research into the Origins of Civilization in the Old and New World*. London: MacMillan, 1876.

Wolfe, Alexander. *Earth Elder Stories: The Pinayzitt Path*. Saskatoon, SK: Fifth House, 1989.

Wotherspoon, Terry L. and Vic Satzewich. *First Nations: Race, Class and Gender Relations*. Toronto: Nelson, 1993.

Wright, Clifford. "Report and Recommendations on Treaty Land Entitlement, Presented to Roland Crowe, Treaty Indian Nations of Saskatchewan and the Honourable Tom Sidden, Minister of Indian Affairs by Treaty Commissioner." Saskatoon, SK: Office of the Treaty Commissioner, 1990.

Wright, James V. *Cree Culture History in the Southern Indian Lake Region: Paper No. 1 (National Museums of Canada Bulletin 232)*. Ottawa: National Museums of Canada, 1971.

_____. "Prehistory of the Canadian Shield." In *Handbook of North American Indians*. Edited by June Helm. Washington, DC: Smithsonian Institute, 1981.

Wuttunee, Deanna. "Indian Act Amendments—Bill C-31." *Saskatchewan Indian*, July 1985: 13.

Yazzie, Robert. "Life Comes Among the People: Torts and Indian Courts." *New Mexico Law Review* 24 (1994): 175–190.

Zieman, Barbara. "Run for Acoose." *Saskatchewan Indian* 12, 7 (September 1982): 59–63.

Zion, James. "Harmony among the People: Torts and Indian Courts." *Montana Law Review* 45 (1984): 265.

Zion, James and Robert Yazzie. "Indigenous Law in North America in the Wake of Conquest." *Boston College International and Comparative Law Review* 20, 1 (1997): 74.

Acknowledgements

There are many people I must thank for their assistance in the completion of this book. First, there are a number of Cowessess members I would like to acknowledge. Much appreciation to Chief Patricia Sparvier and the Band Councillors for allowing me the opportunity to speak to them about the research at a council meeting for which they endorsed the research. Pat Criddle, the executive assistant, was helpful in arranging my meeting with the Chief and Council. Duane Delorme at the Cowessess Urban Office in Regina who provided assistance with locating urban members for the research. Gloria Burgess and Christina Lerat of the Cowessess Health Department who invited me to be involved in a residential school survivor program in which I was able to meet and got to know many band members, many of whom agreed to be interviewed for the research. I would also like to express my gratitude to the First Nations University of Canada, Regina campus, for allowing me to spend time interviewing band members. A special thanks to Terrance Pelletier for all of his assistance. Finally, I would like to extend my appreciation to all the members of Cowessess, especially the Elders who agreed to take part in a focus group interview (and who helped me pull my vehicle out of the snow), who generously agreed to be a part of the research.

This book represents my efforts in meeting the requirements for a PhD in American Indian Studies at the University of Arizona. However, it also represents a culmination of years in obtaining the skills required for a career in this profession. I could not have done this alone. Many people have assisted me in a variety of ways. As a person who did not do well in high school and failed to graduate, I was fortunate to be accepted into the Transitional Year Program at the University of Toronto. The faculty at TYP, Keren Braithwaite, Aggie Lukacs, Maureen FitzGerald, Tom Mathien, Horace Henriques, Keith Allen, and others, provided me with the support and training I needed to experience academic success for the first time. TYP instilled in me a confidence in my academic abilities I had never possessed. Though after my year in TYP I still had many skills to learn and master, without TYP I would have never considered a career in the academy as a truly obtainable goal. It was difficult to learn how to learn in an academic setting, but along with the TYP faculty, I was able to look to fellow students for support and as role models. I was particularly drawn to other Aboriginal students in who had been in the program before, during, and after my time in the program, including Carol Couchie, Tammy Gordon, Isabel Oswamick, Bernie Robertson, the late Dorothy Migwans, and others. Carol and Tammy in particular were important sources of support and some pretty good meals too.

I am also thankful for the presence of First Nations House at the University of Toronto, which provided academic and cultural support, and was a place I made numerous friends, some of whom are colleagues of mine today. FNH offered a haven of sorts to Aboriginal students who utilized the space in a university that had, when I started, a small Aboriginal student population and no Aboriginal faculty. I would especially like to thank Diane Longboat, the late Rodney Bobiwash, and Anita Benedict who served as directors of FNH while I was a student. Also, thanks to the always helpful Jennifer Wesley. Over the four years I spent at FNH, I met many other Aboriginal students as we took part in countless social, political, and cultural activities. Whether it was organizing trips to Elders' conferences, protest marches, speakers' series, feasts, participating in the Native Students' Association, or just hanging out in the lounge or in the Native Students' Association loft, the Aboriginal students formed a much needed support network. Alan Corbiere was one of the first people I met when I went to the Native Students' Association office. Even though he always mocked me for being a history major, as he was doing environmental "science," we developed a longstanding friendship. Alan put his degree to good work, as he is now highly sought after by historians of Ojibwe history and is considered one of the leading experts in that area. Alan worked tirelessly to revive the Native Students' Association and was able to obtain a banner for the association to hang in FNH. Both are still present nearly twenty years later. First Nations House employed student tutors to assist Aboriginal undergrads. I was very lucky to have Deborah McGregor and Gina Luck as my tutors. Both spent many hours tutoring me on my writing. They did a pretty good job considering what they had to work with. I am grateful for their efforts as my writing improved tremendously with their help. Jason Pennington, the first Native person I ever meet who could speak fluent French, is one of those people who is truly nice to the core and who was so very easy to make fun of. Jason is now a practicing medical doctor, and no doubt, an excellent one at that. Atik Bird was in TYP the same year as I, and once the University of Toronto accepted us as undergraduate students we took many classes together—usually the only other person I knew in the class was Atik. Not that we were over our heads, but we spent many hours ruminating over what words like ruminating meant. I was really lucky to be able to go to those classes with Atik. Atik and her husband Gomo George welcomed me into their family and I got to know their children, Ben, Jonathon, Abyomi, and Oji, which is something I will always cherish. Other students I spent significant time with included Edward Doolittle (who I run into quite often as he is now with First Nations University of Canada in Regina), John Dorian, Derek Chum, Jonathan Blackstar, and many others.

The University of Toronto is a big school and though I had excellent professors, it was difficult, for me at least, to develop any meaningful rapport with most. However, I was fortunate enough to have taken classes from Carl Berger and Sylvia Van Kirk. Both allowed me the freedom to explore research topics I was most interested in and provided me with excellent guidance on how to approach those topics. Their enthusiasm for my research topics, for research in general, was instilled in me and is something I carry with me to this day. When I was in TYP I went to hear Dr. Bea Medicine give a public lecture. At the reception afterwards, I was standing by myself as I didn't know anyone there (I really only went for the food), when Dr. Medicine came over and talked to me. She was extremely friendly and encouraging. I left feeling pretty good that I had the chance to meet and talk to her. The next year as a first-year student, I was able to take a third-year Native women's course with her as she was a visiting lecture. Atik had successfully argued that even though we were first-year students we should be allowed to take the course as the university had no Aboriginal faculty. As the only male in the class, I may have been the teacher's pet—at least that is what the only students said. Nonetheless, it was a great experience and I felt extremely lucky to have been allowed to take it. My interaction with Dr. Medicine has had a great influenced on me.

In the master's program in the Department of Native Studies, University of Saskatchewan, I further developed the skills I learned at the University of Toronto. I soon realized, however, that working with Frank Tough and Jim Waldram—who after seeing a draft of my proposal remarked in class, incredulously, "what the hell is this?"—I would be pushed to become a better scholar, and for that I am thankful. I am extremely grateful to have had opportunity to work with my initial thesis advisor, the late F. Laurie Barron, who was a true gentleman and a scholar. Much appreciation goes to Jim Miller, who willingly agreed to become my advisor at the tail end of my studies. As well to my fellow students Brenda Macdougall and Karyn Recollect (Drane), who have since launched successful academic careers, not only was it a pleasure to be in the program with you, but equally so to see your careers develop. I have known Brenda since I first arrived at the University of Saskatchewan in 1996, when I enrolled in a class she taught for the department. A year later, we became students together in the grad program, me as a MA student, her as PhD student, and later were colleagues in the department until she left for the University of Ottawa. When the department first hired me, Brenda was a role model for me, and, as her career has flourished, she continues to be a role model and a friend.

I am deeply indebted to my PhD advisor, Tsianina Lomawaima in the American Indian Studies Program at the University of Arizona. She facilitated the completion of the dissertation with her close attention to detail that demanded that I meet or exceed the scholarly standard. She provided me, and continues to provide me, with guidance and mentorship that has benefitted me throughout my professional career. Without a doubt, selecting Professor Lomawaima to be my advisor was the right decision. That she agreed to be my advisor was an honour. Much appreciation goes to my committee member, Robert Williams Jr., who agreed to be on my committee even though he said upon hearing my attempt to articulate my original thesis statement, "that ain't a thesis, that's a bitch!" Professor Williams was not only one of the best profs I had taken a course with, as a committee member he pointed me towards looking at the notion of tribal customary law as a means to make sense of the persistence of traditional kinship practices among Cowessess people, which became focal point of my whole argument. Also thanks to committee members Robert Martin and Winona Wheeler who both made significant contributions to the final product. I thank all my committee members for the time, encouragement, and direction they gave me. I would also thank Neil

Soiseth for his expertise in copy-editing the original dissertation. I am very appreciative of the financial support from the Cowessess Education Authority and from the Hubert E. Carter Graduate Interdisciplinary Fellowship that supported me during my PhD studies.

I was given much support and encouragement from a number of American Indian Studies faculty members. I first heard about the program when Jay Stauss registered to attend a conference in Saskatoon that I helped organize. Jay, who was the director of the program at the time I started, had such a great sense of humour and used it as a means to direct students to new insights. I very much appreciated his selflessness and eagerness to help. Nancy Parezo, who I spent many hours talking to as she provided her insights on many topics and, in one class, unknowingly bestowed upon me the moniker "good job Rob," a name that some students relentlessly called me after that. I really enjoyed my time with Nancy. Thanks to Luci Tapahonso, for her gentle way, for being as tough as nails. My thanks go to Sheila Lowe for her assistance in navigating the bureaucracy of a graduate program. Thanks to my fellow American Indian Studies PhD and MA students Diana DeLeon, John Dillon, Julie Hailer, Elizabeth Nesbit, Spintz Harrison, Angelica Lawson, Michelle Hale, Ray Austin, Amy Fatzinger, Reuban Naranjo, Ray Cardinal, Joseph Brewer, the late Sarah Welch, Peter Morris, Yuko Matsuno, and so many more that I simply can not list. I spent significant time with all these people. They were all intelligent, funny, and a joy to be with. Sharon Milholland, who always has a place for me in the warmth of Tucson. I also spent much time with Ferlin Clarke, whose humour I very much welcomed and whose ability to complete assignments in mere hours I utterly resented. Louellyn White started the program at the same time as me. We were both TAs and I will never forget her standing beside one of her students, the current NBA player, the seven-foot Channing Frye—priceless! I first met Kevin Wall when I went on school visit and he has become one of my closest friends. We lived at his house in Lansing, Michigan, for a while and he has taught for us in Saskatoon for a year. Many in Saskatoon could not understand his accent and he could not understand many of their Saskatchewan accents. I always look forward to a spot on his porch in the backwoods of Virginia. Through miracle of Facebook, I still maintain contact with many of my former classmates.

Also, I am greatly indebted to the American Indian Studies Program at Michigan State University, which offered me the opportunity through their

Pre-Doctoral Fellowship to make significant progress on the writing of the dissertation. In particular, the late Susan Applegate-Krouse, head of the AIS program, was extremely helpful to me. Susan was a tremendous supporter of young scholars and of AIS, and the perfect person to head the AIS program. I cherish the time I spent with her. Susan's husband Ned Krouse, along with Susan Sleeper-Smith, and others, made my stay in East Lansing a pleasant and productive experience.

Once I joined the Department of Native Studies, University of Saskatchewan, former and current faculty members gave me much support. Thank you to Roger Maaka, Brenda Macdougall, Caroline Tait, Bonita Beatty, Denise Fuchs, Priscilla Settee, Ron Laliberte, Miriam McNab (who was one of my first professors at the University of Saskatchewan and now I sit on her PhD committee and with whom I worked with organizing two conferences), Lesley McBain and Laurie Meijer Drees (who both thrilled my mom by including her in their research project and interviewed her about her experience as a nurse's aide in La Ronge), the incomparable Michelle Jarvin, and Winona Wheeler. I am so grateful to have you as colleagues. My relationship with Winona kind of mirrors that of Forest Gump and Jenny. Since 1996, like Gump did with Jenny, Winona has popped into my life at different stages of my development. Over that time, she has imparted much wisdom and guidance and has been a steady influence on me both professionally and personally. Luckily, unlike Jenny, I'm OK and am now able to enjoy working with Winona as a colleague on a daily basis. Other colleagues I have worked with over the years in the department include that I have benefitted so much from include Sherri Swidrovich and Yale Belanger. I have to also mention Andrew Peters, who I meet when he came to Saskatoon as an Australian exchange student and lived with my mom and I for four months. We have maintained our friendship and plan on working on some projects in the future. I have also worked with Aboriginal student support staff, Lori Delorme, Kathleen Makela, Charlotte Ross, and Lori Peters-Whiteman, whose commitment to improving Aboriginal students' experience is inspirational. To the students I have had the pleasure of working with closely since joining the department as a faculty member, Allison Piché, Rebecca Major, Sabrina Mullis, John Swift, Jennifer Campeau, Roberta Desnomie, Swapna Padmanabha, Albert Berland, Bobby Henry, Michelle Hogan, Deanna Raymond, Lindsay Knight, Dana Carriere, Emma Sim, and Erica Lee, you amaze me with your determination for learning and inspire me with your commitment to improving the lives of Aboriginal people.

The University of Manitoba Press, David Carr, Glenn Bergen, Ariel Gordon, Cheryl Miki, Jean Wilson, and Jarvis Brownlee, and their exceptionally patient copy editor, have been a delight to work with. Everyone has been extremely encouraging, helpful beyond belief, and demonstrated a deep commitment to this book. I am very thankful to be associated with this press and to be included in the exceptionally strong Critical Studies in Native History series; what an honour! I thank the anonymous reviewers whose insightful and encouraging comments helped me rethink aspects of the book making it, I hope, stronger.

At the University of Saskatchewan, I have had the great pleasure to work with a number of excellent people, including Nancy Van Styvendale, Loleen Berdahl, Verna St. Denis, David Natcher, Jim Miller, Keith Carlson, Bill Waiser, and Ryan Walker, to name a few. I've been involved with the Native American and Indigenous Studies Association for a number of years. As a result, I have come into contact with many nationally and internationally renowned Indigenous Studies scholars, who individually and as a collective, have had a profound impact on me as a scholar: Robert Warrior, Jeani O'Brien, Chris Andersen, Audra Simpson, Mary Jane McCallum, Sue Hill, Aroha Harris, Theresa McCarthy, Kim Tallbear, Noenoe Silva, Brendan Hokuwhitu, Niigaan Sinclair, Keavy Martin, and many others.

Others who have had a significant impact on my life include James Froh and Cindy Doxtator and their children Wilson and Starr, Judy Anderson and Larry Gaultier and their children Cruz and Riel, Nancy Cooper and Janet Smylie and their children Quinn and Jay, and Elders Wil Campbell and Danny Musqua. I also have to acknowledge Kim Anderson who I have known number of years. On a personal level we have attended many ceremonies together and I have gotten to know her family—husband David, and son Rajan, and daughter Danica. On a professional level, Kim has gracefully invited me to be a part to two significant research projects. I have been fortunate to have met, listened and participated in ceremonies with many different Elders over twenty years. These Elders presented me with new understandings for how to live life that I had never known. This new direction gave me a different outlook on life and a different reason for being alive. Maria Campbell has also been a very special person in my life. As an Elder, mentor, grandmother to my sons, friend, and as a boarder, Maria has filled many roles in my life.

I could not have met the arduous demands of graduate school without the support of family. To the MacKay family, Don and Gerri, Dawn and Henry,

Bill and Louise, Jason, Ben and Adrienne—and their twin boys Solomon and George, and Ben, who always made me feel welcomed and respected. Thanks to my aunt Veronica for her support. My brothers Paul Christiansen and Brian Innes, his wife Genni, son William and daughter Jessica, you have always been close to my heart. I am lucky to have a big brother like Brian. My sons, Anthony and Samson, give me a sense of purpose and fulfillment. It is a simply the most satisfying aspect of my life to be their father. I enjoy so much watching both my sons grow into young men. For many years I had the love and support of Gail MacKay and for that I will always be grateful. I truly could not have perservered through my years as a student and in my early years as a faculty member without Gail. Finally, this book is dedicated to the memory of my mother, Muriel Doris Innes (née Pelletier), who from the time I was young made sure I always knew who I was and where I came from. A residential school survivor who only was able to reach grade seven before she started to work as a nurse's aide, my mom always stressed the importance of working hard and the need to obtain an education. My mom worked at the University of Manitoba for years, spending most of that time with the Engineering Access Program. She had always hoped one of her sons could graduate from university. I realized how important it was to her when I saw her at my undergraduate convocation ceremony. My mom instilled in me many of her traits. These traits were useful to me in my journey to complete my education and move forward in my life. I am thankful to have had such wonderful and committed mother and I miss her every day.

Index